2=

Global Equity
Investing

Global Equity Investing

Alberto Vivanti

Perry Kaufman

McGraw-Hill

New York   San Francisco   Washington, D.C.   Auckland   Bogotá
Caracas   Lisbon   London   Madrid   Mexico City   Milan
Montreal   New Delhi   San Juan   Singapore
Sydney   Tokyo   Toronto

Library of Congress Cataloging-in-Publication Data

Vivanti, Alberto.
    Global equity investing / Alberto Vivanti, Perry Kaufman.
        p.   cm.
    Includes index.
    ISBN 0-07-067519-8
    1. Electronic trading of securities.   2. Investments, Foreign.
I. Kaufman, Perry. II. Title.
HG4515.95.V58   1997
332.63'22—dc21   97-7450
                                                CIP

McGraw-Hill

A Division of The McGraw·Hill Companies

1 2 3 4 5 6 7 8 9 0 FGR/FGR 9 0 2 1 0 9 8 7

ISBN 0-07-067519-8

The sponsorimg editor for this book was Allyson Arias, the editing supervisor was Jane Palmieri, and the production supervisor was Pamela Pelton. It was set in Palatino by Renee Lipton of McGraw-Hill's Professional Book Group composition unit.

Printed and bound by Quebecor/Fairfield.

McGraw-Hill books are available at special quantity discounts to use as premiums and sales promotions, or for use in corporate training programs. For more information, please write to the Director of Special Sales, McGraw-Hill, 11 West 19th Street, New York, NY 10011. Or contact your local bookstore.

This publication is designed to provide accurate and authoritative information in regard to the subject matter covered. It is sold with the understanding that the publisher is not engaged in rendering legal, accounting, or other professional service. If legal advice or other expert assistance is required, the services of a competent professional person should be sought.   *—from a declaration of principles jointly adopted by a committee of the American Bar Association and a Committee of publishers*

This book is printed on recycled, acid-free paper containing a minimum of 50% recycled, de-inked fiber.

To Marisa, for being by my side for the past twenty years, and for caring enough to look past those long weekends of work so that I can deliver this gift to you.

A.V.

To Barbara, for just being you.

P.J.K.

Contents

Preface

Even before we welcome the next millennium, the borders of international trade have fallen and the buying habits of consumers have changed. The bulk of everything we buy is manufactured elsewhere. Instead of repairing their shoes, many people discard them and buy new ones. This is the first time in the history of civilization that we can manufacture a product anywhere in the world and easily ship it to any other location. This growth phenomena will seek out the cheapest labor and redistribute wealth around the world.

Compared to most countries, the United States is no longer the choice for manufacturing; instead, it provides creativity, technology, and services. It is the first to design and develop a new generation of electronics; intentionally or inadvertently, it is just as quick to export this technology to countries that can manufacture it at a fraction of the cost.

For investors this means that the greatest growth and investment opportunities—and the greatest risk—may lie outside their borders. For U.S. investors we are not downplaying the spectacular returns of Microsoft, Intel, or other companies that have rapidly become Internet giants. Many investors have participated in their profits; however, it is not easy to recognize their potential in advance and to invest enough to benefit from their growth.

It is easier to select a world geographic zone, or an economic region, that holds potential rather than having to decide specifically which countries or which companies will perform the best. It seems evident that during the next 20 years China will emerge as a formidable economic power. More than that, the people of China, nearly one-quarter of the world's population, will become active consumers. How will that affect the world economy? It would appear that their impact will be nothing short of explosive.

During this growth period, all of the countries that are geographically near China will benefit from its economic expansion. Proximity is important. In the United States it is easily forgotten that Canada is their biggest trade partner, because the media focuses on Mexico, Japan, and China. Trade flows to those nearest; therefore, it is most of the Far East that will profit as China blossoms.

There is no area of potential growth greater than Asia. To complement that further will be the emergence of India, another massive market. How can we in the West ignore the significance of this change to the world economy? If we limit our investments to domestic companies, we will be playing the same old game with less and less opportunity. When imports increase, investors have nothing to counterbalance the resulting inflation. As more products are manufactured elsewhere, a domestic financial portfolio increases in risk.

The only way to protect your future is to participate in this growth and change. It is necessary to invest in the United States, Europe, Asia, and India and to benefit from their expansion and their new roles. Because we cannot know that Asian firms will yield a better return than those of Europe or the United States in any given year, we do not make that choice, but rather create a simple plan to diversify safely across the world markets. It should not matter which region is the winner each year; as long as the world economies are expanding, your investments should grow at a very satisfactory rate. Investors have always understood that diversification reduces risk; now they must understand that true diversification means participation beyond their borders. It is not just an opportunity, it is imperative.

This book will show how to build a global portfolio without unnecessary complication and risk. There are many individual investors, along with institutions and public funds, that need a way to invest in international economies. The financial markets have responded by listing many large firms on exchanges in more than one country. They have also created index markets on regional economies that can be traded as easily as a stock. You can build your own multinational portfolio of individual stocks or buy and sell whole economies. This approach is still new, but so essential to investment survival that more products are rapidly entering the market, increasing selection and expanding participation.

This is a "how-to" book, with simple, practical steps for selecting and evaluating your portfolio. The method presented here is sensible but not trivial. We have added background on various economies to show how the investors of each country or region see their own market. History often shows the reasons for strong underlying diversification, and why it is likely to continue. We have explained the entire process so that you can do it yourself and continue to monitor and change your portfolio. We have tried to show you our thought process and hope that you find investing in world markets as valuable as we have.

Alberto Vivanti and Perry Kaufman
April 1997

Global Equity Investing

1

Introduction: Thinking of Risk before Reward

If you are looking for investment returns, the biggest payout can be a hit Broadway show, an oil exploration company that finds an enormous reserve in southern China, or a partnership in a successful restaurant with Michael Jordan. The monetary rewards and the personal satisfaction would be high, but the uncertainty is too great for most people. Even a small investment may seem too much. If so, you understand the importance of business risk, yet you may overlook a very significant risk when you choose investments that are all based in the United States, or all in Germany or Japan.

For most investors, it is the return, or capital appreciation, that is the most important part of an investment. Everyone wants to be part of a big winner, and no one would like to admit to having missed the 20-year rally in the U.S. equities markets. When looking for a place to invest, it is more reasonable to expect a company that has just given high returns to continue into the future, than to pick one that did poorly and expect it to change. But the solution is far from simple. Yesterday's best performers, whether an applauded producer such as Andrew Lloyd Weber or a government bond that yielded 12%, do not guarantee the same success tomorrow; yesterday's failures are more often a worse choice. Investment quality is not decided by profits alone.

The chance of a good profit means nothing without considering the risk. Risk underlies the investment decisions made by most people, and justifiably so. Even the most successful investors may not always be aware of their sensitivity to risk, yet it is an important part of every decision. If many people feel comfortable with a modest return from U.S. Treasury bills, rather than the "sure thing" 200% return of the International Grommet Company, they are exercising their preference for "risk aversion."

The Time Horizon Changes Your Perception of Risk

Institutional investors, who have a professional and legal responsibility to ensure the safety of their investments, place about 60% of their funds in the stock market. At the same time, the small, conservative investor sees too much risk in stock market fluctuations. The reason for this conflict is the way that they view market movement over different time frames. During any one day or week it is not surprising to see the Dow Jones Industrial Average go up or down by 50 points, or 1%. Over 50 years it has steadily gone up.

A Matter of Perspective

On October 19, 1987, the Standard and Poor's 500 Index (S&P), a broader market indicator than the Dow Jones Industrial Average (DJIA or Dow), dropped 30% in one day, yet the Index showed a profit for the year. Also, in 1987, the Lehman Brothers Treasury Index (LBTI) posted seven losing months and still yielded a positive return for the year, representing the performance of the fixed-income market.

Table 1-1 gives a recap of the monthly changes during 1987 with a cumulative index value representing an investment of $100 that began January 1, 1987. In the stock market, the Standard & Poor's 500 dropped 30% on Monday, October 19, but had recovered to show a loss of only 8.4% by the end of the month. If you had deposited your funds on January 1, you had gained 36% by the end of August, and the October plunge could be considered only a temporary loss of profits. By the end of the year, the Standard and Poor's 500 investment yielded a 4.7% return.

The short-term is very different from the long-term perspective. If you had been unlucky enough to invest in September 1987 and you had financed the position, then you could have lost everything on the Monday the market dropped 30%.

In the long run, the stock market performance represents economic growth. If the country moves forward, stock prices rise. This increase can be expected to exceed any returns possible from government-"guaranteed" interest rates. By accumulating shares over a long period and storing them in a locked chest for appreciation, you will not see the months, or even years, of market weakness. You may not even realize that it affected your investment. And when you open that chest in 30 or 40 years, history has shown that you will find much more than you expected.

For most individual and institutional investors, a fully funded buy-and-hold (also called a *passive*) strategy is not enough. Over time some markets atrophy and new markets replace them in the public's eye. It is remarkable that, by most investor standards, the stock market is too volatile and risky; yet to the profes-

Table 1-1. Looking at 1987 Investment Returns from Different Time Horizons

End of month	S&P 500 % Change	S&P 500 Index	LBTI % Change	LBTI Index
Dec. 1986		100.00		100.00
Jan. 1987	13.44	113.44	1.37	101.37
Feb. 1987	4.13	118.13	0.66	102.04
Mar. 1987	2.20	120.72	−0.54	101.49
Apr. 1987	−0.88	119.66	−2.67	98.78
May 1987	1.03	120.89	−0.44	98.34
Jun. 1987	4.99	126.93	1.24	99.56
Jul. 1987	4.98	133.25	−0.22	99.34
Aug. 1987	3.85	138.38	−0.57	98.78
Sep. 1987	−2.19	135.35	−2.15	96.65
Oct. 1987	−21.55	106.18	3.75	100.28
Nov. 1987	−8.19	97.48	0.63	100.91
Dec. 1987	7.40	104.70	1.37	102.29

sional investor, the near-catastrophic risk of 1987 is easily forgotten in the sustained bull market rally of the past 20 years.

There are good statistical reasons to say that your final capital, on average, will be well rewarded after many years. But, if you need stability and you do not accept sharp and sometimes prolonged capital declines, or "drawdowns," then a simple buy-and-hold strategy cannot work.

The U.S. and many world equity markets, as analyzed in the chapters ahead, have provided a very good place for investments, but this is easy to say looking back at past performance. Unfortunately, we can never go back and know what would we have done at the end of 1974, after a two-year bear market decline had pushed the Dow Jones Industrial Average to under 600 from the level of more than 1000 recorded in January 1973. Hopefully, we looked at the long-term appreciation and held on. Afterwards, we looked back and saw that the Dow Jones Industrial Average had gained 145% from December 1966 to December 1986, a period that not only included the extended drop of a bear market, but one that was characterized by many years of market choppiness.

Looking inside the Index

We all know that the Dow Jones Industrial Average (DJIA or Dow) or the Standard and Poor's (S&P) 500 are indices that represent a basket of stocks; their numbers give a rough but good idea of where the market is heading. We also know that even in a declining period some stocks, or group of stocks related to one economic sector, often move in a different way. For example, during the 1970s the Dow performed badly, moving mostly sideways, hovering below the 1000 level but dropping 40% from 1972 to 1974. One of the reasons was an inflationary oil crisis. Therefore, within a general market decline, the oil-related stocks rallied based on increasing energy prices. This type of diversification, relating to groups of stocks influenced by unique economic factors, opens the door to valuable ways to avoid undesired capital drawdown.

Comparing World Market Movements

The same concept of independent movement that we see in single markets applies to the world stock markets as a whole. One clear example involves Japan during the decade beginning in 1971. The Nikkei, Japan's major stock index, progressed almost 250% while the Dow Jones Industrial Average gained only slightly more than 15%. In more recent years the relative performance of those two markets has been completely reversed, with the Nikkei plunging from nearly 40,000 at the end of 1989 to 15,000 in mid-1992 (a drop of 62%), while the DJIA moved from 2750 to 3400 during the same period (a gain of 23%).

Even on the surface, this argues that we should always pay attention to both the U.S. and Japanese markets. From 1971 to 1995 the Japanese Nikkei 225 index increased by about 900% (ignoring currency considerations) despite the 60% drawdown of the early 1990s, while the Dow Jones Industrial Average increased about 500% in a more orderly and consistent manner (with a "small" dislocation in October 1987). Often a negative period for one market occurs while there is a positive one for the other. Without analyzing the fundamental reasons that caused that market behavior, some form of global diversification would appear to be a wise investment philosophy.

Influence of Currency Shifts

The world financial scenario is changing dramatically. One main factor has been the orchestrated depreciation of the U.S. dollar against the other main currencies. It took more than four Swiss francs to buy one U.S. dollar in 1971, and it takes only a little more than one Swiss franc for the same purchase in 1995. This does not mean that the trend is endless. We witnessed a strong dollar rally in the early 1980s and this could happen again, but these biggest movements are based on economic policies and last many years, leaving ineffaceable marks in the financial world.

There continue to be several important changes, and chances, occurring in the world economy as we come to the end of the twentieth century. Emerging markets top the list. A few years ago, their market capitalization was absurdly low, but now they are increasing in value and growing at a dramatic pace. Cheap labor caused by socioeconomic gaps makes them very competitive and highly attractive to manufacturers, which in turn raises the importance of their economies to investors.

The Japanese market, once considered emerging, is now enormous; yet it is facing ripeness problems. Europe, which struggled for union and is now stalled by a structural and historical heterogeneity, is composed of several different equity markets the behavior of which is so different that some of them have characteristics of less-developed markets.

Once, the market capitalization of the United States was far higher than the rest of the world combined. Now, the weight of the U.S. equity markets has declined from more than two-thirds to about one-third of the world scale. These major changes cannot be ignored. They explain the increasing number of foreign stocks and country funds being traded on Wall Street and the steadily growing allocation of world stocks within most institutional portfolios.

Throughout this book we will see how world markets differ from one another and how many chances one gets, not just for profit hunting, but for improving returns and reducing the risk of loss through a simple and practical approach to international diversification.

2

Buy-and-Hold Does Not Mean Low Risk

Historic Returns of the Stock Market: A Century of Expansion

By now, the long-term upward trend of stock prices on Wall Street has attracted the attention of every investor. The modern age has been characterized by a human progress never witnessed during the previous centuries. Despite wars, political tensions, and economic recessions, wealth has increased dramatically and social conditions have improved at a pace never seen before. For most of us, the worst case is not very bad. This expansion has been reflected in the stock market through the evolution of corporate assets.

Each phase of this progress is led by a particular sector of the economy. Once the railroad companies were the main force that created wealth in the country, tying together production and the source of resources. After that early stage of industrialization several other sectors drove economic progress: automobiles, electric tools, domestic appliances, computers, airlines, specialized retailers, aircraft, biotechnology, and now communications and computer software. The stock value of the companies in those expanding sectors had their own period of dramatic increase. For each there has been a shining period in the stock market, and many of them still participate in new market expansion phases.

The secular trend of the equities market is up. This is especially true for U.S. equities, pushed by the driving force of the United States for world progress in the twentieth century and an undeniable vein of creativity and ambition. That key role is still very important on both political and economical fronts. For those reasons, the investors who committed their savings to the stock market as a whole, through mutual funds or diversified programs, have been well rewarded throughout the years.

A Long Way Up

In order to have a sound understanding of our investment choices, we need to quantify and evaluate the stock market's performance over the last half-century. To get the full picture of the market as a whole, we use an average of representative stocks; the value that is universally accepted for this purpose is the Dow Jones Industrial Average. Created by Charles Dow more than one century ago simply to have a general measure of market direction, it still does its job well. The Dow Jones is composed of 30 industrial stocks, of which all except General Electric have been replaced through the years. Those companies are an excellent proxy for the performance of the whole exchange because they represent a large part of U.S. business output. We will use the DJIA, which we will also call the "Dow," throughout the book because it relates closely to other broader and more modern indices, such as the S&P 500, and its history goes farther back and is readily available.

Table 2-1 shows the performance of the Dow Jones Industrial Average during the half-century from 1945 to 1995. In Figure 2-1 we can see the unusually rapid growth beginning in the early 1980s, compared to the previous 40 years, even though prices are charted on a logarithmic scale, a technique that is commonly used to show "normal" growth. It took 35 years for a $100 investment to reach $500 and only 15 years to go from $500 to $2653.

Comparison with a Risk-Free Investment

During the same 50 years, a risk-free investment in three-month U.S. Treasury bills would have produced a 915% return (based on the yield at the beginning of each year, taxes ignored). This is equivalent to a compounded rate of 4.7%, two full percentage points below the 6.8% rate given by the stock market and shown in Figure 2-2.

If it so easy to beat a risk-free rate investment, then why do so many investors prefer to place their money in a fixed-income deposit and avoid such a rewarding alternative? To understand the concerns of investors, we must look at shorter time periods of Dow performance. As we pointed out in Chapter 1, shorter intervals carry greater risk. While growing 2553%, the DJIA has had periods of very erratic performance. In Figure 2-1 we see that there were no bear markets following World War II that remotely approached the same magnitude as the one that began the Great Depression (which declined almost 90% from 1929 to 1932). But for an investor who could have chosen a risk-free U.S. bond, the period from the early 1960s to the beginning of the 1980s had no gain and provided a regular reminder of risk with some distressing drawdowns. We must be realistic enough to admit that the good performance of the equity market has been achieved over a rough road. It is easy to judge, after the fact, that equities are the best possible investment.

The most sensible way to justify our long-term position is by relating the success of the stock market to the economic health of the nation. When the economy expands, the market rises; when productivity increases, the market rises. The government expends considerable effort to ensure that the economy maintains a slow,

Table 2-1. Fifty Years of Investment Returns for the Dow Jones
Industrial Averages and U.S. Treasury Bills

Table 2-1 and Figure 2-1 show a total gain of 2553% for the Dow over
50 years, without reinvesting dividends. That corresponds to the
compounded rate of return of 6.8%. If you had invested $100 in 1945 at
6.8% and reinvested the interest each year at the same rate, you would
have received the same result as the DJIA, equal to $2653. During the
same period, U.S. Treasury bills, shown in Table 2-1, gained 915.1%,
for a compounded return of 4.7%.

	Year-end value of DJIA	% Change DJIA	$100 Invested in DJIA	Year-end % change T-bills	$100 Invested in T-bills
1945	192.84		100.00		100.00
1946	175.77	−8.9	91.15	0.37	100.37
1947	179.23	2.0	92.94	0.37	100.74
1948	177.30	−1.1	91.94	0.37	101.11
1949	200.13	12.9	103.78	0.95	102.07
1950	235.41	17.6	122.08	1.15	103.25
1951	268.52	14.1	139.24	1.08	104.36
1952	288.23	7.3	149.47	1.38	105.80
1953	280.90	−2.5	145.66	1.87	107.78
1954	404.39	44.0	209.70	2.23	110.19
1955	488.40	20.8	253.27	1.57	111.92
1956	496.41	1.6	257.42	1.17	113.23
1957	432.90	−12.8	224.49	2.69	116.27
1958	572.73	32.3	297.00	3.22	120.01
1959	679.36	18.6	352.29	3.17	123.82
1960	615.89	−9.3	319.38	2.74	127.21
1961	720.87	17.0	373.82	4.52	132.96
1962	651.43	−9.6	337.81	2.15	135.82
1963	762.95	17.1	395.64	2.59	139.34
1964	874.13	14.6	453.29	2.89	143.37
1965	969.26	10.9	502.62	3.52	148.41
1966	785.69	−18.9	407.43	3.87	154.16
1967	905.11	15.2	469.36	4.46	161.03
1968	952.51	5.2	493.94	4.75	168.68
1969	797.65	−16.3	413.63	4.99	177.10
1970	838.92	5.2	435.03	6.28	188.22
1971	890.20	6.1	461.63	7.80	202.90
1972	1020.02	14.6	528.95	4.83	212.70
1973	848.02	−16.9	439.75	3.73	220.63
1974	602.16	−29.0	312.26	5.11	231.91

(*Continued*)

Table 2-1. Fifty Years of Investment Returns for the Dow Jones Industrial Averages and U.S. Treasury Bills (*Continued*)

	Year-end value of DJIA	% Change DJIA	$100 Invested in DJIA	Year-end % change T-bills	$100 Invested in T-bills
1975	859.81	42.8	445.87	7.35	248.95
1976	1004.65	16.8	520.98	6.96	266.28
1977	831.17	−17.3	431.02	5.34	280.50
1978	805.01	−3.1	417.45	4.30	292.56
1979	838.91	4.2	435.03	6.15	310.55
1980	966.38	15.2	501.13	9.34	339.56
1981	875.00	−9.5	453.74	12.07	380.54
1982	1046.50	19.6	542.68	14.99	437.59
1983	1258.60	20.3	652.67	11.69	488.74
1984	1204.20	−4.3	624.46	7.98	527.74
1985	1543.00	28.1	800.15	8.94	574.92
1986	1930.40	25.1	1001.04	7.75	619.48
1987	1938.80	0.4	1005.39	7.02	662.97
1988	2168.60	11.9	1124.56	5.49	699.36
1989	2753.20	27.0	1427.71	5.73	739.44
1990	2629.20	−4.5	1363.41	8.22	800.22
1991	3101.52	18.0	1608.34	7.77	862.40
1992	3301.11	6.4	1711.84	6.52	918.62
1993	3754.09	13.7	1946.74	3.92	954.63
1994	3834.44	2.1	1988.40	3.15	984.71
1995	5117.00	33.4	2653.50	3.09	1015.13
50-Year % return			2553.50		915.13
Compounded rate of return			6.78%		4.74%
Average yearly return			7.96%		4.79%
Best year			44.0%		15.0%
Worst year			−29.0%		0.4%
Standard deviation of returns			16.0%		3.2%
Number of winning years			35		50
Number of losing years			15		0

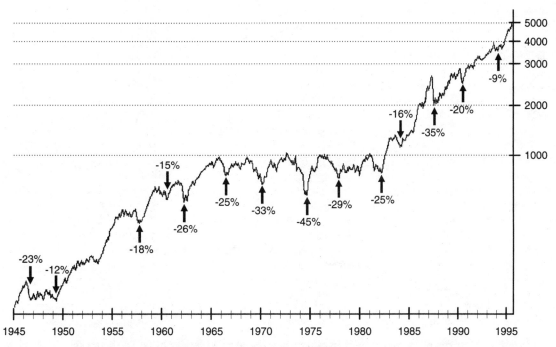

Figure 2-1. The Dow Jones Industrial Averages, 1946–1995. Despite a 2500% return over 50 years, the long bull market has often been interrupted by negative periods. The arrows on the chart indicate the largest drawdowns. Most are concentrated in the 1970s. Drawdowns are calculated on weekly closing prices. Note that the more recent 1987 crash does not appear unusual when seen with past performance and plotted on a logarithmic scale.

steady growth. When we invest for the long term, we need to remember this sound footing because there have been several long periods over which market performance has been quite disappointing. The government orchestrates economic growth and encourages the country to finance it by offering tax incentives and protective legislation. Although the results of these efforts are far from uniform, they are reflected in the stock market. This is one case in which we are certain that the government is on our side—if growth falters, we can expect the government to fix the problem, as it did in 1987.

It is important to remember that even a "risk-free" investment is not always risk-free. If we buy and hold a Treasury bill to maturity, which is usually only three months, we always get a positive return equal to the yield at the time of purchase. If we needed to liquidate that investment shortly after purchasing, our return is not guaranteed. The pro rata yield for 10 days may be offset by a sharp rise in interest rates, resulting in a loss. For example, we buy a one-year $10,000 Treasury bill yielding 4.0% for 9600. The next week, according to the Producer Price Index, inflation jumps and the Federal Reserve responds by raising interest rates $\frac{1}{2}$ point. At the same time you have a personal emergency that requires the liquidation of the Treasury bill that you just purchased. At the current rate of $5\frac{1}{2}$%, you get back

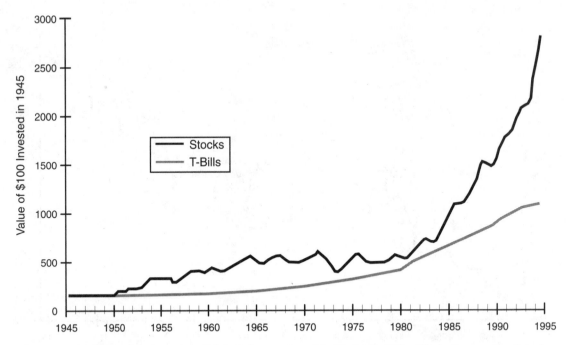

Figure 2-2. Returns of an investment in stocks compared to Treasury bills. The better results of stocks are evident, but the equity curve for the risk-free investment is very smooth.

about $9500, without transaction costs; therefore, your "risk-free" investment lost ½% in a few days.

The Bumpy Road of the Stock Market

We can understand more about equity investments by looking at the way that the Dow Jones Industrial Average moved before reaching the level of 5000 at the end of 1995 (shown in Figure 2-1). According to the Dow, 35 out of 50 years were winners for Wall Street. That means you have a 70% chance of a profitable year had you begun your investment at any time. Of those years, 50% produced double-digit gains.

The most rewarding year was 1954 with an increase of 44%, followed by 1975 (42.8%) and 1995 (33.4%). The worst years, those with a double-digit percent decrease in the Dow, were 1974 (−29%), 1966 (−18.9%), 1977 (−17.3%), 1973 (−16.9%), 1969 (−16.3%), and 1957 (−12.8%). If you are surprised not to see 1987 among the largest drops, remember that the market was very strong during the first nine months of 1987 and recovered enough after the October plunge to show a gain of 0.4% in the Dow by the end of the year. Three years out of the worst six were in the 1970s and also four of the six if we also consider the eve of the decade, 1969. That period was, as a matter of fact, especially disappointing for the equity investor. It is sometimes more difficult for an investor to bear a long unsatisfactory period rather than a single very bad year.

At the end of 1981 the Dow Jones Industrial Average was 8% below its 1968 level. The years between had shown very erratic and volatile market performance. From 1969 to 1972 the market increased 28% and then plummeted almost 41% in the following two years. It recovered 66% during 1975 and 1976 and lost ground again (−20%) in 1977 and 1978. It was a decade when many investors developed a "risk-averse" attitude. While the stock investor was struggling, those who chose Treasury bills had more than doubled their capital (+126%) without any drawdowns, thanks to historically high interest rates toward the end of the 1970s. That was equal to a compounded rate of return and an average yearly yield of 6.5%.

The worst drawdowns of the DJIA are shown in Table 2-2. Of the fourteen decreases greater than 10%, three of them are in the 1970s. The worst, and also the longest, was a drop of 45% from January 1973 to December 1974. The 1987 "crash" is the second worst period but lasted only four months.

The beginning of the 1980s showed a surge of young portfolio managers, especially in Europe, without any stock market experience. Until the renewed strength in the market attracted their attention, they had only considered fixed-rate investments for their clients. Having never seen a bull market during their professional life, they watched, along with their clients and other small investors, while the market climbed in the early 1980s. Small savers in particular lacked the confidence to enter the market and missed much of the first leg of this move. Many foreign investors were finally convinced that stocks were a good alternative, entering the market just ahead of the 1987 crash.

Table 2-2. Largest Drawdowns of the Past 50 Years

Period	% Drawdown
Jan. 73–Dec. 74	−45
Aug. 87–Dec. 87	−35
Nov. 68–May 70	−33
Sep. 76–Feb. 78	−29
Nov. 61–Jun. 62	−26
Feb. 66–Oct. 66	−25
Apr. 81–Aug. 82	−25
May 46–May 47	−23
Jun. 90–Oct. 90	−20
Mar. 56–Dec. 57	−18
Jan. 84–Jun. 84	−16
Jan. 60–Oct. 60	−15
Jun. 50–Sep. 50	−12
Jan. 53–Sep. 53	−11
Feb. 94–Apr. 94	−9

This look at the patterns of performance is to show that higher returns involve higher risk. The equity market suffers, with a certain cyclical recurrence, periods of poor performance that cause significant drawdowns for the investors. While those periods are part of the success of a 50-year investment portfolio, they are very hard to live through.

Measuring Market Risk

The level of risk that is part of the market should be as familiar to us as the rate of return, but we somehow manage to remember profits and opportunities and disregard risk. Consistent with this, the most common way to measure risk in the equities market is to use a calculation based on a long-term investment. Professional analysts have decided that the variation of yearly returns, rather than monthly or weekly, measured using a standard deviation, gives a good overall indication of risk and allows everyone to use the same language.

Risk, as with profits, is not usually pinpointed as a single value, but is normally given as a range of values or a probability. For example, we say there is a 5% chance that you will have a loss greater than 24% in the Dow in a single year. In general, the standard deviation measures how widely values vary from the average. The standard deviation of 50 yearly returns for the DJIA is about 16%, twice the 6.8% average compounded rate of return shown in Table 2-1.

When you apply the standard deviation formula to the change in prices, the result is a value called 1 *standard deviation*, which represents a clustering of 68% of all data around the average. For the 5-year example, 1 standard deviation of the Dow from 1990 to 1995 is approximately 420 points; therefore there is a 68% chance that the Dow will *rise or fall* 420 points from last year's level of 5117, a range of 4697 to 5537. Continuing further, there is a 95% chance that prices will vary less than 820 points this year (equal to 2 standard deviations) and a 99% chance it will remain within plus or minus 1230 points (3 standard deviations). Remember that these numbers give the probability of an event happening. The Dow can move anywhere; however, the chance of it moving above 6357 or below 3877, more than 3 standard deviations, is considered to be less than 1%. For those readers who do not use the standard deviation regularly, the next section gives some additional information on its calculation and use.

The Standard Deviation and Probability. The standard deviation is an accepted measurement for finding the likelihood of a price move and is used for determining the chance of a profit or loss of a certain size. In programming notation, this calculation is

standard deviation = @sqrt(@sum(list of (price change^2))/number of changes)

where the square root and summation functions are preceded with the symbol @ and the notation ^2 indicates that we are squaring the individual price changes (raising to the power of 2). Most computer software programs provide a built-in function that calculates the standard deviation, which will look similar to standard deviation = @StDev(price changes)

This may be understood more easily if we look at the steps needed to find the standard deviation using a spreadsheet. Assuming that column A, from 1 to 50, holds the year-end Dow values, then

Column B, row 2:	+A2 − A1	The price changes
Column C, row 2:	+B2^2	The square of the price changes
Column C, row 51:	@sum(B2 . . B50)	The sum of the squares of the price changes
Column C, row 52:	@sqrt(C51)	The value of 1 standard deviation

Again, we are not likely to go through this exercise because spreadsheet programs provide a standard deviation function that will give you the value in a single step:

| Column A, row 51: | @std(A1 . . A50) | The value of 1 standard deviation |

We use this value to find the probability that prices will remain below a specific level. Most often, we only look at the probabilities given by 1, 2, and 3 standard deviations:

- There is a 68% chance that prices will remain within the range given by the average plus or minus 1 standard deviation.

- There is a 95% chance that prices will remain within the range given by the average plus or minus 2 standard deviations.

- There is a 99% chance that prices will remain within the range given by the average plus or minus 3 standard deviations.

Using 50 years of the Dow given in Table 2-1 and applying the standard deviation calculation to the column 3, "% Change DJIA," we get an annual standard deviation of 16%. From this value of 1 standard deviation, we can create a simple list, Table 2-3, that shows there is less than a 2.3% chance that the Dow will rise more than 32% in one year or fall more than 32% in one year. Looking back at Table 2-2, there were 4 out of 50 years in which the index did rise more than 32%, and no years in which it fell more than 32%. Therefore, in reality, the Dow exceeded 32%

Table 2-3. How the Standard Deviation Relates to Price Moves

Standard deviation	Chance of a move up	Percentage Dow move	Expected range with +8% bias
0.5	30.8%	8%	+0% to +16%
1.0	15.9%	16%	−8% to +24%
2.0	2.3%	32%	−24% to +40%
3.0	0.1%	48%	−40% to +56%

in 8% of the cases, but taking the gains and losses together, we get 4 out of 100 cases, slightly lower than the 4.6% expected using the standard deviation.

The standard deviation also says that there is less than a 0.2% chance that the Dow will rise or fall more than 48%. Because there were no years in which that happened, the statistics seem accurate.

The standard deviation measures the way in which prices are grouped around the average. When we use price changes, rather than actual prices, then the average will be zero, provided prices have not changed much over time. Because the stock market has gained steadily, its average will be +7.96 for the past 50 years. This is called an *upwards bias*. The last column of Table 2-3 shows the range of probable movement in the Dow based on a positive 8% bias.

Plotting the Standard Deviation Distribution. The probabilities given by the standard deviation measurement always assume that price changes are distributed evenly in a normal bell-shaped curve, as seen in Figure 2-3, where the average price change is in the center. The values of 1, 2, and 3 standard deviations are measured from the average in both positive and negative directions.

Two points should be remembered when applying the standard deviation. Although calculations use price changes, rather than original prices, the bell-curve result is symmetric and does not show that stock market gains tend to be larger and more frequent than losses. This will be seen when we use the frequency distribution to look at price distribution in the following section. Also, price volatility has been increasing, even when price changes are expressed in percent; therefore, a more sophisticated measure, such as a logarithmic ("log"), should be considered if you are going to evaluate long periods of performance. To do this, the logarithm of each change in the Dow is used instead of the raw value. The result is then expressed as a logarithm and must be converted back to be useful.

Frequency Distributions. It is even easier, and just as useful, to view returns as a sorted bar chart or *frequency distribution*. In Figure 2-4 we see the 50 yearly returns sorted with the lowest on the left. The middle value, called the *median*, is 7.34% and is below the average of 8.0%. This is because the very large returns on the far right raise the average. We consider the median value more representative of the return that is likely to occur each year. As with the standard deviation, the median is available in all spreadsheet programs as the function @median. Unlike the standard deviation, the frequency distribution clearly shows the upwards bias of stock market returns, because the losing years fall far left of center.

The frequency distribution can also be used to decide the chances of a profit or loss during any year. In Figure 2-5 we have regrouped the yearly returns to show how many times the profits or losses fell within a range of returns. The total range from −29.0 to +44.0% was divided into 20 parts. We then counted the number of yearly returns that were below the value under the bar, but above the previous value. On the bar marked 7 along the bottom, there were five yearly returns that were no greater than 7% and above 4%. Because there are two years that were above 40 and below 44, we can say that history shows there is a 2 out of 50 (4%)

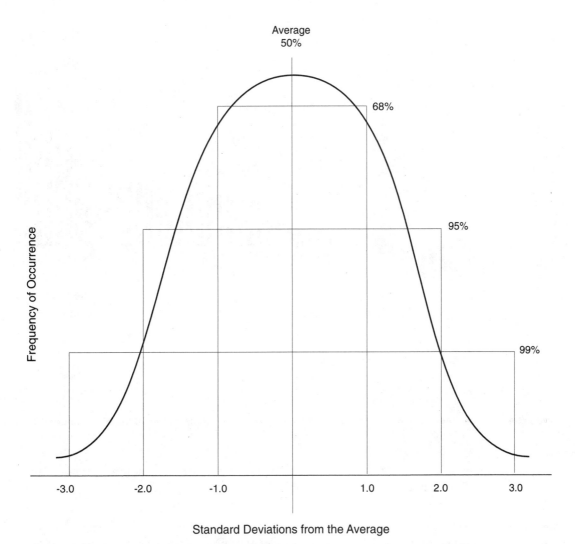

Figure 2-3. Bell curve representing the standard deviation of the Dow and the probability of change. This standard industry measurement assumes that returns are symmetrical, which is not the case.

chance of a return greater than 40%. There is also a 1 out of 50 (2%) chance of a loss below 25%.

If we draw a bell curve on the same chart (solid line), which shows the way the standard deviation would view the probability of returns, we see that the actual returns are skewed to the right. This is apparent from the two largest bars, which are both to the right of center, and by the positive extreme, which is nearly double the negative value. A dotted line has been drawn to approximate the shape of the skewed distribution. The amount of skewness tells us the upwards bias of the

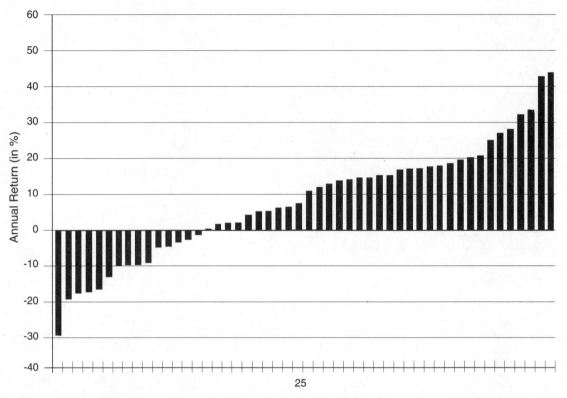

Figure 2-4. Sorted bar chart of Dow returns, 1946–1995. The middle value, falling at 25, shows that returns are noticeably skewed to the positive side.

market. For this type of chart, 50 years is not a lot of information; therefore, two smoothed lines show how this might look over time.

Risk and Return

The ratio of the average rate of return to the standard deviation of returns, called a *risk-adjusted ratio,* is a useful way of viewing profits relative to risk (more on this topic can be found in the book *Smarter Trading* by Perry J. Kaufman, McGraw-Hill, 1995). This method gives you a way of comparing two investments by finding the amount of profit for each unit of risk; therefore, we can also call it a *risk-adjusted return.*

$$\text{Risk-adjusted ratio (RAR)} = \frac{\text{Annualized rate of return}}{\text{Standard deviation of annualized returns}}$$

For example, an investment in company A has yielded an annualized return of 10% with a risk of 4% (1 standard deviation of the annual returns). Company B has a spectacular history of 25% returns but with a risk of 10%. Which is better? Of course, they are both the same, with a risk-adjusted ratio of 2.5 (10:4 and 25:10), or

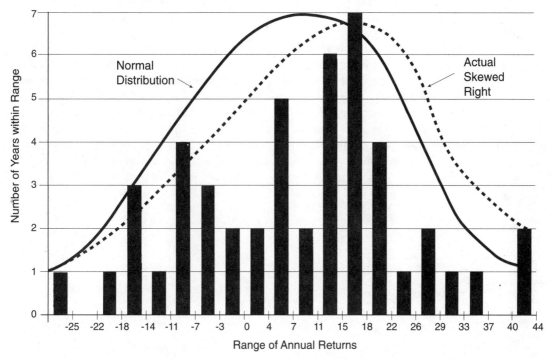

Figure 2-5. Frequency distribution of Dow returns, 1946–1995. By grouping the returns we can see that the most frequent returns are from 11 to 18%. Rather than a symmetric, bell-shaped curve, the distribution of real returns is skewed to the right.

2.5 units of profit for 1 unit of risk. On the other hand, if company C is a high-tech stock showing a three-year return of 35% and fluctuations resulting in a risk of 20%, while company D posted a gain of only 15% with a risk of 6%, then company D is clearly the best choice. Its risk-adjusted ratio is 2.50 compared to a 1.75 ratio for company C. Company D offers more profit for the same unit of risk.

As the risk-adjusted ratio gets smaller, the potential risk increases. A better ratio can come from either a higher return, without increasing the risk, or a lower risk (standard deviation), without decreasing the returns. You can choose an investment with both lower returns and lower risk and still be making a sound choice. A value of RAR = 1 means that there is a 68% chance (1 standard deviation) that the profit or loss in one year will be 16% for the Dow, equal to the rate of return itself. Because the Dow itself has an RAR of only 0.42 (using the compounded rate of return 6.8%, divided by the standard deviation of 16%), this can be our benchmark for risk and return. As this indicator gets closer to zero, the investment becomes more volatile and the risk becomes extremely large compared to the potential profit. The investment is not worth the risk.

We can see that the risk-free Treasury bill had a very high ratio of 1.48 (4.7% divided by 3%), compared to 0.42 for the Dow, despite the lower returns of

Treasury bills. The equity market is therefore more rewarding in the long run, but considerably riskier.

Ranking Stocks by Risk-Adjusted Ratio.   By dividing the annualized rate of return by the standard deviation of annual changes we get a ratio that shows the amount of profit for each unit of risk. This allows us to select which investment is best. Because one stock with a return of 15% and a risk of 20% is the same as another stock with a return of 7.5% and a risk of 10%, the final decision becomes one of *risk preference*. Is a higher return and higher risk more attractive than a lower return and a lower risk? No one can answer that question for you.

Figure 2-6 shows how return and risk can be plotted to see the comparative ranking of stocks. When choosing a stock using this method, those higher and to

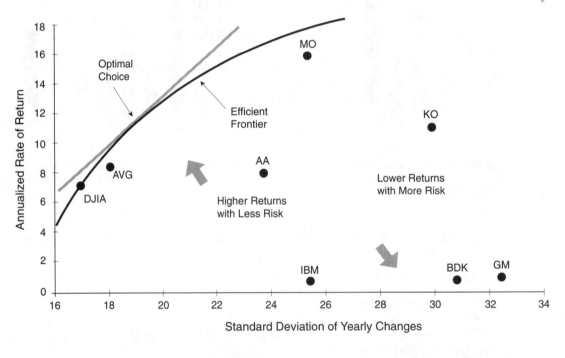

	DJIA (DJIA)	General Motors (GM)	IBM (IBM)	Coca-Cola (KO)	Philip Morris (MO)	Black & Decker (BDK)	Alcoa (AA)	Stocks Average (Avg.)
Average Yearly Return	8.8%	5.7%	4.5%	17.3%	20.1%	6.8%	9.7%	10.7%
Standard Deviation of Returns	17.0%	32.2%	25.3%	29.7%	25.2%	30.7%	23.6%	17.9%
Risk-Adjusted Ratio	0.425	0.045	0.049	0.386	0.637	0.041	0.350	0.474

Figure 2-6. Risk vs. reward of selected stocks and averages. Each stock is positioned by its annualized return (left axis) and risk (bottom axis), and form a curve across the upper left part of the chart, called the *efficient frontier*. This curve usually goes up sharply at the lower far left, then flattens out as it moves higher and to the right, indicating that risk grows faster than returns. Although Philip Morris has the highest risk-adjusted return, traditional asset allocation will choose stocks from that area of the efficient frontier where a straight line drawn from the current risk-free rate of return touches a point on the top of the curve.

the left are better choices. The curve drawn across the top of the best performers is called the *efficient frontier* and represents the best choices at all levels of return. The curve flattens out as it moves to the far right, because there are no stocks that have unlimited returns, and those with very high profits also have very high risk. A "rational" investor, who must select between one of two stocks, will always choose the one that is higher than and to the left of the other.

Because it is a relative measure, you can get more information using the standard deviation of monthly returns, rather than annual. Traditionally, however, analysts compare yearly figures.

We can compare the plot of risk and return with a simple list of risk-adjusted ratios (RARs) to see two slightly different views of the same issue. According to both presentations, General Motors, Black & Decker, and IBM fall at the bottom of the choices. The RARs are all below 0.05 and the stocks fall in the far lower right portion of the chart. Philip Morris, on the other hand, has the same risk as IBM, but a return of 16.0% instead of 1.2%. Based on history, any rational investor would choose Philip Morris over IBM.

The choice between the Dow and Philip Morris is not as clear. Let us say we could trade the Dow by using the S&P 500 or some other available index market. Then we need to choose between the Dow, with a 7.25% return and a risk of 17%, or Philip Morris, with a 16.0% return and a risk of 25.2%. One has lower risk and lower return, while the other has higher risk and higher return. The RAR favors Philip Morris, with a ratio of 0.63 compared to the Dow ratio of 0.42, but the final choice is the investor's. At some level, no one wants to take a high risk, regardless of the potential returns.

Other Useful Calculations

We have used certain values in the previous pages that you should be able to calculate yourself. Fortunately, we are in an era of computers, and most of the formulas in this book can be solved by using a spreadsheet program or most hand-held calculators. Still, it is important to understand the method in order to recognize an error. The following calculations are given in a form easily adapted to both computer programming and spreadsheets.

Compounded Rate of Return. When you have the starting and ending values of your equity you can calculate the compounded rate of return (see Table 2-4), in whole percent, for the period that the investment has been held.

Compounded annualized rate of return =
((Ending value/Starting value)^(1/Years)−1.0)*100

where the symbol ^ is the computer spreadsheet notation for "raising to a power" or "exponentiation."

The *return to risk ratio* is simply the ratio between the compounded rate of return, or the annualized return, and the standard deviation of yearly returns. This

Table 2-4. Calculating the Compounded Annualized Rate of Return
The figures below can be used to check your calculations of compounded annualized rate of return and standard deviation. Note that column B calculates the standard deviation on the raw prices, giving a much higher value than column C in which the standard deviation was calculated from the price changes. Using price changes "detrend" the data, making the average close to zero over the long term, and gives a more accurate picture of price fluctuation around the trend. Column D shows the same values as C in percent, and column E gives the value of the Dow by applying the calculated CROR to the starting value of 2629.20. The risk-adjusted returns (RAR) are 14/10.9 = 1.28 for these five years, far above the historic returns because there are no declining years.

Row	A	B	C	D	E
1	Year	DJIA	Change	% Change	Estimated value
2	1990	2629.20			
3	1991	3101.52	472.32	0.180	3003.74
4	1992	3301.11	199.59	0.064	3431.63
5	1993	3754.09	452.98	0.137	3920.48
6	1994	3844.44	80.35	0.021	4478.96
7	1995	5117.00	1282.56	0.334	5117.00
8					
9	**Average**	3622.89	497.56	0.147	
10	**StDev**	780.72	419.93	0.109	
11	**CROR**	14%			

value allows you to compare the results of different items as though each one began with the same size investment and all of them had the same risk. Examples of this were given in Chapter 1.

Spreadsheet Notation. If you have a column of numbers on a spreadsheet, representing the account value at the end of each year, as shown by the DJIA from 1990 to 1995, then you can calculate the basic values for risk and return (in whole percent) by using the following code:

Compounded rate of return $((B7/B2)^{(1/(@count(B7 .. B2)-1))}-1)* 100$
Standard deviation   @STD(C7 .. C3)
RAR = Return/risk (in %)   +B9/C10

If you are using monthly returns, rather than yearly, simply divide the number of rows (less 1) by 12 for the annualized rate of return. The standard deviation, however, does not translate as easily. The annualized standard deviation, that is, the standard deviation resulting from using the change in the DJIA each year, is not 12 times the size of the standard deviation of the monthly prices. Risk does not double when the time period doubles but flattens out as shown by the efficient frontier in Figure 2-6. Because the relationship between daily and monthly price variation is not very consistent, it is always best to begin with the values you want to use in your calculation.

Performance of Individual Stocks

So far, we have looked at the performance of the market through the eyes of an index, the Dow Jones Industrial Average. A market index contains prices for a basket of stocks, 30 for the case of the Dow. Thus the analysis, based on the index, is similar to an investment in a portfolio of somewhat diversified stocks. Is it better to diversify than to choose only one or a few stocks? Of course, the answer is *yes!* The purpose of this book is to show how broad diversification is so important for reducing risk. To begin, we are going to review the results of few stocks separately and compare their performance to the market as a whole.

Table 2-5 shows the performance of a few large capitalization stocks of very popular U.S. companies, the same ones used in our previous example of risk and return. It covers a 25-year period from 1971 to 1995 and includes General Motors (GM), International Business Machines (IBM), Coca-Cola (KO), Philip Morris (MO), Black & Decker (BDK), and Aluminum Company of America (Alcoa)(AA). They were chosen because of their obviously different business focus.

It may be that the patterns of the individual stock prices will be a surprise to you. Nevertheless, our aim is not to analyze the fundamental reasons that allowed the consumer industry and related stocks to far outperform giants such as General Motors and IBM. Despite highly different returns, all of them show a common factor: a standard deviation of yearly results that is nearly twice the size of the Dow. A stock with a disappointing performance, such as General Motors, which only rose 44% in 25 years, has almost the same standard deviation of returns as Coca-Cola, which rose more than 2000%. Philip Morris, with sustained growth that yielded a total compounded rate of return of 18% in 25 years, has a lower standard deviation of returns (see Figure 2-7).

The profit to risk ratios, or risk-adjusted returns, of these stocks are very different from one another. For the worst performers the ratios are close to zero, indicating very little return for a lot of risk. A high deviation may be offset by an excellent return, as in the case of Philip Morris, whose profit to risk ratio is at a reasonable 0.7.

The investment profile of the Dow is, in most cases, much better than those of the single stocks. The Dow shows a 17% standard deviation compared to 28% for the average standard deviation of the six individual stocks. The risk-adjusted returns for the Dow are the highest, with the exception of Philip Morris. It is particularly interesting to compare the Dow with Coca-Cola, which had nearly twice the rate of return and twice the deviation in yearly results. Therefore, the risk-adjusted ratio gives values that are similar to what we would expect.

Table 2-5. Twenty-Five Year Performance of Six Selected Stocks

	DJIA (DJIA)	General Motors (GM)	IBM (IBM)	Coca-Cola (KO)	Philip Morris (MO)	Black & Decker (BDK)	Alcoa (AA)	Stocks average (AVG)
1971	6.1%	−0.1%	5.9%	43.7%	41.3%	36.3%	−23.8%	17.2%
1972	14.6%	0.9%	19.5%	21.9%	68.5%	39.5%	22.0%	28.7%
1973	−16.9%	−43.2%	−23.3%	−14.7%	−2.7%	−7.4%	36.7%	−9.1%
1974	−29.0%	−33.2%	−31.9%	−58.1%	−16.4%	−37.0%	−38.5%	−35.8%
1975	42.8%	87.1%	33.5%	54.9%	10.3%	10.7%	29.3%	37.7%
1976	16.8%	41.6%	24.5%	−4.0%	16.6%	−13.4%	48.1%	18.9%
1977	−17.3%	−20.0%	−2.2%	−5.4%	0.3%	−21.8%	−18.5%	−11.3%
1978	−3.1%	−13.6%	9.2%	17.6%	14.0%	5.6%	2.4%	5.9%
1979	4.2%	−7.6%	−13.3%	−21.3%	2.0%	38.3%	14.9%	2.2%
1980	15.2%	−9.9%	5.0%	−0.6%	20.2%	−20.1%	8.7%	0.6%
1981	−9.5%	−14.4%	−16.2%	4.1%	12.6%	−17.7%	−14.1%	−7.6%
1982	19.6%	61.4%	69.2%	49.6%	23.2%	19.8%	21.0%	40.7%
1983	20.3%	19.3%	26.8%	2.9%	19.6%	45.5%	44.8%	26.5%
1984	−4.3%	8.2%	0.9%	16.6%	12.4%	−10.9%	−17.6%	1.6%
1985	28.1%	−8.1%	26.3%	35.5%	9.6%	−8.5%	4.1%	9.8%
1986	25.1%	−6.2%	−22.8%	34.0%	62.6%	−24.4%	−12.0%	5.2%
1987	0.4%	−7.0%	−3.8%	1.0%	18.8%	16.2%	38.0%	10.5%
1988	11.9%	36.0%	5.5%	17.0%	19.4%	22.5%	19.8%	20.0%
1989	27.0%	1.2%	−22.8%	73.1%	63.4%	−15.7%	33.9%	22.2%
1990	−4.5%	−18.6%	20.1%	20.4%	24.3%	−51.9%	−23.2%	−4.8%
1991	18.0%	−16.0%	−21.2%	72.6%	55.1%	81.2%	11.7%	30.6%
1992	6.4%	11.7%	−43.4%	4.4%	−3.9%	6.6%	11.2%	−2.2%
1993	13.7%	70.2%	12.2%	6.6%	−27.9%	8.9%	−3.1%	11.1%
1994	2.1%	−23.2%	30.1%	15.4%	3.4%	20.3%	24.8%	11.8%
1995	33.4%	25.5%	24.3%	44.2%	57.0%	48.4%	22.1%	36.9%
% Return, 25 years	510.0	43.6	43.8	2065.4	5722.6	86.1	453.7	798.4
Compounded rate of return	7.2	1.5	1.2	11.5	16.0	1.3	8.3	8.5
Average yearly return	8.8%	5.7%	4.5%	17.3%	20.1%	6.8%	9.7%	10.7%
Standard deviation of returns	17.0%	32.2%	25.3%	29.7%	25.2%	30.7%	23.6%	17.9%
Risk-adjusted ratio	0.425	0.045	0.049	0.386	0.637	0.041	0.350	0.474

Diversification Is the Key

We can combine the six stocks of our example into a single portfolio to show the benefit of diversification. Assume that we bought an equal number of shares (only one share will be used in this example) in each company. This portfolio of only a few equally weighted equities would have doubled the performance of the index. Should we be pleased with the results? Not until we look at the risk. And, do not forget that these stocks were chosen arbitrarily; you should not be satisfied with these returns until you have compared them against a broader sample. Another set

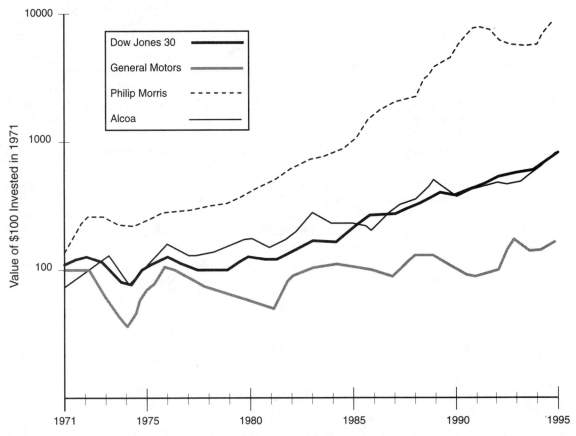

Figure 2-7. Three blue-chip companies compared to the Dow. Based on stock appreciation only, $100 invested in 1971 in Philip Morris would be $5800 at the end of 1995. The same investment in General Motors would be $143.

of stocks, which represents a selection of very different sectors, could give even better returns; choosing only one company from each sector is not the best approach.

As it turns out, the standard deviation of the yearly returns for our sample portfolio is also higher than the Dow. Because our sample portfolio return was also higher, the return to risk ratio remains at 0.47, a good level, and a little above the Dow ratio of 0.425. However, we will see that smaller portfolios have more uncertainty than larger, more diverse ones.

Put Your Eggs in Several Baskets

Diversification is a valuable tool to reduce risk for the buy-and-hold investor. Take the case of the best performer of our example, Philip Morris. It gave excellent results that frequently beat the market. Nevertheless, in 1993, the stock lost 27% while the index rose 14%—a difference of 41%.

In the same year one of the stars of Wall Street was General Motors (GM), rising 70%. Even though GM was one of the worst performers over the 25 years that we studied, it was occasionally a bright star when other stocks were dark. In 1975, General Motors was up 87% while the Dow rose 43% and Philip Morris gained only 10%; over the past 50 years, there are many other interesting combinations.

Diversification is a precious tool to smooth out investment ripples, but it does not fix all of the problems. During a broad bear market, when nearly every stock is down over a period of years, it is hard to find a single investor or portfolio that produced a profit by owning stocks. Of course, hindsight allows us to find stocks that would have profited in any market; however, that is unrealistic, and we will avoid using that method here. We will remember that if the investment objective is long term, then good diversification should reduce the volatility of an investment, whatever its exposure.

A typical portfolio mix of stocks and fixed income will also be improved by diversification (see Figure 2-8). A 50-year investment, from 1945 to 1995, one half in stocks and the other half in Treasury bills, produced a 1792% return, corresponding to a compounded annual rate of return of 6.1%. The standard deviation of yearly results was 8.3%; therefore, our return to risk ratio is 0.72, well above that

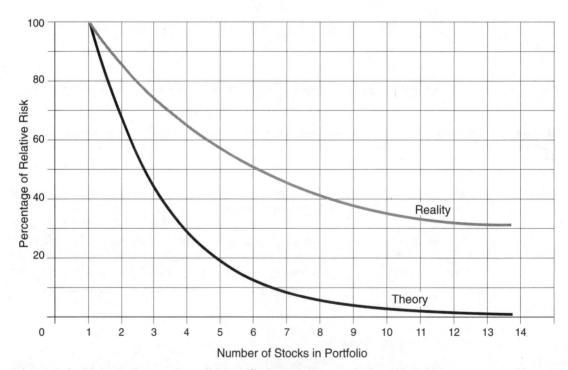

Figure 2-8. Risk vs. the number of diversified stocks. In an ideal world, risk drops as you add more diversification to your portfolio. In reality, the amount of risk reduction is based on the similarity of the stocks that are selected, and how the market moves as a whole during the next economic crisis.

of stocks alone. More often, a stock and bond portfolio has 60% stocks and 40% fixed income, which then increases both risk and return expectations.

Diversification, by adding fixed income to equities, significantly reduces the risk of drawdowns, but the potential reward decreases as we make the risk-free portion larger. The investor, in this case, should choose the solution that best fits his or her degree of risk preference.

Risk Here and Risk There

The secular trend of the equity market, throughout most industrialized countries, has been up for nearly 20 years, and the strength of that trend seems to be increasing. That is good news for most investors, and in particular for those who are in the market for the long term. But even the past has shown sideways and bear markets that cause even the staunch, veteran saver to take notice. After ten years of sideways stock prices, fixed income begins to be tempting; just as now, with returns reaching unprecedented high levels, the stock market is drawing in many investors who would have previously thought it too risky.

We are all prepared to accept a certain amount of increased risk to get much better returns. Most of us can look back at October 1987 painlessly, because the sharp plunge in the market was followed by a quick recovery. The government has shown that it will try to protect us from another seriously volatile period, and we tend to believe it (which seems strange, because we believe so little else of the government). But can we really be protected as much as we would like? With a 50-year view, does it matter if the market drops for five years? We will see that diversification is the most reliable tool for beating market risk and limiting portfolio volatility. It is better for a small investor to buy an index-related mutual fund than a few individual stocks. It is even better to buy a variety of index markets.

When the U.S. market fell in 1987, so did other major world markets. When the United States lowers interest rates, other industrialized nations follow. Money flows from country to country in order to get the best returns, net of interest income, inflation, and foreign exchange rates. But there are other countries besides the United States that are financially strong. The value of the German mark strongly influences the European economies; therefore, the Bundesbank must consider the impact of its policies on its neighbors in the European Community. It may raise rates if inflation is high, even if U.S. rates remain unchanged. If the United States is refinancing its debt, it may be forced to raise rates to attract investments that might move away from the German bund. On the other side of the world, what happens in Japan, China, and Australia affects everyone. If the business climate changes in China or trade sanctions are put in place, then many U.S. companies would be hurt. If the London stock market falls, so will others. We are no longer in financial isolation.

Globalization of financial markets has added vulnerability to our investments. We may not be able to see the risk that begins in another part of the world, and we may not profit from economic expansion in other time zones. As an investor in U.S. stocks, we get most of the world risk but little of its advantage. While even professional portfolio managers in the United States have moved at least 20% of their holdings outside of the United States, most investors only look for opportunities in their own familiar territory. We will take you outside that boundary and show how easy it is to take advantage of world stocks to gain opportunity and to reduce national and world risk.

Riding the Wave of International Expansion: The Results of a Buy-and-Hold Portfolio of International Markets

Being and Becoming

If Wall Street is universally recognized as the biggest and most prestigious stock market, other countries deserve special attention because they represent a large part of the total wealth in the world. In the evolution of our society, its historical events and social changes generate continuous switches in the role and importance that each country plays in the world economy.

Before the twentieth century, the United States was an emerging market. The undisputed sovereign in finance and wealth was the United Kingdom. It was not Wall Street but the City of London that represented the most important location for exchanges and the center of trade. Thanks to its colonies around the world, the British Empire had control over the importing of a wide range of raw materials to trade throughout Europe.

This marks the origin of modern futures markets. Because of the exceptional length of the sea journeys, goods were traded before their arrival. The high risk of shipwreck stimulated an entire financial support network—insurance—which created the fortunes of Lloyds of London. The movement of raw materials by sea, and their trade, was the most important driving force for the preindustrial economies. The Mediterranean powers all owed their affluence to sea trade. Among the great trade centers, such as Athens, Istanbul, and Venice, it is not a coincidence that Genoa, the city of Christopher Columbus, was where the insurance industry developed.

These references to history are a reminder of how often wealth has changed hands and how many centuries this process has continued. Our time may be different from that of the past because technology, mainly communications, has caused everything to change faster. While it may be that our view of rapid changes only applies to small, less important segments of the world economy, there is reason to think that the flow of wealth is moving across the world, distributing more evenly than during the days when the United Kingdom ruled and changing hands more rapidly.

Japan is the best example of recent change. Its economy was desperately poor in 1945, when World War II ended. In less than ten years, the 1950s represented a flourishing decade for the Nipponic industries and Japan became a fast-growing emerging market. In the 1980s, only 40 years after economic devastation, this country shared the rule of world economy with the United States. Now, after a severe financial crisis, including economic deflation, many giants of the international electronic and auto industries are looking outside of Japan and exploiting other, new favorable environments for production. In turn, the countries of southern Asia are growing at an unprecedented pace, and the financial centers of the world wait to see how the role of China will develop.

Europe is also witnessing important changes. The ex-communist countries are now benefiting from western European investments, especially those of Germany. And Germany's situation is quite similar to that of Japan. Its recovery, following the war, has been so fast and strong that it is again one of the most powerful economies in the world. Now, at the end of the twentieth century, Germany is facing postindustrial problems that are pressuring its prestigious multinational industries to invest abroad, where plants and wages are cheaper. This, in turn, redistributes wealth.

For the first time in the history of the world, manufacturing now moves to the source of the cheapest labor, where before it had been located at the point of natural resources. A product can be made anywhere in the world and delivered to any other place. This process will cause a shift of wealth, raising the standards of the poorest nations. These continuous changes among countries and their economies are causing shifts in different investment environments around the world. Often, when one market is sluggish there is another that offers a desirable opportunity.

A World of Differences

In the long run, all markets tend to go up, and when the major markets temporarily move down they affect almost all other countries. Nevertheless, there are times when, for very different reasons, some markets will move their own way and keep their independence for years. Usually, this detachment is the result of radical changes in the social or economic environment of a country, such as the development of a strong policy to correct internal inflation or stimulate growth.

This potential economic independence of world markets is the most important reason for choosing international diversification when investing rather than a single market. Table 2-6 and Figure 2-9 show the returns of six important world equity markets over the 25 years from 1971 to 1995. All of them, the United Kingdom, Germany, Japan, Switzerland, Italy, and the United States, reflect expanding economies with market growth. The U.K. market was the best performer, posting a 1204% total return, corresponding to an annualized compounded rate of return of 10.8%. This was followed by Japan, which netted 910% in 25 years for a yearly return of 9.6%. The least appealing market, based on pure return, is Switzerland with 273%.

Adding Currency Changes

Those results, nevertheless, cannot be compared to one another because they all required the use of local currency. While the British investor would have had a 1204% return on his or her pounds sterling, the Japanese trader would have yielded 910% in yen. A German investor, however, must have converted his or her

Table 2-6. Yearly Results of Six Main Equity Markets, Calculated in Local Currencies

	U.K.	Germany	Japan	Switzerland	Italy	U.S.
1971	38.7%	5.6%	36.6%	13.1%	−15.8%	6.1%
1972	10.5%	13.6%	91.9%	18.5%	7.9%	14.6%
1973	−30.8%	−21.1%	−17.3%	−22.0%	17.7%	−16.9%
1974	−54.4%	−0.1%	−11.4%	−35.8%	−29.1%	−29.0%
1975	141.3%	35.7%	14.2%	42.4%	−6.5%	42.8%
1976	−1.0%	−7.7%	14.4%	4.9%	−9.5%	16.8%
1977	41.4%	8.4%	−2.4%	5.1%	−25.7%	−17.3%
1978	4.7%	6.9%	23.4%	−3.4%	23.6%	−3.1%
1979	5.2%	−11.6%	9.5%	7.8%	19.8%	4.2%
1980	27.1%	−2.1%	7.5%	1.8%	108.8%	15.2%
1981	5.7%	−0.7%	8.8%	−13.9%	13.2%	−9.5%
1982	21.9%	14.4%	4.4%	9.8%	−14.8%	19.6%
1983	19.9%	39.1%	23.4%	24.2%	15.4%	20.3%
1984	23.2%	8.3%	16.7%	2.1%	20.3%	−4.3%
1985	14.7%	64.3%	13.3%	57.0%	98.4%	28.1%
1986	18.8%	8.0%	43.9%	6.5%	58.1%	25.1%
1987	2.0%	−37.1%	14.6%	−31.0%	−32.5%	0.4%
1988	4.7%	29.3%	39.4%	19.8%	20.8%	11.9%
1989	35.1%	34.7%	29.5%	18.1%	16.6%	27.0%
1990	−10.8%	−18.6%	−38.7%	−21.3%	−24.9%	−4.5%
1991	12.0%	6.2%	−3.6%	14.4%	−1.7%	18.0%
1992	17.0%	−5.8%	−26.4%	15.6%	−12.1%	6.4%
1993	20.7%	40.6%	2.9%	47.3%	38.8%	13.7%
1994	−10.3%	−7.4%	13.2%	−8.3%	2.1%	2.1%
1995	20.3%	4.0%	0.7%	21.9%	−6.8%	33.4%
Total return	1203.6%	335.2%	899.8%	273.4%	404.5%	510.0%
Compounded rate of return	10.8%	6.1%	9.6%	5.4%	6.7%	7.5%
Standard deviation of returns	33.6%	22.5%	25.5%	22.6%	35.4%	17.0%
Average yearly return	15.1%	8.3%	12.3%	7.8%	11.3%	8.8%
Risk-adjusted ratio	0.32	0.27	0.38	0.24	0.19	0.44

funds from Deutschemarks to pounds sterling in 1971 to take advantage of that market and then converted them back into Deutschemarks in 1995 to fully realize the profits. During these 25 years there were many changes due to inflation, politics, and interest rates in Germany, England, and Japan, all of which affected the rate at which these currencies changed hands. The currency exchange rate becomes an inseparable part of investing in world markets.

The 1970s and early 1980s have been characterized by high inflation and high interest rates in countries such as Italy and the United Kingdom, and very much

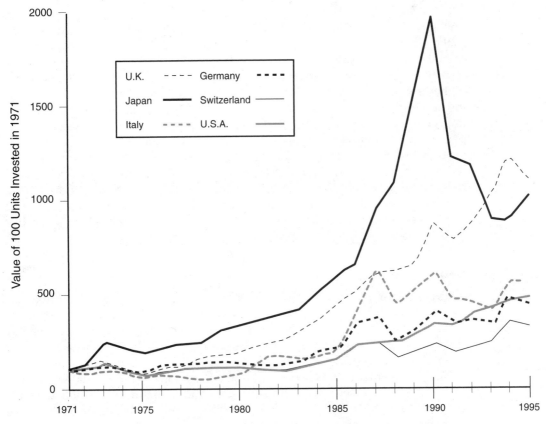

Figure 2-9. Performance of six major world equity markets, 1971–1995, in local currencies.

lower rates in Germany, Switzerland, and Japan. These latter countries have kept tight control over the fluctuations in their economies, and this has resulted in stronger currencies. The economic weakness of the United Kingdom and Italy, while far from the extremes of Mexico, has nevertheless caused a decline in trade and a generally lower exchange rate. The average three-month deposit yield for the 15 years from 1980 to 1995 has been 5.6% in Switzerland and 10.7% in the United Kingdom, reflecting the contrast in management and need for prolonged economic control in Great Britain.

The similarity of interest rates to the compounded rate of return of the two equity markets could seem to be a pure coincidence, yet it is not surprising. Strong economic growth, reflected in the value of equities, is watched carefully by governments for signs of inflation. To control this, a responsible central bank will raise interest rates until a satisfactory balance between growth and prices is reached. Therefore, a strong equity market is often accompanied by increasing interest rates.

Adding in Volatility

The analysis of yearly returns and their standard deviation better explains the *quality* of results, that is, why investors choose one market over another. The standard deviation of yearly returns, which shows the volatility of the market, tends to be higher for those countries that posted the best rates of return. Of course, the highest returns are counterbalanced by the deepest retracements, as seen by looking at the standard deviation and returns in Table 2-6. There is always an exception, and Italy shows the highest deviation despite a disappointing historic performance. Its market returned less than 7% annualized, despite double-digit yields in risk-free investments for almost the entire last quarter century. Thus, the risk-adjusted ratio, as described in the first section of this chapter, is the lowest for Italy. The best reading for this ratio, among the markets selected, is the United States at 0.44, with Japan and United Kingdom ranking next at 0.38 and 0.32, respectively. Our observation tells us that there is a minimum level of risk in all of these markets, regardless of returns.

The Charts Tell the Story

It is very important to study the individual markets by looking at their financial charts. This will help us to develop an understanding of the forces that act upon each, and it will allow us to form expectations of how each can be used effectively as we blend them together. In some cases, such as the British Financial Times 100 Index (FTSE-100), the past 20 years can be seen to have had exceptionally low volatility. Even though this period has lasted this long, it is unreasonable to expect such a uniform pattern to continue. You might compare that period with the Japanese Nikkei during the 15 years from 1975 through 1989. Although these two similar events were the result of very different economic situations, no one pattern can be sustained.

Figures 2-10 through 2-14 show the performance of each of the major markets with the most significant drawdowns indicated by arrows. The largest drawdowns, those over 15%, are summarized in Table 2-7. For every country, the 1970s were disappointing and the 1980s were bullish. The 1987 crash left a trace on the charts that can be compared to the footprint of an earthquake on the planet's seismographs.

It is quite clear that every equity market is dominated by different economic considerations. Even during a bull or bear market that influences the whole world, somewhere there is an economy moving independently. Even among highly interactive countries that are strong trading partners, global events impact each differently. During the Middle Ages, which were unenlightened centuries for Europe, other, distant cultures were experiencing a Renaissance. From the eleventh to the fifteenth century, the world's major advances were led by the Arabs, whose scientists, astronomers, poets, and artists flourished.

Throughout 1995, while Wall Street was collecting new highs, other markets were not performing as well. Germany, considered the driving economy in Europe, reflected investors' concerns about the ability to win over stagnation in

Figure 2-10. German equity index, FAZ, 1971–1995.

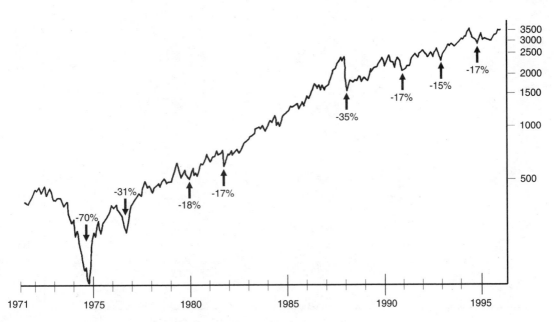

Figure 2-11. British equity index, FTSE-100, 1971–1995.

Figure 2-12. Japanese equity index, Nikkei 225, 1972–1995.

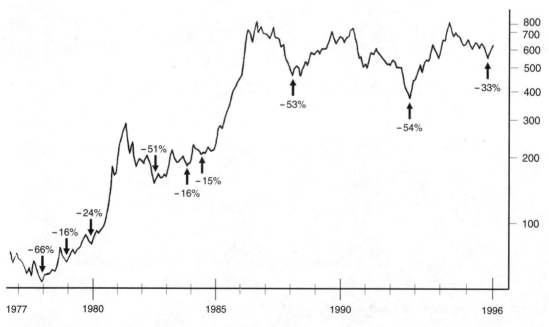

Figure 2-13. Italian equity index, COMIT, 1976–1995.

Figure 2-14. Swiss equity index, SMI, 1971–1995.

private consumption, exports, and employment that became serious obstacles to its economic recovery. Switzerland faced very similar problems due to an over-valued currency and its refusal to join the European Community in an environment strictly dependent upon trade with Europe.

In sharp contrast, the Japanese equity market, after some years of decline, began a recovery from historical lows that were equal to price levels witnessed ten years earlier. Italy's economy was, if not excellent, at least in better shape than others in Europe. Yet even its strong improvement in exports that followed a significant devaluation in their currency could not offset the negative effects of an exhausting political crisis. Figure 2-13 shows the result of Italy's internal struggle—nearly ten years of sideways markets.

Great Britain, because it is both an Anglo-Saxon country and an island, has an economy far less dependent upon the European Community and Germany and maintains many similarities to America. The movements of the British exchange, surprisingly, show a stronger correlation with Wall Street than with its neighbors.

These differences allowed room for unique market patterns in 1995, among even the strongest "globalized" countries. If we look a little further into the past we can find more significant divergences. For those readers who believe that glob-

Table 2-7. Market Drawdowns Greater Than 15% for Six Principal International Equity Markets, 1971 through 1995

United Kingdom		Germany		Japan		Switzerland		Italy		United States	
Period	%	Period	%	Period	%	Period	%	Period	%	Period	%
Sep. 72–Jan. 75	–70	Apr. 86–Jan. 88	–47	Dec. 89–Jul. 95	–65	Aug. 72–Dec. 74	–52	Jun. 73–Dec. 78	–66	Dec. 72–Dec. 74	–45
Jul. 87–Dec. 87	–35	Aug. 72–Oct. 74	–35	Feb. 73–Oct. 74	–34	Oct. 87–Dec. 87	–37	Jun. 90–Sep. 92	–54	Aug. 87–Nov. 87	–35
Apr. 76–Oct. 76	–31	Mar. 90–Sep. 90	–32	Oct. 87–Jan. 88	–20	Aug. 89–Jan. 91	–32	May 86–Feb. 88	–53	Sep. 76–Feb. 78	–29
May 79–Jan. 80	–18	Feb. 70–Nov. 71	–27	Aug. 81–Aug. 82	–15	Feb. 81–Aug. 82	–24	Jun. 81–Jul. 82	–51	May 81–Jun. 82	–25
Aug. 81–Aug. 82	–17	Oct. 78–Mar. 80	–22			Feb. 94–Mar. 95	–21	May 94–Dec. 95	–33	Jul. 90–Oct. 90	–20
Jan. 90–Sep. 90	–17	Mar. 76–Oct. 76	–16			Jan. 78–Nov. 78	–16	Oct. 80–Nov. 80	–19	Nov. 83–May 84	–16
Jan. 94–Jun. 94	–17	Dec. 93–Mar. 95	–16					Oct. 79–Dec. 79	–18		
May 92–Aug. 92	–15							Apr. 83–Dec. 83	–16		
								Feb. 84–Jun. 84	–15		

alization is a one-way street we can suggest that emerging economies will still offer these opportunities far into the future. And, as demonstrated by the Soviet Union, there are occasional setbacks, even on a one-way street. Figure 2-15 shows the astonishing market rally that occurred in Italy between 1985 and 1986. Italy experienced a surprising and remarkable boom after years of deep crisis. Its performance outpaced all other world markets.

A very familiar example can be seen by comparing the U.S. Dow Jones Industrial Average with the Japanese Nikkei. Figure 2-16 shows the two markets between 1986 and 1992. Until 1990, the Nikkei was clearly outperforming the Dow. During the four years ending in 1989, it gained nearly 200%, while the Dow increased only 80%. The market plunge of October 1987 was less than half the depth for the Nikkei as for the Dow Jones Industrial Average. It took only six months for the Japanese market to recover to its precrash level and record new highs. It took almost one year for Wall Street to do the same. From 1990 the relationship between the two markets was entirely reversed. While the Dow Jones continued its bull move, the Nikkei fell steadily.

History is filled with similar examples. The result is a heterogeneity of moves, allowing investors a wealth of opportunity, especially for risk reduction, which we

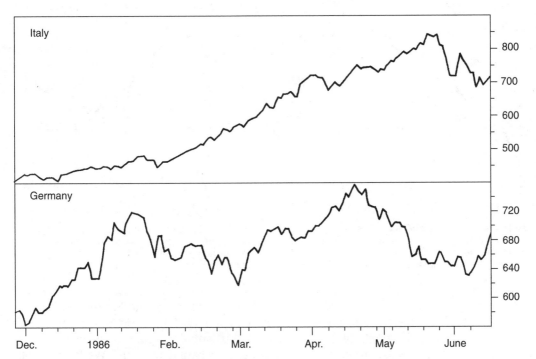

Figure 2-15. Contrasting Italian and German market performances. In 1986, Italy sharply outperformed the other European markets, despite a disappointing longer-term performance. The comparison between the Italian and German indices shows the strong recovery of the Italian market that produced a three-digit return, while Germany could hardly generate an uptrend.

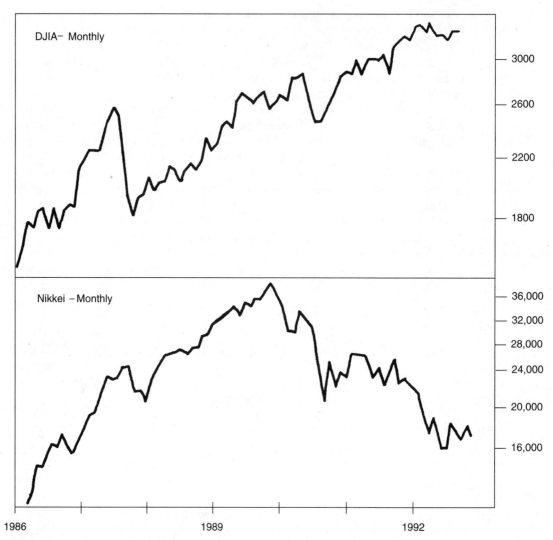

Figure 2-16. The U.S. and Japanese markets. Until 1990, Japan was clearly outperforming the United States. During the four years ending in 1989, the Nikkei returned 200% while the Dow yielded only 80%. This was partly due to the Nikkei's much smaller drop in 1987 and its faster recovery. From 1990, the relationship between the two markets has reversed. While the Dow continued in its bull market, the Nikkei fell.

consider possibly better than profits. Even if the global market trend is up, the results are often reached over different time periods. Highs and lows displace each other, and the length of the moves differ substantially. Again we choose an example of different market behavior during a particular moment. We look at 1987 because of the combination of a strong rally followed by extreme market volatility that accompanied the October drop. Table 2-8 compares those moves for the six markets used in our examples. The differences are seen not only in the yearly per-

Table 2-8. Comparison of Market Reactions to the 1987 Crash

	U.K.	Germany	Japan	Switzerland	Italy	U.S.
	Price Levels					
Year ending 1986	1679	676	18821	678	723	1930
Highest precrash level	2443	677	26646	734	767	2747
Lowest precrash level	1565	400	21036	454	476	1638
Year ending 1987	1713	425	21564	467	488	1939
	Percentage Price Moves					
Highest 1987 from 1986 end	45.5	0.1	41.6	8.3	6.1	42.3
Maximum 1987 high to low range	−35.9	−40.9	−21.1	−38.1	−37.9	−40.4
Lowest 1987 to end 1987	9.5	6.3	2.5	2.9	2.5	18.4
1987 Year-end performance	2.0	−37.1	14.6	−31.1	−32.5	0.5

formances, but also in the way they were reached. The U.S. market, together with the British and the Japanese, had soared more than 40% before the crash, while Germany, Switzerland, and Italy were almost flat. The size of the crash was very uniform, with the exception of Japan, which dropped only 21%, half as much as the other markets. By the end of 1987 the Dow had recovered 18% from the lows while other countries were still very near the lows reached after the crash.

The Importance of Foreign-Exchange Changes on Returns

The individual market history, as shown by the indices of the country, is always reflected in local currency. When we acknowledge that the German FAZ (Frankfuter Allgemeine Index) gained 335%, we know that return was denominated in German marks. In order to participate in the German market, we must make our purchases in marks, in the same way that any business normally takes in only its own currency. If investors do not systematically protect themselves from the change in foreign-exchange rates, they are exposed to currency risk. This becomes an important added uncertainty that can only increase the volatility of their equity.

Foreign-exchange risk is an old problem. Most businesses involved in foreign trade adopt a policy of neutralizing this risk by purchasing foreign currency equal to their future obligations. In that way they lock-in the value of the currency at the current exchange rate. This enables them to ensure their expected profit on the business deal. Some firms choose to hedge only part of their obligations, but only if they have a strong opinion on the direction of the currency movement during the period they are exposed. This is often a successful and profitable decision, and little is heard of it. Occasionally, a Volkswagen or Metallgesellschaft proves that unprotected currency risk, or aggressive speculation in exchange rates, can far exceed the rewards.

The size of currency moves can be dramatic and often overwhelms those of the equity markets. Two-digit percent swings in a few months are quite likely in the foreign exchange, even between currencies representing solid economies. The U.S. dollar to German mark ratio moved in a 15% range in 1995, down from 25% in 1992 and 40% in 1985. Imagine the difference in your returns when you invest in German stocks with full currency risk protection or no protection at all. Currency movements can add gain to gains, offset gains, cancel losses, add losses to losses, turn losses into profits, or do the reverse.

The Latin American markets are particularly good examples because their enormous inflation in recent years has inflated stocks prices while at the same time devaluing their currencies. What was gained in the equities was offset in currency shifts. In 1995, the Mexican stock index rose 17% and the Venezuelan index almost 50%, based on local currencies. Those same indices, translated into U.S. dollars, produced losses of 23% and 11%, respectively, due to declines in currencies of 40% and 61% against the dollar. The European and Japanese currencies performed very differently. The Nikkei rose through 1995 along with the yen vis-à-vis the dollar, compounding equity holdings for the U.S. investor who remained unhedged in yen. The effects on the stock holdings for American investors changed significantly from the values we analyzed earlier.

Are Stocks or Currencies the Object of Your Foreign Investment Decision?

Techniques for handling foreign currency movements will be covered later in this book; however, this is a good time to think about the effects of currency changes on foreign equity holdings. Table 2-9 puts the change in a buy-and-hold equity position into U.S. dollars, rather than local currency, which was shown in Table 2-6. Four of the five other markets posted higher profits than Wall Street when seen in U.S. dollars. The sharp differences with the results in Table 2-6 may cause an immediate reaction that currency hedging is not advisable for the American investor because a large part of gains abroad were made selling the dollar. Japan, Switzerland, and Germany allowed the investor to get double-digit yearly compounded returns with only a small increase in the volatility of each market. Thus the risk-adjusted ratio for those markets, when translated into U.S. dollars, is much better than before and competitive with that of the Dow.

The most disappointing performance is seen in the Italian market. The lira is one of the few western currencies that did not appreciate against the dollar. Except for specific years such as 1980, 1985, and 1986, the stock market also did not perform well. This combination of high volatility and mediocre appreciation gives it the lowest risk-adjusted return. Because the British pound is related more closely to the dollar, the currency change did not do much to affect the relative returns. For an American investment in London, both returns and volatility declined slightly, leaving the risk-adjusted returns very similar.

Table 2-9. Yearly Results of Six Principal Equity Markets, Calculated in U.S. Dollars

	U.K.	Germany	Japan	Switzerland	Italy	U.S.
1971	46.8%	19.5%	54.8%	24.4%	−11.8%	6.1%
1972	1.8%	16.1%	100.4%	22.9%	10.0%	14.6%
1973	−31.7%	−6.5%	−11.0%	−9.5%	12.7%	−16.9%
1974	−53.8%	11.9%	−17.5%	−18.2%	−33.5%	−29.0%
1975	107.5%	24.8%	12.6%	38.5%	−11.4%	42.8%
1976	−16.7%	2.5%	19.1%	12.1%	−29.1%	16.8%
1977	59.8%	21.8%	18.6%	29.4%	−25.5%	−17.3%
1978	11.3%	23.3%	53.1%	18.6%	29.6%	−3.1%
1979	14.4%	−7.0%	−11.5%	9.2%	23.8%	4.2%
1980	36.9%	−14.4%	27.2%	−8.5%	80.5%	15.2%
1981	−15.5%	−12.2%	0.5%	−14.4%	−11.8%	−9.5 %
1982	3.4%	7.7%	−2.3%	−2.2%	−25.9%	19.6%
1983	7.3%	21.3%	25.0%	14.5%	−4.5%	20.3%
1984	−1.4%	−6.4%	7.4%	−14.7%	2.9%	−4.3%
1985	43.4%	112.8%	42.4%	98.9%	130.3%	28.1%
1986	21.2%	37.3%	82.0%	36.3%	97.0%	25.1%
1987	30.3%	−23.1%	49.6%	−12.6%	−22.1%	0.4%
1988	0.3%	14.7%	35.1%	1.4%	7.2%	11.9%
1989	20.9%	41.1%	12.6%	15.0%	20.3%	27.0%
1990	6.2%	−7.7%	−35.1%	−4.6%	−15.6%	−4.5%
1991	8.5%	4.1%	4.7%	6.8%	−3.5%	18.0%
1992	−5.5%	−11.6%	−26.3%	6.9%	−31.6%	6.4%
1993	18.3%	30.9%	15.0%	46.3%	19.8%	13.7%
1994	−4.9%	3.9%	26.8%	3.6%	7.9%	2.1%
1995	18.8%	11.9%	−2.8%	38.9%	−4.9%	33.4%
Total return	738.4%	1018.2%	3353.7%	1296.0%	97.7%	510.0%
Compounded rate of return	8.88%	10.14%	15.22%	11.12%	2.76%	7.50%
Standard deviation of returns	31.5%	26.8%	32.1%	25.7%	40.4%	17.0%
Average yearly return	13.1%	12.7%	19.2%	13.6%	8.4%	8.8%
Risk-adjusted ratio	0.28	0.38	0.47	0.43	0.07	0.44

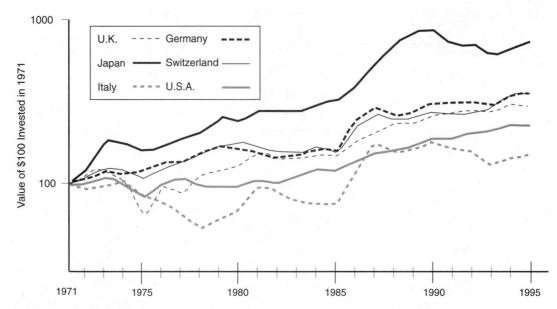

Figure 2-17. Market movement in U.S. dollars. The relative performance of six major equity markets, 1971–1995 (1971 = 100), converted to U.S. dollars and shown on a logarithmic scale. Note the major change in the returns of Japan compared to Figure 2-9.

Figure 2-17 deserves special attention and should be compared to Figure 2-9. It shows the returns of the same six markets, this time expressed in U.S. dollars. The differences between the two charts are enormous. It emphasizes that the foreign-exchange component cannot be disregarded for international investing.

Comparing Volatility

Where Is the Risk?

Many investors fear the equity market because of risk. Although the trend of stock prices is up, the results are reached over a bumpy road. Several well-known periods are characterized by ups and downs in stock prices that cause sharp capital drawdowns to investors. Strong, healthy trends are always followed by declines, cautiously called *corrections* by the financial industry. A correction is a natural retracement of the previous movement and, most of the time, is followed by a further upside move. The size and duration of those corrections are usually limited to periods that make investors nervous but do not cause panic. We have seen them over and over again, and there is nothing to worry about. You only need the patience to wait for the market uptrend to resume.

Periodically, a succession of corrections occurs one after another and we have a *bear market*. Once a bear market exists, the size of its downward slide and length are hard to forecast; its extent always seems to be related to how close to exhaustion you can bring the investor. If we look back at Figures 2-10 through 2-14 and

Table 2-6 we will see that every equity market in the world posted double-digit losses at least three times in a decade; most of those losses are greater than 20%.

The bear market is the true risk of a stock investment. But even bear markets come to an end, usually because of a remedy in government policy, however slow. If we want to benefit from the high secular potential of the market we need to evaluate that risk in order to live with it, or even better, to avoid it. To begin, we need to know the probable size of the market moves, and to do this we must measure the past volatility.

Shifting Returns

The analysis of the past tells us that not all the markets in the world have the same volatility at the same time. So far we have analyzed volatility using the standard deviation of the yearly changes in the market indices. We then compared the volatility to the compounded rates of return for the longer time span of 25 years.

If we separate the analysis into shorter time intervals we will see how the market patterns change from period to period. Table 2-10 shows how the best and the worst performers differ during each five-year period. There is a lot to learn by looking more closely at those periods.

Table 2-10. Comparison of CROR and Standard Deviations of Six World Equity Markets Grouped into Five-Year Periods from 1971 through 1995

There is no consistency in the best and worst countries. It is more likely that the best performer will become the worst and the worst will become the best as in the case of Germany.

	U.K.	Germany	Japan	Switz-erland	Italy	U.S.	Best	Worst
				Yearly Compounded Rates of Return				
1971–1975	3.1%	5.1%	17.0%	−0.9%	−6.7%	0.5%	Japan, Germany	Italy, Switzerland
1976–1980	14.4%	−1.5%	10.1%	3.2%	15.8%	2.4%	Italy, U.K.	Germany, U.S.
1981–1985	16.9%	23.0%	13.1%	13.5%	21.6%	9.8%	Germany, U.K.	U.S., Japan
1986–1990	8.9%	−0.8%	12.8%	−3.9%	2.5%	11.2%	Japan, U.S.	Switzerland, Germany
1991–1995	11.3%	6.2%	−3.6%	16.8%	2.7%	14.2%	Switzerland, U.S.	Japan, Italy
				Standard Deviations of Yearly Returns				
1971–1975	76.3%	20.7%	44.2%	31.7%	18.6%	28.0%	Italy, Germany	U.K., Japan
1976–1980	18.1%	8.8%	9.5%	4.3%	52.0%	14.1%	Switzerland, Germany	Italy, U.K.
1981–1985	7.1%	26.4%	7.3%	26.8%	42.5%	16.6%	U.K., Japan	Italy, Switzerland
1986–1990	17.6%	30.8%	33.5%	23.3%	37.0%	14.2%	U.S., U.K.	Italy, Japan
1991–1995	12.9%	19.4%	14.6%	19.9%	20.1%	12.1%	U.S., U.K.	Italy, Switzerland
				Risk-Adjusted Ratio				
1971–1975	0.041	0.247	0.385	−0.029	−0.358	0.018	Japan, Germany	Italy, Switzerland
1976–1980	0.798	−0.175	1.071	0.734	0.303	0.168	Japan, U.K.	Germany, U.S.
1981–1985	2.367	0.870	1.793	0.503	0.507	0.590	Japan, U.K.	Italy, Switzerland
1986–1990	0.504	−0.024	0.381	−0.170	0.067	0.795	U.S., U.K.	Germany, Switzerland
1991–1995	0.874	0.321	−0.245	0.846	0.133	1.174	U.S., U.K.	Japan, Italy

During the early 1970s the Japanese market grew at a 17% yearly compounded rate while the U.S. market was almost flat. That growth pace dropped to 10% for Japan in the second part of the decade, while Italy and the United Kingdom showed better results and Wall Street still remained confined to a wide-ranging sideways market. The bullish 1980s saw all of our sample markets reach double-digit yearly returns in the first part of the decade, but the United States, with a yearly 10% return, underperformed the market of Germany (23%) and Italy (22%). The situation changed substantially in the late 1980s when the U.S. market outperformed all but Japan, which was immediately followed by the Japanese market sharply reversing its position to become the worst performer of the early 1990s.

Positioning Markets by Volatility

Looking at these markets in terms of volatility, instead of only returns, will confirm this shifting of dominance. We see that the standard deviation of yearly returns for the British FTSE-100 was among the highest in the 1970s, and among the lowest in the 1980s and 1990s. However, neither returns or volatility alone determines the best investment. The risk-adjusted ratio, a comparison between the annualized compounded rate of return and the standard deviation of results (described in the first part of this chapter), combines performance and risk. When markets are less volatile they have less risk and are considered a better investment. The risk-adjusted ratio shows that markets have a longer cycle of favor with investors. Japan ranked at the top for 15 years, but has now become a poor return for risk and ranks last. Wall Street showed the opposite trend, as it rated high from 1986 to 1995, changing from being among the worst during the 1970s.

Diversification Flattens Volatility

These changing scenarios should first bring to mind some thoughts about how investments in these various countries would work together in a diversified stock portfolio. Would international diversification improve our profit and risk expectations? Once again, the answer is "yes," the same as we asserted in the section entitled "Diversification Is the Key," earlier in this chapter, where we concluded that a multistock choice is far less volatile than a single stock investment. Diversification reduces volatility and smooths the equity curve of our investment while still maintaining good yearly return.

If we had invested equally in the six countries given in the example, we would have had a 778% return over the 25 years from 1971 to 1995. This equally weighted portfolio corresponds to an investment at a compounded rate of 9.1% per year. This result is better than the performance of the Dow and only slightly lower than the result of the best performing markets, but it is achieved through a far lower volatility (as shown in Figure 2-18). This is particularly good because we did not have to decide, in advance, which markets to choose—we simply used them all.

The standard deviation of combined yearly returns is 18.4%, well below those of the single markets, only a little higher than the United States. And, while the United States has a smaller equity fluctuation, it also had lower returns of 510%

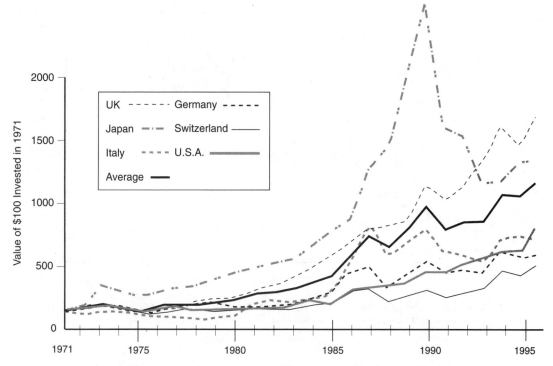

Figure 2-18. Comparing the performance of six sample markets with equally weighted diversification. Equal weighting gives each market the same relative importance and can serve as a benchmark for other allocation methods.

compared to 778% for the portfolio. Remember that this approach is still incomplete because it has not included the fluctuations of the original currencies of the foreign markets. It is as if we had not converted our dollars into those currencies but systematically covered the currency risk, creating a *fully hedged* portfolio, with no currency exposure.

The risk-adjusted ratio for the equally weighted portfolio is therefore better than any single market investment in our example, with a value very close to 0.5 (see the left column of Table 2-5). It is easy to conclude that a diversified international stock portfolio is better than any single market choice in terms of return; however, we can see its greatest value when we compare the risk.

The standard deviation of returns for the average (an equally weighted portfolio) is lower than that of most foreign markets and similar to that of the United States. The compounded rate of return is therefore a little smaller. We can get a clear idea of how such a diversification reduced the risk by comparing the drawdowns of the portfolio with those of the individual markets for the worst periods, those that produced a decline greater than 15% of the stock price. Figures 2-10 through 2-14, which have the individual drawdowns marked, were summarized in Table 2-6.

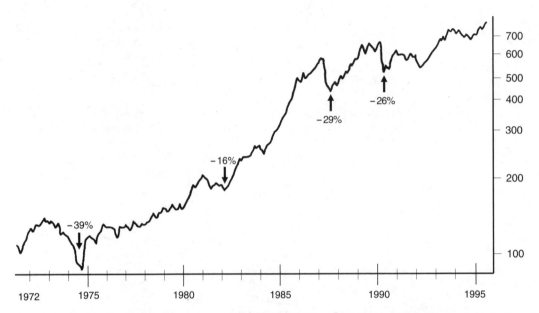

Figure 2-19. Equity curve for an equally weighted diversified portfolio of six international indices, showing largest drawdowns. Drawdowns are all smaller than those of the individual markets.

Figure 2-19 plots the course of the average investment in those five markets plus the United States, where each market represents one sixth of the global investment. Currency considerations are not taken in account. Despite three considerable plunges, one in the early 1970s (−39%), another due to the 1987 crash (−29%), and the last during the Persian Gulf crisis (−26%), none of these declines were as large as any of the largest drawdowns of the individual markets, shown on the top line of Table 2-6. The greatest portfolio drop of 39% is far lower than that of the United Kingdom, Italy, or Switzerland, even though those markets are included equally in the results. International diversification gives the investor more comfort than using any one market alone, without his or her having to decide in advance which market to choose.

Changing the Weighting Rules

This analysis, nevertheless, is overly simplified. First, we have arbitrarily chosen five markets to use with the United States. In fact, we did not consider other important markets such as France, Canada, the Pacific Rim, Scandinavia, and Latin America. The reason was to create a representative sample of the three blocs, America, the Far East, and Europe (where Italy and Switzerland are less important markets than others, such as France). Furthermore, we weighted those six markets equally, giving the same importance to Switzerland and Italy, whose capitalization is very small, as we did the United States and Japan, which together represent nearly two-thirds of the entire world capitalization of stocks. Finally, we looked at a very long period of 25 years and evaluated the results using only a few simple rules rather than a comprehensive profile. We are now going to examine the reliability of our conclusions by evaluating the effects of international diversification from different approaches.

Weighting the Markets by Importance. As an alternative to the equally distributed investment, it seems reasonable to consider an international portfolio weighted by the importance that each market or group of markets represents in the world economic scenario. A simple and significant example, consistent with the previous section, is to allocate one-third of the portfolio equity to the U.S. markets, one-third to Japan, and the remaining third to be distributed among the four European markets, the United Kingdom, Germany, Italy, and Switzerland, which are still part of our example. The result of this allocation, called a *geographically weighted portfolio,* is compared to the equally distributed portfolio in Figure 2-20 and shown in Table 2-11.

This simulated case produces even better results than the equal distribution, in terms of both return and risk. The yearly compounded rate of return is a little higher, the standard deviation of yearly returns is lower, and thus the risk-adjusted ratio is better. Therefore, global results are not very different. This so-called *continental weighting* does not significantly improve or deteriorate the

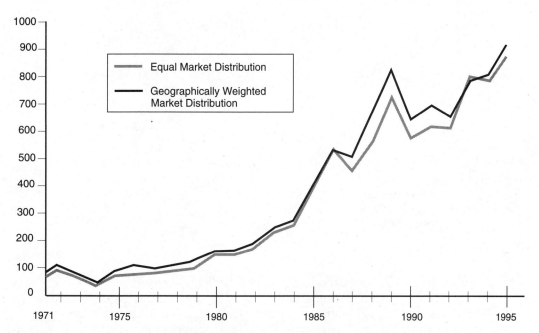

Figure 2-20. Comparison of equally weighted diversification and a geographically weighted portfolio. Results improve when selections are geographically diverse.

Table 2-11. Comparison of Equally Weighted Diversification and a Geographically Weighted Portfolio

	Equal market distribution	Geographically weighted market distribution ⅓ U.S. ⅓ Japan ⅓ Europe
	100.00	100.00
1971	114.05	117.70
1972	143.89	164.43
1973	122.20	137.99
1974	89.65	105.69
1975	129.96	144.50
1976	133.84	157.95
1977	135.96	151.42
1978	147.75	165.64
1979	156.34	176.11
1980	197.60	209.35
1981	198.78	209.61
1982	217.09	231.82
1983	268.55	284.61
1984	298.23	309.12
1985	435.37	412.26
1986	551.78	538.44
1987	474.86	521.12
1988	574.48	642.50
1989	728.61	819.37
1990	584.30	649.69
1991	628.35	697.47
1992	622.85	659.67
1993	793.03	777.22
1994	781.65	801.53
1995	877.62	919.23
25-Year return	777.6%	819.2%
Compounded rate of return	9.1%	9.3%
Standard deviation of returns	18.4%	17.0%
Average yearly return	10.6%	10.6%
Risk-adjusted ratio	0.493	0.545

results given by an equally distributed investment. This is a simple, commonsense way to confirm the robustness of the diversification concept. Nearly any diversification will improve results, and specific weighting can create large variations.

We can explain the benefits of diversification in the following way: If markets behave differently, as we have seen so far, then when one is going down there is another that is likely to be going up or going sideways. When all the markets are going up or down, some are more dynamic than others. The average of these movements has inevitably less extremes than a single investment. The result is a smoother, more stable pattern of growth.

Other Ways to Measure Volatility.   Volatility is therefore the main cause of concern to equity investors, and diversification is a good tool to reduce volatility. The way we have measured volatility so far has been to use the standard deviation and frequency distribution of yearly results. These methods let us know how far values can move from their average or median, giving us an idea of how a market is susceptible to fluctuations.

Another measure that gives us a valid approximation of investment swings is the range in which prices vary during a specific past period. This is the ratio between the highest and the lowest price during that period. There is a good chance that future price moves will be contained in a range of similar size, but when markets move fast, and especially when they reach new high levels, volatility often changes and the range increases.

To see how the yearly fluctuations differ from one market to another, we can look at Figure 2-21 and Table 2-12, which show the yearly percent fluctuation of

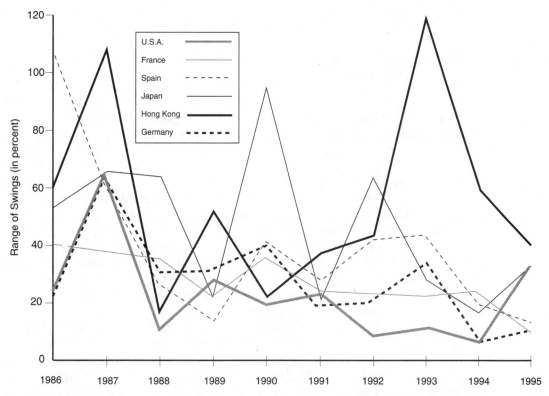

Figure 2-21. Comparison of volatility changes among six markets, 1986–1995. Volatility is very different and very changeable.

Table 2-12. Comparison of Changes in Volatility among Six
Markets, 1986 through 1995 (Percentage of High–Low Range)

	U.S.	France	Spain	Japan	Hong Kong	Germany
1986	32.2	58.1	108.8	47.0	64.7	29.1
1987	67.7	70.3	63.3	43.7	109.4	69.2
1988	18.9	68.5	33.8	41.8	24.7	38.8
1989	32.1	29.9	22.3	29.5	58.1	38.3
1990	29.0	43.4	47.9	96.9	30.1	46.1
1991	30.9	31.6	35.3	29.1	44.1	25.8
1992	11.2	31.9	48.6	68.4	49.9	28.2
1993	18.7	30.4	50.1	35.8	119.9	42.2
1994	13.7	31.4	27.8	25.1	64.3	15.8
1995	38.9	18.3	21.2	40.1	46.2	19.5

the six indices from 1986 to 1995. The percentage fluctuation for each year is given
by the calculation

$$\text{Percentage fluctuation} = \text{Highest(year)}/\text{Lowest(year)} - 1$$

where *Highest(year)* is the highest index value for *year* and
      Lowest(year) is the lowest index value for *year.*

For this example, we substituted France, Spain, and Hong Kong for Switzerland,
Italy, and Great Britain. The reason for this is to show how markets with changing
dynamics and more potential volatility behave in an international equity portfolio, compared to bigger and more traditionally representative world markets.

From Hong Kong one could expect higher fluctuations because of its status and
characteristics as an emerging market. Even without this classification, knowledge
of the imminent turnover to China would be a sure candidate for uncertainty and
potential volatility. This is reflected in the chart. Hang Seng price fluctuations
topped 100% twice in the past ten years, 1987 and 1993.

It is interesting that the extreme volatility varies from one market to another in
our example. First look at 1990 in Figure 2-21. This was a troubled year for all
world financial markets because of the invasion of Kuwait that was a prelude to
the Gulf War. Hong Kong's fluctuation range had been among the lowest in our
sample of markets and, surprisingly, the U.S. index was also low despite its deep
involvement in a major international crisis. The highest volatility in the example,
nevertheless, was reached by the Japanese market, the fluctuation of which was
close to 100%, more than double the average of the other markets in the example.
In retrospect, we know that Japan is most severely affected by interruptions in oil
imports. During the years when Hong Kong recorded the highest range of fluctuation, Japan, usually very volatile, ranked among the lowest.

This example reinforces arguments in favor of diversification. If volatility alternates from one market to another, then an average investment in a broad sample of different markets can shrink equity swings.

Effects of Market Efficiency and Liquidity. Apart from the cyclical changes due to reversals in global trends, there is a tendency in less liquid markets for prices to continue too far in both upwards and downwards directions. We call a market "efficient" when prices quickly (and correctly) adjust to reflect changes in economic or market conditions, such as a rise in interest rates or announcement of dividend earnings. Sometimes the release of news causes a market reaction that is contrary to expectations. It is well known that a market expecting an increased dividend of 4% will rise ahead of the announcement, then drop sharply if the dividend turns out to be only 3%.

An active stock exchange is used by a large number of participants with different interests and financial objectives. There are institutions, such as Merrill Lynch, that buy and sell for mutual funds or growth funds, private banks placing orders for large individual investors, long-term position traders, and simple savers, all entering the market at different times for different reasons. This generates a steady flow of buy-and-sell orders that adds liquidity to a marketplace. The prevailing side of all the combined trades will determine the direction of prices.

If a resource or company ownership is in the hands of a few traders and shareholders, their action will be almost undisputed. Therefore, if one person wants to buy a large number of shares and there are very few sellers, prices can increase sharply. The more a market is in the hands of a few traders and shareholders, the lower the liquidity and efficiency and the greater the chance of wide swings.

Although lack of liquidity increases the size of price swings, it is not the main reason for high volatility. There are many domestic and international factors that influence each market. The combination of these factors causes price movements. It is almost impossible to forecast the size of a market movement by simply analyzing the multiple reasons that could cause such a move. The volatility component of each market, which depends on economic conditions, efficiency, and liquidity, is only one of them. In 1993, when Hong Kong experienced a three-digit high to low range, as did Spain in 1986, the reason was probably its market inefficiency. But in 1988, when the German stock index moved in a range wider than that of either Hong Kong or Spain, efficiency and liquidity had little to do with the cause. Instead, it was the changing political environment preceding the fall of the communist bloc and the anticipation of economic problems associated with unification.

Further Considerations about Volatility

Until now we considered volatility as an undesirable effect of market movement. Nevertheless we must remember that volatility represents the energy needed for the investment to increase in value. We could not see a 25% gain if the market volatility was not at least that great. In order to obtain a good return from an investment, we need some volatility in the market. The risk is the increasing likelihood that the market reverses to our disadvantage. No pain, no gain! For this and other reasons it is not advisable to avoid the more volatile markets.

We need our investment choices to be volatile from time to time if we want them to produce a positive return. At the same time, we know that we cannot forecast the changes in volatility. Markets tend to increase or decrease the size of the volatility swings at unpredictable, cyclical intervals; therefore, if we choose a less volatile market after reviewing the recent history, we take the risk that our selection is on the eve of the turnaround. We need a way of appraising the *potential* swings of the global investments in order to feel comfortable with the degree of risk to which we will be exposed.

Volatility as a Measure of Swings.   A useful measurement of volatility is the sum of all changes, up or down, taken as positive numbers, that occurred over a particular time period. This is more sophisticated than simply measuring the high to low range because it also includes the concept of market choppiness. On a spreadsheet, this sum would use the absolute value function:

$$\text{Volatility} = @sum(@abs(\text{List of price changes}))$$

where

$$\text{Price change} = \text{Current price} - \text{Previous price}$$

Figure 2-22 shows the three basic methods for calculating volatility. The first simply measures the price change over a fixed period of time (for example, one year). The second takes volatility as the high to low range over the same one-year period (which we called the percent range method). The third calculation sums each of the monthly changes as positive numbers or absolute values.

Prices can rise by 20% by going straight up or through a frantic sequence of up and down moves that span a range of 20% from high to low. Both cases can be considered to have the same volatility but the second one is far less desirable for an investor. The sum of all the absolute moves given in the third method of calculation is more meaningful when related to the final results of the period because it gives us the market tendency for price swings.

The ratio between the absolute yearly change and the sum of the absolute values of the twelve monthly returns is a value ranging between zero and one, which we will call the *efficiency ratio*. If the reading for the value is one, it means that the result for the year has been reached with a consistent move in the same direction. While this case is unusually good, it is also unlikely; however, the closer the indicator to the value one, the less tendency towards choppiness, and the more "efficient" the price move.

$$\text{Efficiency ratio} = @abs(\text{Yearly change})/@sum(@abs(\text{Monthly changes}))$$

When the ratio value nears zero, we would expect to see a pattern of extreme market noise, causing prices to be exceptionally erratic, and that the net gain or loss at the end of the year represented only a small fraction of their sum. In this case the market performance was very inefficient and unpleasant for an investor looking for stability. Figures 2-23 and 2-24 show the efficiency ratio plotted along

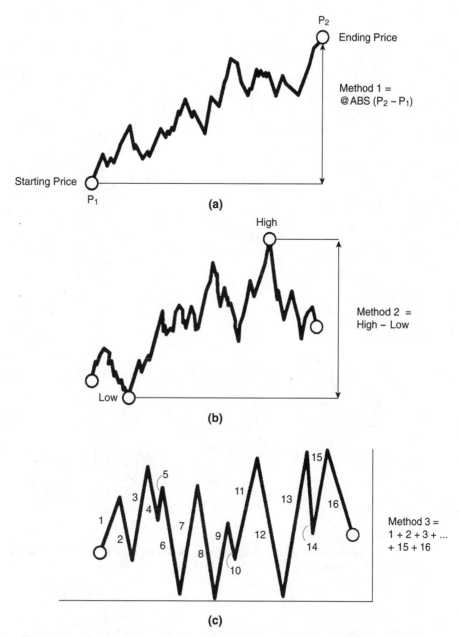

Figure 2-22. Three methods of calculating volatility. (a) Volatility = Ending price − starting price. (b) Volatility = Highest price−lowest price. (c) Volatility = Sum of each price change, taken as positive numbers. (*Adapted from* Smarter Trading: Improving Performance in Changing Markets *by P. Kaufman, McGraw-Hill, 1995.*)

Figure 2-23. Dow Jones Industrial Averages (top), with efficiency ratio (bottom) calculated over twelve monthly price changes.

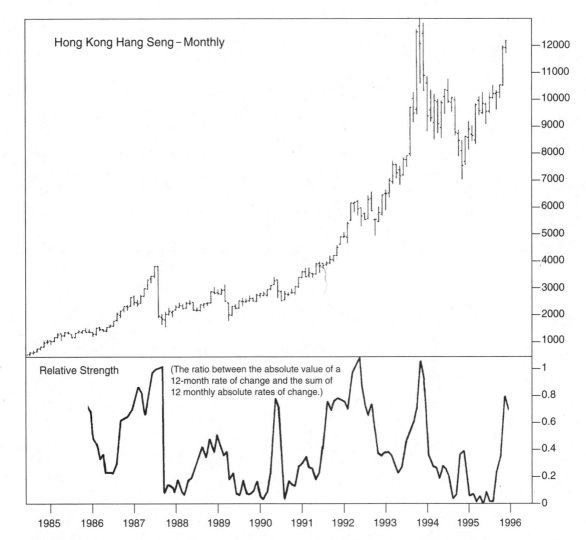

Figure 2-24. Hang Seng indices (top), with efficiency ratio (bottom) calculated over twelve monthly price changes.

the bottom for U.S. and Hong Kong markets over the past decade. The charts show that market choppiness, as with other volatility indicators, is also cyclical. Periods of straight moves alternate with periods of uncertainty and contradiction.

The conclusion is that volatility, as measured in several ways, is not a peculiarity of one market. It changes constantly and reflects the effects produced by all the factors that influenced the market during any one period.

3
Different Market Behavior

How the United States Compares to Other World Stock Markets

Historical Analysis of Different Investment Attitudes

While American investors have been committing a substantial part of their savings to the stock market, Europeans have been distrustful of equity investment for equally as long. This basic divergence in attitude underlies the difference in the patterns and performance of these markets.

The United States owes its role of world leadership to its freedom—freedom of men and trade. Even today America is seen by people from other countries as a big and fertile territory, one that only a few decades ago (from the European perspective) was mostly unexplored. Immigrants look past the partisan issues of politics and debates over education and health services, and see the country as a new world in which to build their fortunes—"the American dream."

The European heritage is at the root of American culture. During the nineteenth and twentieth centuries, Europe exported the best of the human progress to America. Among these exports were the steam engine, the radio, and the railroad. But America had the advantage of being free of the heavy chains of secular power and overwhelming monarchies that have created a tradition of inhibiting social progress in Europe. America broke these undesirable bonds with Europe by declaring independence through the Revolutionary War. Europe had its war for independence, the French Revolution, but that progress soon failed with the rise and defeat of Napoleon. The Austro-Hungarian empire then ruled in the prerevolutionary style for almost a century.

While Europe struggled under the worst expression of oppressive feudalism that was finally defeated in 1945, America, waving its flag of freedom, could attract and use the best of its human resources and transform itself into a bastion of strength and independence. The economic expansion of the United States during the twentieth century has been astonishing. Its free financial structure has allowed everyone to participate in the increasing wealth through the equity market. In turn, equities have become very popular and easy to access; investors at all levels are encouraged to participate. The equity companies listed on U.S. exchanges represent most of the nation's economic activity.

On the other hand, state governments intervene very little in business affairs. This further encourages business because individuals, who need to take certain risks to improve their condition, are free to expend their effort to achieve progress. Based on these freedoms, the U.S. society is greatly entrepreneurial and not averse to taking risks when choosing among investment opportunities. In this light, the equity market is not considered to be an unbearable risk by the American investor. It is considered a good chance to increase capital, it is encouraged by government policy, and it is worth the risk.

Changing demographics is another significant factor that encourages equity investment. Both longevity and the quality of life have been steadily increasing. The need for individual retirement capital expands with everyone's good health and added free time. The long-term growth of equity value is evidence that the stock market is a good place to obtain a better long-term investment return. Because the future pensioners will not draw on this capital for many years, they can disregard any market tumbles. Those occasional drops can even be an advantage. With their wealth built through constant payments, the periods of lower equity prices are considered opportunities to buy cheaper.

Yet there are other considerations, based on the analysis noted above, that speak in favor of the equity market. An open financial structure makes the access to the stock exchange easy and competition keeps costs low. Even the individual stock shares in America are rarely priced higher than $100, reflecting the intention to encourage participation by smaller investors. This is in sharp contrast to Switzerland, where many blue-chip stocks are priced at over $1000. The U.S. system provides easy access, low cost, and government support, all focused on using the stock market to build pension capital.

Different History, Different Markets

Europe is characterized by a different social, political, and, by consequence, economic environment. The European investor is traditionally unfamiliar with the equity market. A free-trade mentality never developed broadly among individuals in Europe, despite a community strongly dependent on free trade during the Middle Ages. But it is unrealistic to draw inference from so far back in history. The primary factor is that the European political environment has been dominated by strong, traditional monarchies until the beginning of the twentieth century.

A social transformation in Europe was inspired by technical progress during the mid-nineteenth century, and a desire for a better quality of life appeared. At that time the most powerful continental state was the Austro-Hungarian empire, and its structure, essentially feudalistic, could not survive world change. It was defeated in World War I but left a leadership void that allowed political aberrations to develop. Fascism and communism followed, both committed to reestablishing a new order with a different type of dictatorship, and were inspired by an ideal of social equalization, in sharp contrast to a free economy.

The defeat of Nazi fascism could still not give way to complete freedom because the presence of a strong communist bloc at the eastern border of Europe had an equally strong influence on political thinking. The result was a state-dominated economy in almost all European countries.

Even today, the main services and utilities in Europe are normally managed by the governments. No railway, telephone, electric company, airline, or television network was in private hands until the 1980s. Even certain automakers, banking groups, and oil companies were state owned.

The Old Continent Renews

At long last, there is a slow change occurring. The privatization process that started in the 1980s has continued. The European governments that had contributed to a welfare mentality of its citizens now encourage savers to subscribe to stock issues and place their funds in private hands. The practical side of this change of attitude is that they can no longer sustain the former budget policy and need to reduce debt. It is quite common in Europe to see commercial advertising aimed at showing the advantages of being shareholders of a formerly state-owned bank, telephone company, or oil company.

The European free-trade market continues to progress despite historical, cultural, and social diversities. The fall of the communist bloc, an epic event that has removed many psychological fences, has also helped to expand business throughout the continent.

Another driving factor that encourages an equity-investing mentality among the Europeans is the new course of the retirement system. As in most European countries, this important economic sector is controlled by the state. The increasing age of the population, together with serious budget problems, does not allow the governments to increase their contribution to social funds. Instead, they favor the development of a new structure, similar to those adopted in the Anglo-Saxon countries. New laws are being promulgated in order to deregulate pension plans and substitute private savings designated for retirement. In some European countries, such as Switzerland, a compulsory retirement insurance system has already been implemented. It is managed by private institutions that invest the subscriber contributions in financial markets, according to strict allocation criteria aimed at preserving the capital.

These changes will make savers more interested in "investing" money, with some risk but with higher expectations, rather than "lending" money to the state or other institutions.

Structural Changes in the World Equity Markets: How Market Capitalization Evolves

A clearer idea of the effect of those slow but deep structural changes is seen in an analysis of the size of equity markets around the world. The *market capitalization* is the total value of all the stocks listed on one exchange, and it is obtained by multiplying the number of outstanding stock shares by their current market price. The market capitalization changes as each price changes, and it grows when new issues are listed. In the case of markets not denominated in dollars, the fluctuation of the local currency is also a variable when we express the market capitalization in U.S. dollars.

Capitalization is increased not only by prices but also when new business activities are financed through the market. This has the effect of making participation more popular and efficient. The entire world market capitalization at the end of 1994 was US$15,185,600,000,000, or about 15 trillion U.S. dollars. Ten years before it was US$3,442,240,000,000, about 3½ trillion; therefore it grew 341%.

The pattern of growth during these ten years has been quite different among countries, as shown in the comparison of G7 nations ("Group of 7") with emerging economies and other industrialized countries given in Table 3-1. Table 3-2 and Figure 3-1 show the capitalization expressed as a percentage of the world total.

In the United States, equity market capitalization grew by 173%, less than the world average but still representing the largest share of the total equity worldwide (33.5%) at the end of 1994; its relative weight is smaller than the 54% ten years earlier, giving way to the expansion of all other countries. While Canada had a pattern of growth similar to that of the United States (gaining 134%), it is the only other country from the G7 that declined in its total position. Japan and the United Kingdom, the most active financial centers outside America, posted a growth near the world average (458 and 375%, respectively).

The other European countries among those of the G7 were much less developed as marketplaces in 1984, and by consequence, in this context of evolution, gained more ground. Germany increased 500% in the dollar value of its stocks, Italy 600%, and France 1000%.

The case of Japan is worth special attention. It is the second most important market after the United States and represented one-fourth of the world equities in 1994. In the years 1988 and 1989, Japan became the biggest market on Earth, counting for about 40% of the total, with a value exceeding 4 trillion U.S. dollars. Japan achieved this position simply because of an overvaluation of stock prices. When the bubble was punctured in the early 1990s, stocks prices dropped to nearly one-half their peak value, and Japan came back to a more realistic relative size.

Emerging Countries. The emerging countries would not be so named if they were not in a period of exceptional evolution. The value of stocks traded in those countries was nearly 2 trillion U.S. dollars at the end of 1994, up 1222% from ten

Table 3-1. Market Capitalization in Millions of U.S. Dollars

	United States	Canada	Japan	United Kingdom	Germany	France	Italy	Other industrialized countries	Emerging countries	World total
1984	1,862,940	134,700	667,049	242,700	78,400	41,100	25,700	243,781	145,870	3,442,240
1985	2,324,650	147,000	978,663	328,000	183,765	79,000	58,502	396,930	171,260	4,667,770
1986	2,636,600	166,300	1,841,785	439,500	257,677	149,500	140,249	643,979	238,300	6,513,890
1987	2,588,890	218,817	2,032,952	680,721	213,166	172,048	119,559	1,484,917	319,320	7,830,390
1988	2,793,820	241,680	3,906,680	771,206	251,777	244,833	135,428	899,936	483,130	9,728,490
1989	3,505,700	291,328	4,392,597	826,598	365,176	364,841	169,417	1,059,983	738,060	11,713,700
1990	3,099,650	241,920	2,917,679	867,599	355,073	314,384	148,766	867,409	611,660	9,424,140
1991	4,180,210	266,874	3,130,863	1,003,184	393,454	348,083	154,126	970,736	852,070	11,299,600
1992	4,497,830	243,018	2,399,004	838,579	348,138	350,858	129,191	1,155,882	883,900	10,846,400
1993	5,223,770	326,524	2,999,756	927,129	463,476	456,111	136,153	1,931,701	1,591,080	14,055,700
1994	5,081,810	315,009	3,719,914	1,151,646	470,519	451,263	180,135	1,886,334	1,928,970	15,185,600
	173%	134%	458%	375%	500%	998%	601%	674%	1222%	341%

Table 3-2. How Market Capitalization Compares to World Totals

	United States	Canada	Japan	United Kingdom	Germany	France	Italy	Other industrialized countries	Emerging countries	World total
1984	54.1%	3.9%	19.4%	7.1%	2.3%	1.2%	0.7%	7.1%	4.2%	100%
1985	49.8%	3.1%	21.0%	7.0%	3.9%	1.7%	1.3%	8.5%	3.7%	100%
1986	40.5%	2.6%	28.3%	6.7%	4.0%	2.3%	2.2%	9.9%	3.7%	100%
1987	33.1%	2.8%	26.0%	8.7%	2.7%	2.2%	1.5%	19.0%	4.1%	100%
1988	28.7%	2.5%	40.2%	7.9%	2.6%	2.5%	1.4%	9.3%	5.0%	100%
1989	29.9%	2.5%	37.5%	7.1%	3.1%	3.1%	1.4%	9.0%	6.3%	100%
1990	32.9%	2.6%	31.0%	9.2%	3.8%	3.3%	1.6%	9.2%	6.5%	100%
1991	37.0%	2.4%	27.7%	8.9%	3.5%	3.1%	1.4%	8.6%	7.5%	100%
1992	41.5%	2.2%	22.1%	7.7%	3.2%	3.2%	1.2%	10.7%	8.1%	100%
1993	37.2%	2.3%	21.3%	6.6%	3.3%	3.2%	1.0%	13.7%	11.3%	100%
1994	33.5%	2.1%	24.5%	7.6%	3.1%	3.0%	1.2%	12.4%	12.7%	100%

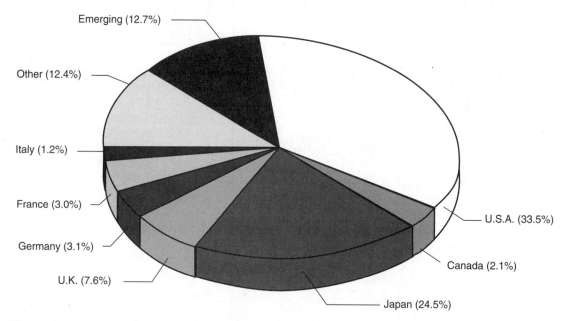

Emerging (12.7%)

Other (12.4%)

Italy (1.2%)

France (3.0%)

Germany (3.1%)

U.K. (7.6%)

U.S.A. (33.5%)

Canada (2.1%)

Japan (24.5%)

Figure 3-1. Shares of world market capitalization, 1994. Combined, the United States and Japan have 58%.

years before. These countries are growing at an explosive pace, and the financial world is investing in the emerging countries to take advantage of their volatility and potential. Their relatively low costs of labor and real estate together with the demographic impact on the demand are key ingredients that favor a booming expansion. These countries allow advanced economies to be more competitive and open a gap that can be filled with massive investments.

The fastest growing emerging countries can be classified in two important geographical areas: Southeast Asia and Latin America. Both are characterized by a strong relationship to the U.S. dollar. Many Asian countries, such as India, have the advantage of being familiar with the Anglo-Saxon financial world because they were former English colonies and have a developed free-trade mentality. Latin America is strictly linked with North America for trade and exchange of human resources.

A look at Figure 3-2 gives a clear idea of the increasing importance of emerging markets and the rate at which they are gaining a share of the total world equity. In fact, they represented a little more than 4% of the total in 1984, and ten years later they counted for 12.7%—half of the Japanese market, or almost all of the markets of the United Kingdom, Germany, and France together.

The industrialized countries, other than those in the G7, also are important in this transformation process. These developed economies in countries such as Spain, Belgium, and Austria provide a resource and an investment depository similar to the emerging countries. The increase in their market share was signifi-

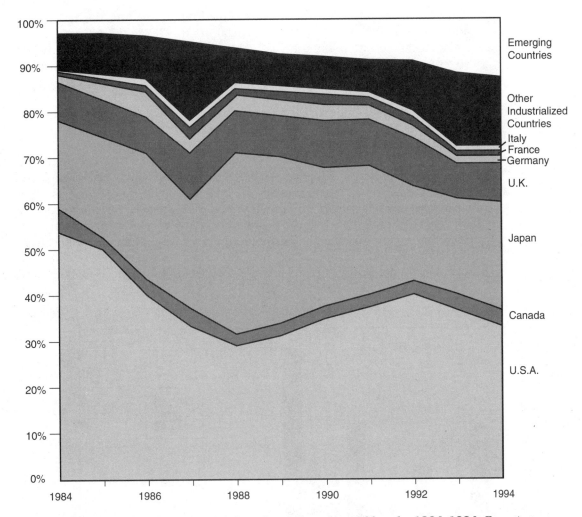

Figure 3-2. How market capitalization has changed on the world scale, 1984–1994. Emerging markets have increased from 4% to 12.7%, reducing the importance of other major markets.

cant during the past ten years, although only half that of the emerging markets, and can be also seen in Tables 3-1 and 3-2 as well as Figure 3-2.

Market Size versus Economy

The importance that the equity markets represent in each country can be measured by comparing the market capitalization to the gross domestic product (GDP). The stock exchange should depict the heart of the financial activity and mirror the real and complete economy of the country. Therefore, the more an economy is modern and efficient, the more its activities are represented by the financial markets.

For the United States, Canada, Japan, and the United Kingdom, the free-market tradition is well established, and more than 50% of the GDP in 1994 is represented by market capitalization. But other G7 countries such as Italy and France, which also represent very important economies, have only a small stake of their business activities reflected in the stock market. The U.S. market capitalization accounted for 75% of its GDP at the end of 1994 (up from 49% in 1984). By comparison, in Italy, one of the most industrialized countries with a GDP that is 15% that of the United States, the value of the stocks only represents 18% of the domestic product. In 1984 this share was as low as 6.9%.

Figure 3-3 shows how those ratios changed from 1984 to 1994 among the G7 countries and provides evidence for the clear division within the group. The United States, Canada, Japan, and the United Kingdom represent high usage of the financial markets, while Germany, France, and Italy show a very low level. The latter three countries, however, did post significant progress. France and Italy witnessed the best improvement in the decade, but their ratios at the end of 1994 were still well below those of the biggest markets, as was Germany. The size of these economies do not justify such relatively small use of the financial markets, and

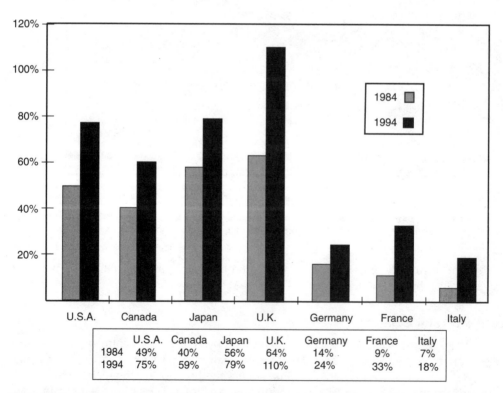

	U.S.A.	Canada	Japan	U.K.	Germany	France	Italy
1984	49%	40%	56%	64%	14%	9%	7%
1994	75%	59%	79%	110%	24%	33%	18%

Figure 3-3. Equity market capitalization as a percentage of GDP. More developed countries use the stock market actively for financing. Germany, France, and Italy are lagging far behind.

they should continue to expand as a natural consequence of the political, social, and economic transformations.

An impressive example of the speed at which a stock market may expand can be seen in Israel, whose GDP grew from 41.7 billion U.S. dollars in 1988 to US$73.9 billion in 1994. But what is more interesting is the growth of its equity market capitalization, which increased from $5.4 to $32.7 billions of U.S. dollars in the same period. The Israeli economy almost doubled, but the stock market grew 500% and represented, in 1994, a good 44% of the GDP. This is a ratio that is close to the North American standards and has not been reached by either Germany or France.

Economic expansion is everywhere in the world but most active in the emerging countries, where there is more room for growth. The equity markets are gaining in popularity, especially in those areas where they were underutilized, and because they are a vehicle for a free-trade economy that is slowly penetrating every country. The need for places that provide cheaper manufacturing and investment opportunity causes the more developed countries to reach out to those less developed nations. This makes it likely that the equity markets will grow at a faster pace than the economies themselves.

This pattern has no end in sight. For the first time in the history of the world a product can be manufactured in any country and sold anywhere else. There are no bounds on free trade. When the current emerging economies have moved into the mainstream of industrialized nations, they will themselves seek out other nations who will provide cheaper labor and become the next generation of emerging markets.

Comparing International Markets

The Markets of the World Are Often Related

World equity markets are usually linked by the strong undercurrent of international economic policy. Even if domestic events and local concerns determine the individual current market trends, the influence of international economic developments is so overwhelming that most markets take on the same global direction. For example, the prolonged period of upward trend that constituted the bull market of the 1980s was experienced, each in its own way, by every market in the world. It is rare when a negative shock to the U.S. markets, such as the 1987 collapse, the 1990 bear market reaction to Gulf crisis, or the interest rate pressure of 1994, does not have a global echo.

Domestic Factors Create Sharp Differences

The domestic component, nevertheless, is the clear element that provides the unique patterns that create investment diversification. Those domestic peculiarities can have very strong positive or negative effects so that the behavior of one market can be quite different from the global trend of the world's stocks over a short time period.

In the first two sections of Chapter 2 we concluded that diversification is a valuable tool for improving the quality of results of an equity investment. In fact, diversification allows us to participate in all of the individual markets that are overperforming, and to smooth the negative effects of those that are underperforming.

We can never presume to know which market is about to be the best or the worst performer. Furthermore, the effect of a global event may differ from one market to another. On Sunday, August 16th, 1991, for example, the old Communist Party in Russia tried to stop the new policies of openness and rebuilding, called *glastnost* and *perestroyka*, by abducting President Gorbachev. The German market, represented by companies that had the most to benefit from new investments in Eastern Europe, fell 9.5% on the following day, while Wall Street only recorded a 2.4% loss.

Political events are crucial to market performance. Figure 3-4 compares the U.S. and Hong Kong stock markets from 1988 to 1991. A quick glance at the charts gives the impression of homogeneity between the two markets; there are sustained upward trends with the peaks and drops in much the same places—except for June of 1989. During June, Hong Kong suffered a loss of one-third of its value, not seen elsewhere, because of a political event limited to that country, the bloody Chinese reaction to democratic overtures in Beijing. This event raised serious concerns about the nature of freedom in Hong Kong after 1997.

Examples of market differences are usually the result of unexpected and sudden events with deep but short-lived effects. When a structural change affects one market, its behavior will be different from the others until that news is fully absorbed. During this adjustment period, which could last for a relatively long time, we say that the market is less *correlated* to the others.

The Correlation Coefficient

A good way to measure the degree to which markets are interrelated is to study their *correlation coefficient.* The correlation coefficient is a statistical function that results in a number ranging from +1 to −1. It tells us, in the extremes, that over a certain time interval the prices of two markets have moved in perfect unison (every gain in one corresponding to a proportional *gain* in the other) or in a perfectly opposite manner (every gain in one corresponding to a proportional *loss* in the other). This calculation, which is available on all spreadsheet programs, is widely used in many fields, and is a simple and reliable measure of the similarity of relationships. If you were a medical research analyst, you could take the historic levels of pollution and the subsequent occurrence of various diseases and if the correlation results are above 0.50 quickly conclude that there is a likely causal relationship.

Calculation of the Correlation Coefficient. There is an easy and a difficult way to get the correlation coefficient for two series of values. The easy way is to simply use the built-in function CORREL in your spreadsheet program. The hard

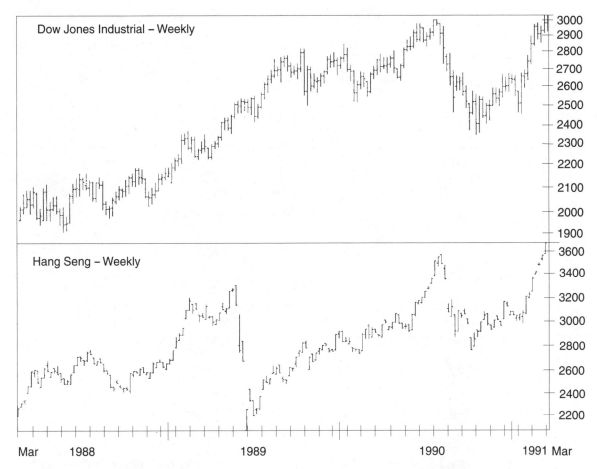

Figure 3-4. The DJIA and Hang Seng, March 1988–March 1991. Local political events can cause important differences in price moves.

way is to calculate the answer from the formula or from the set of steps that follow. Nevertheless, it is important to understand the process, even though we will always choose the shorter method.

Step 1. Calculate and compare the variance of each market to determine whether the direction is the same (this is commonly called *covariance*).

Let us suppose that we have the following returns, in percent, for two stock index markets over five months:

	Month 1	Month 2	Month 3	Month 4	Month 5	Average
Index *A*	0.050	0.030	−0.025	0.070	−0.014	0.0222
Index *B*	0.060	0.040	−0.013	−0.035	0.001	0.0106

Part *a*. For each monthly return, calculate the difference from its average:

	Month 1	Month 2	Month 3	Month 4	Month 5
Index *A*	0.0278	0.0078	−0.0472	0.0478	−0.0362
Index *B*	0.0494	0.0294	−0.0236	−0.0456	−0.0096

Part *b*. Multiply each pair of monthly changes in part *a*:

	Month 1	Month 2	Month 3	Month 4	Month 5
Multiply and divide	0.00137	0.00023	0.00111	−0.00218	0.00035

Part *c*. Add the five values together, and divide by the number of months minus 1:

$$\text{Covariance} = \text{sum}/(\text{observations} - 1)$$

$$= 0.00088/4$$

$$= 0.0002211$$

Step 2. Calculate the standard deviation of the two series of monthly returns.

The standard deviation measures how widely values vary from the average, in this case we can see the variation of monthly index returns. This technique can be found in Chapter 2. Following this method, we get

Standard deviation of index *A*   0.04079
Standard deviation of index *B*   0.03883

Step 3. Multiply the two standard deviations together:

$$0.04079 \times 0.03883 = 0.0015843$$

Step 4. Divide the covariance (Step 1, Part *c*) by the product of the two standard deviations (Step 3) to get the correlation coefficient:

$$0.0002211/0.0015843 = 0.13955 \text{ (correlation coefficient)}$$

Spreadsheet Solutions. Fortunately, many spreadsheet programs have a built-in function for providing a painless way to find the correlation coefficient. In Microsoft *Excel* and in Borland *Quattro*, the form is identical:

$$\text{correl(series1, series2)}$$

Figure 3-5 shows an *Excel* spreadsheet with a "running" correlation coefficient calculation. The first two columns represent monthly prices, both with an upward trend. The correlation value in column *C* uses all the available prices; therefore it gets more accurate toward the bottom of the page. Columns *C* and *D* are the price changes based on the first two columns *A* and *B*. The correlation coefficient using those two series appears in column *E*.

The correlation coefficient is always a number from +1 to −1 and is interpreted as

	A	B	C	D	E	F	G
1							
2	Price		Percentage Changes	Correlation			
3	Value A	Value B	Value A	Value B	Coefficient		
4	1225	9357					
5	1276	9320	4.16	-0.40			
6	1259	9894	-1.33	6.16			
7	1221	10196	-3.02	3.05			
8	1155	10031	-5.41	-1.62			
9	1165	10929	0.87	8.95	-1.00		
10	1171	10982	0.52	0.48	-0.75		
11	1105	9940	-5.64	-9.49	-0.01		
12	1132	10378	2.44	4.41	0.20		
13	1115	9999	-1.50	-3.65	0.14		
14	1224	10584	9.78	5.85	0.48		
15	1207	10649	-1.39	0.61	0.51		
16	1207	11253	0.00	5.67	0.51		
17							
19	Running correlation in column 14: =+CORREL(C5:C14,D5:D14)						

Figure 3-5. An Excel spreadsheet example of the correlation coefficient.
Values in column E become more stable as additional data are used.

- *+1 means a perfect positive correlation,* when two series move exactly the same way (proportionally).

- *−1 means a perfect negative correlation,* where two series move in the exact opposite direction (proportionally).

- *0 means no correlation,* either positive or negative. One market does not show any pattern that depends upon the other market.

In Figure 3-5 the correlation values are lower when the price changes are compared instead of the raw prices. A strong underlying trend in a market, which is typical of many stock indices, will obscure the smaller price patterns and cause two markets to seem highly correlated when the short-term price fluctuations are very different. It is important to point out that we must always compare the price *changes* of the two markets and not the prices themselves to get an accurate correlation coefficient. These numbers can be expressed as raw values, such as the DJIA at the end of February minus the DJIA at the end of January, or as a percentage change. By using changes rather than prices, we are "detrending" the data.

Interpreting the Results

If you would like to visualize how the correlation works, select a time period and draw a straight line through each of the two markets representing the trend of the entire period. It does not matter whether the straight-line trend is at the same angle in each case. Now look at the peaks and valleys above and below the straight lines in the two markets. Do they occur at about the same place and are the peaks

Table 3-3. Comparison of U.S. and Hong Kong Indices

	a. Comparison of weekly data					*b.* Comparison of monthly data				
	Weekly Returns						Monthly Returns			
	Dow Jones (U.S.)		Hang Seng (H.K.)				Dow Jones (U.S.)		Hang Seng (H.K.)	
Date	Price	Change	Price	Change		Date	Price	Change	Price	Change
12/30/88	2168.6		2687.4			12/30/88	2168.6		2687.4	
01/06/89	2194.3	0.012	2766.7	0.030		01/27/89	2322.9	0.071	2957.0	0.100
01/13/89	2226.1	0.014	2844.0	0.028		02/24/89	2245.5	−0.033	3114.2	0.053
01/20/89	2235.4	0.004	2897.9	0.019		03/31/89	2293.6	0.021	3005.0	−0.035
01/27/89	2322.9	0.039	2957.0	0.020		04/28/89	2418.8	0.055	3116.0	0.037
02/03/89	2331.3	0.004	3106.0	0.050		05/26/89	2493.8	0.031	2765.7	−0.112
02/10/89	2286.1	−0.019	3184.2	0.025		06/30/89	2440.1	−0.022	2273.9	−0.178
02/17/89	2324.8	0.017	3106.3	−0.024		07/28/89	2635.2	0.080	2526.8	0.111
02/24/89	2245.5	−0.034	3114.2	0.003		08/25/89	2732.4	0.037	2516.8	−0.004
03/03/89	2274.3	0.013	3056.6	−0.018		09/29/89	2692.8	−0.014	2758.3	0.096
03/10/89	2282.1	0.003	3046.8	−0.003		10/27/89	2596.7	−0.036	2668.0	−0.033
03/17/89	2292.1	0.004	3136.9	0.030		11/24/89	2675.6	0.030	2808.5	0.053
03/24/89	2243.0	−0.021	3049.6	−0.028		12/29/89	2753.2	0.029	2836.6	0.010
03/31/89	2293.6	0.023	3005.0	−0.015						
04/07/89	2304.8	0.005	3024.1	0.006		Correlation coefficient of 12 monthly returns:			0.407	
04/14/89	2336.7	0.014	3082.7	0.019						
04/21/89	2409.5	0.031	3109.2	0.009						
04/28/89	2418.8	0.004	3116.0	0.002						
05/05/89	2382.0	−0.015	3262.9	0.047						
05/12/89	2439.7	0.024	3278.4	0.005						
05/19/89	2501.1	0.025	3145.6	−0.041						
05/26/89	2493.8	−0.003	2765.7	−0.121						
06/02/89	2517.8	0.010	2675.4	−0.033						
06/09/89	2513.4	−0.002	2268.4	−0.152						
06/16/89	2486.4	−0.011	2342.4	0.033						
06/23/89	2531.9	0.018	2219.0	−0.053						
06/30/89	2440.1	−0.036	2273.9	0.025						
07/07/89	2487.9	0.020	2375.9	0.045						
07/14/89	2554.8	0.027	2516.1	0.059						
07/21/89	2607.4	0.021	2495.7	−0.008						
07/28/89	2635.2	0.011	2526.8	0.012						
08/04/89	2653.5	0.007	2579.1	0.021						
08/11/89	2684.0	0.011	2613.4	0.013						
08/18/89	2688.0	0.001	2573.2	−0.015						
08/25/89	2732.4	0.017	2516.8	−0.022						
09/01/89	2752.1	0.007	2508.9	−0.003						
09/08/89	2709.5	−0.015	2620.6	0.045						
09/15/89	2674.6	−0.013	2612.8	−0.003						
09/22/89	2681.6	0.003	2706.4	0.036						
09/29/89	2692.8	0.004	2758.3	0.019						
10/06/89	2785.5	0.034	2826.2	0.025						
10/13/89	2569.9	−0.077	2782.3	−0.016						
10/20/89	2689.1	0.046	2704.0	−0.028						
10/27/89	2596.7	−0.034	2668.0	−0.013						
11/03/89	2629.5	0.013	2739.8	0.027						
11/10/89	2625.6	−0.001	2776.9	0.014						
11/17/89	2652.7	0.010	2804.3	0.010						
11/24/89	2675.6	0.009	2808.5	0.001						
12/01/89	2747.6	0.027	2756.9	−0.018						
12/08/89	2731.4	−0.006	2754.1	−0.001						
12/15/89	2739.6	0.003	2896.6	0.052						
12/22/89	2711.4	−0.010	2921.0	0.008						
12/29/89	2753.2	0.015	2836.6	−0.029						

Correlation coefficient of 52 weekly returns: 0.005

at relatively the same distance above the lines whenever they occur? The greater the similarity, the closer the correlation result will be to the value +1.

As the value of the correlation coefficient moves closer to +1 the two series have a greater *positive* correlation and they are likely to move together, both up or both down. A *negative* correlation, close to −1, means that their movement is in tandem, but opposite; when one series goes up, the other is likely to go down. A correlation of zero means that there is no identifiable relationship between the two markets. Their movements are not related to each other, either positively nor negatively; the two move independent of one another.

If you change the time interval over which the correlation coefficient is calculated, you will get different results. Comparing two markets over longer periods will usually show a lower correlation, while short periods may have similar movements by coincidence. Therefore, more data tend to give more reliable answers. For the same reason, the frequency of the observations is also important to the result. If we calculate the correlation coefficient using monthly or weekly periods, we get very different results than when daily data is used.

Table 3-3 is a comparison of the U.S. Dow Jones Industrial Average and Hong Kong's Hang Seng Index in 1989; these markets were charted in Figure 3-4 where it was pointed out that, with the exception of the drop in the Hang Seng Index from May through June 1989, these markets appeared to be very similar. To understand how this one drop affects the results of the correlation, we compared 52 weekly returns during 1989 and got a correlation value very close to 0. This means that, viewed weekly, the price changes are so different that a common pattern cannot be found. We expect that, in addition to small weekly price differences, the two months in which prices moved in opposite directions was an overwhelming factor in the results.

If we reevaluate the correlation using monthly data, the resulting correlation coefficient is 0.41, which is a much more positive relationship between the two indices, despite the June 1989 divergence. This means that, on the medium-term monthly horizon the two markets have common movement, even though the weekly movements are very different. When we casually view the two charts, the similar price swings that we instinctively see must then be the larger, monthly ones.

This result is quite understandable because the domestic factors are more likely to affect short-term movements while the global trend of the world's stocks will influence the medium-term course. Technically speaking, the market movements contain a certain underlying level of noise that is proportionally larger for data representing shorter time intervals. If we filter out that noise by reducing the number of observations in the same time span, then the correlation will increase.

The Historical Correlation of the World Markets

Table 3-4 contains two correlation matrices relating the returns of eleven equity markets in the ten years from 1986 to 1995. The correlation matrix is simply a convenient way to look up the relationship between any two markets. Part *a* of Table 3-4 shows

Table 3-4. Correlation Matrices for 11 Markets from 1986 through 1995

Yearly Returns

	Hong Kong	Spain	France	Netherlands	Canada	U.S.	Italy	Switzerland	Japan	Germany	U.K.
United Kingdom	0.49	0.43	0.57	0.61	0.72	0.81	0.47	0.69	0.32	0.63	1.00
Germany	0.59	0.39	0.77	0.95	0.75	0.58	0.74	0.88	0.42	1.00	
Japan	−0.04	0.65	0.65	0.35	0.49	0.46	0.65	0.17	1.00		
Switzerland	0.75	0.36	0.65	0.95	0.76	0.61	0.62	1.00			
Italy	0.57	0.85	0.85	0.66	0.58	0.53	1.00				
United States	0.33	0.51	0.60	0.58	0.64	1.00					
Canada	0.63	0.50	0.50	0.82	1.00						
Netherlands	0.66	0.36	0.70	1.00							
France	0.48	0.70	1.00								
Spain	0.56	1.00									
Hong Kong	1.00										

Monthly Returns

	Hong Kong	Spain	France	Netherlands	Canada	U.S.	Italy	Switzerland	Japan	Germany	U.K.
United Kingdom	0.56	0.56	0.56	0.74	0.66	0.75	0.40	0.68	0.35	0.53	1.00
Germany	0.41	0.48	0.68	0.74	0.46	0.49	0.54	0.70	0.31	1.00	
Japan	0.21	0.54	0.36	0.40	0.39	0.38	0.38	0.37	1.00		
Switzerland	0.50	0.54	0.56	0.78	0.63	0.65	0.43	1.00			
Italy	0.23	0.53	0.54	0.46	0.36	0.32	1.00				
United States	0.51	0.59	0.54	0.70	0.79	1.00					
Canada	0.57	0.53	0.47	0.69	1.00						
Holland	0.52	0.57	0.57	1.00							
France	0.39	0.58	1.00								
Spain	0.48	1.00									
Hong Kong	1.00										

the correlation coefficient calculated on ten yearly results; part *b* takes the same markets calculated over the same period using monthly instead of yearly returns. We can compare these two results to find the long-term and medium-term similarities between each pair of markets for the ten years.

Using the matrix of yearly returns it is easy find markets that have been closely linked. Germany and Switzerland, which have been tied by monetary and trade policy, stand out with an exceptionally high correlation of 0.88. The correlation is nearly perfect between Germany and the Netherlands, with a result of 0.95, confirming even closer economic ties. It is interesting that the United States and the United Kingdom, with a correlation of 0.81, have closer relationships to each other than their neighbors, Canada and Europe, respectively. There is also strong commonality among southern European countries such as Italy and Spain or Italy and France, both posting 0.85. Figure 3-6 shows the patterns of the Italian and French

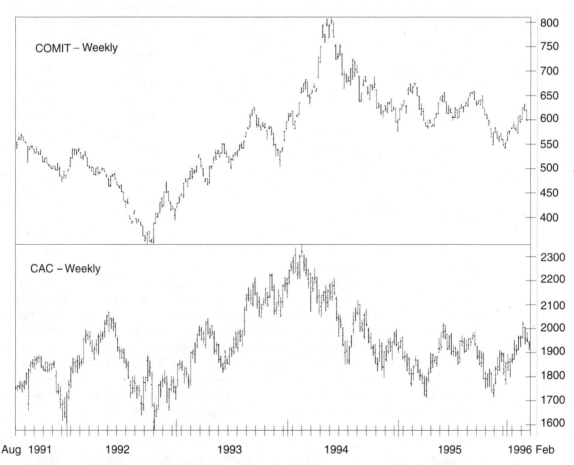

Figure 3-6. The Italian COMIT and French CAC-40 indices, August 1991–February 1996. Countries that have more trade in common have higher positive correlations in their equity markets.

markets from 1991 to 1995, displaying an extremely strong homogeneity, with only a few exceptions in 1992 when Italy was experiencing a severe political crisis. In a manner similar to sector analysis, we find that groups of economies that have more in common also show the highest positive correlation in their equity markets.

The stock markets of the world are all correlated with one another, some more and some less, but always positively. This confirms that the global trend of stocks is generally in the same direction. We would expect this to be true when a country has a public, exchange-traded market; therefore, it is following the capitalistic model set by other nations.

The most extreme contrast within the industrialized countries is Japan, which had the lowest degree of long-term correlation compared to nearly all other markets because of a macro structural change. From 1989 to the mid-1990s, the Nipponic stocks were pushed down because of a loss of competitiveness upon which Japan had built its growth. This corresponded to a period of stronger yen and a dramatic turn in corporate profits, GDP growth, consumer demand, and balance of trade from extremely positive to negative. And while the global trend of the other markets was up, the Japanese economy was down.

Although the overall direction of global markets is the same and the correlations are positive, it might be difficult to see this pattern in the monthly returns, shown in Table 3-3. A positive correlation does not mean that every move in one market is shadowed by a similar move in the others. Some markets may lag, others may have no reaction, and another group will be moving according to its own domestic issues. The correlation among the equity markets can weaken but remain globally positive.

How Correlation Varies over Time

The ten-year correlation matrices are useful for getting a broad view of relative market behavior over the long term but cannot reflect the dynamics of those relationships. A more enlightening picture is Figure 3-7, which gives a "rolling" correlation coefficient calculated over six monthly returns between two markets that have often been in opposition, the United States and Japan. When the rolling value moves to the top of the chart the relationship between the two markets is very strong; in the middle of the chart, from about +0.2 to −0.2 there is no relationship, and below −0.4 we would see a strong opposite pattern.

In Figure 3-7 there appears to be a cyclic pattern in the correlation between the Japanese and U.S. markets. Correlation values move to near 0.80, which shows a very strong, similar movement, then relax back to a moderate correlation, followed by periods of meaningless or even negative correlation.

The negative periods are the most interesting for us. During 1984 and 1986, when Japan was rallying at an unprecedented pace, the U.S. market would undergo small reversals during its sustained bull trend of the 1980s. This was orchestrated by the money-tightening policy of the Federal Reserve Bank, aimed at achieving a specific target of growth and at controlling inflation risks that accom-

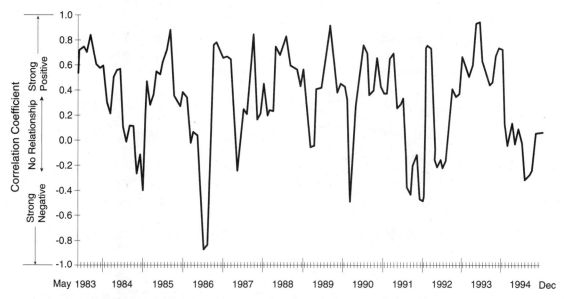

Figure 3-7. Six-month correlation between the U.S. and Japanese stock markets. Using a "rolling" correlation shows the pattern of change.

pany a booming economy. In 1989 and 1991, the Japanese market, now depressed, could not share the bullish sentiment with the United States, and in 1994, a negative year for most markets, Japan saw a technical recovery from its low.

When Things Go Wrong, the Correlation Is High

It is important to realize that, during declining periods and price shocks, the U.S. and Japanese markets have been positively correlated. This observation is enough evidence to prove that, while introducing less-correlated markets into a portfolio reduces volatility under normal conditions, we cannot expect to avoid the risk of market crashes and severe bear markets. If we look at the end of 1987 or 1990 in Figure 3-7 we will find correlation values close to +1. The two markets did not share the same trends but still had the two price plunges in common. Diversification is a useful tool to smooth investment performance, but we should be wary that it may not help in the worst cases.

The relationship among the movements of the European and Asian sectors are shown in Figures 3-8 and 3-9. The first illustrates the United Kingdom, France, Italy, Switzerland, and Germany; the second Japan, Singapore, Hong Kong, and Taiwan. They clearly show that the correlation among monthly market returns is very unstable and changes often. Therefore, if we plan to take advantage of less-correlated markets in our portfolio, we will need to recheck the coefficient often. If our aim is a long-term buy-and-hold portfolio characterized by uncorrelated markets, then we could start with the yearly correlation matrix given in part *a* of Table 3-4.

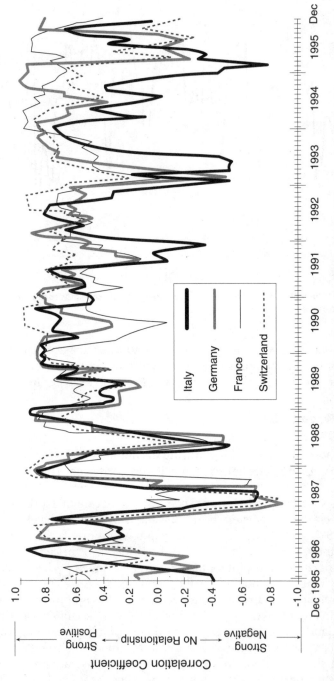

Figure 3-8. Six-month correlations of four main European stock markets versus the U.K. stock market. The significant differences are important for diversification.

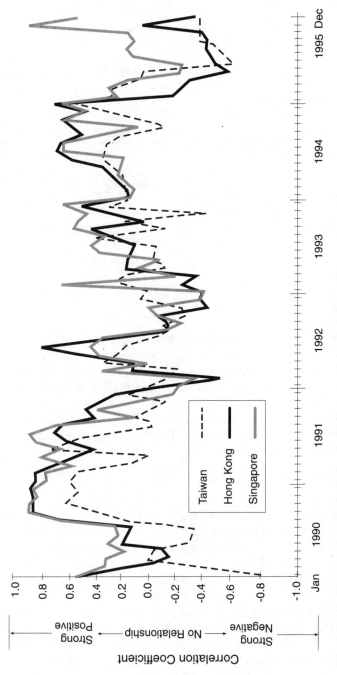

Figure 3-9. Six-month correlations of three main Asian stock markets versus the Japanese stock market. As with the European sector, Southeast Asian markets can differ greatly from Japan.

Table 3-5. Risk Reduction by Diversifying with Different
Levels of Correlation

	Markets			
	A	B	C	D
Return	15%	15%	15%	15%
Standard deviation of returns	3.39%	3.44%	3.36%	3.39%
Correlation coefficient versus A		−0.21	0.29	0.89
Risk-adjusted ratio	4.42	4.36	4.46	4.42
	Diversification results		
	A + B	A + C	A + D
Return	15%	15%	15%
Standard deviation of returns	2.10%	2.70%	3.30%
Risk-adjusted ratio	7.14	5.56	4.55

Building a Portfolio Based on Correlations

The correlation value derived from yearly results provides a valuable tool for creating a diversified portfolio. If two markets have the same global returns and the same standard deviations of returns, the lower their correlation coefficient, the lower the standard deviation of returns for an investment that combines them. This is shown in Table 3-5, where four markets were selected, all with a yearly return of 15% and with the nearly the same standard deviation of monthly results, 3.4%, for a twelve-month period. The correlation coefficient calculated for market A with respect to the three other choices, B, C, and D, for twelve monthly returns, are nevertheless quite different. While market D had a very strong positive correlation of 0.89 with market A, market C had only 0.29, and market B showed a moderately negative correlation coefficient of −0.21.

If market A were combined equally with the highly correlated market D, the diversification did not add much to the result. However, the lowest correlation, market B, proved our contention. When market B was combined with market A, it produced the lowest standard deviation of returns and the highest risk-adjusted ratio, derived by dividing the returns by the standard deviation of results. Risk-adjusted returns were improved by nearly 40%.

We should not forget that the overall positive correlation among the stock markets of the world prevents us from adding a truly uncorrelated element to a diversified portfolio. It is even possible that as world economies become more interdependent there will be no uncorrelated investments of any type. Even real estate and agricultural commodities may be so broadly traded worldwide that they will suffer the same fluctuations. A weak world economy means less global demand and lower prices for everything. For now, we can still take advantage of the fact that equity diversification using world markets can dramatically improve your returns by reducing risk. We will always be able to count on short-term differences, even if there is a long-term similarity.

Relative Strength and Cyclic Lag

Global Trends and Domestic Situations

Each equity market in the world is influenced by a multitude of factors, from strictly domestic issues to international events and politics. The extent to which these factors cause prices to move is directly related to how important and lasting these issues are to that country's economy.

Global events have a way of influencing the world economy, as discussed in Chapter 2, by impacting one after another of the major industrialized countries until we see the results as influencing all the markets as a whole. The characteristics of individual markets, those that remain isolated to one country, are caused by domestic, often localized political factors. A deep restructuring of one country's policies will change the course of its stock market and overwhelm the influence of the global economic environment.

It is the differences in monetary policy and the effect of anticipating changing exchange rates among countries that create different financial environments and profit expectations. This is the main reason for different market behavior.

The Impact of Single Stocks and Sectors

We cannot forget that each market is made up of many single stocks that perform according to how their individual business expectations are interpreted. Generally, a good economic environment favors the whole market; prices rise for companies in all sectors as investor confidence increases. The market index reflects this with a steady climb upwards.

If a special situation turns the trend of a single equity away from the direction of the multitude of market stocks, the effect on the composite index is negligible. Any one stock is a very small part of the whole market. One of the companies in the S&P 500 is, on average, only $\frac{1}{500}$ or 0.2% of the total, and $\frac{1}{225}$ for the Nikkei. In particular, the weight of an individual stock ranges from 0.01 to 2.8% for the S&P 500 and from 0.1 to 3.3% for the Nikkei. If that special situation is one of those that can change the perspective of an entire sector of the economy, then the total market will be influenced to the degree that one sector effects the entire economy of that country.

The stock indices that represent very large markets, such as the United States or Japan, are composed of many stocks that represent a broad range of business sectors; consequently they are less sensitive to those special situations that only affect one or a few companies. This is not true of all countries, where a single "blue-chip" stock can be a large part of the total value of the index, and of their total market. Even in the highly industrialized and developed Germany, 11% of the *DAX* (Deutsch Aktien Index) is weighted by the single stock Allianz, a main European insurer. In Spain we find that the same situation exists, where the telephone company Telefonica and the energy company Endesa taken together represent a 25% share of the Spanish index *IBEX*.

The case of Switzerland is very special. This small alpine country is the home of a few of the world biggest multinational groups for drugs, food, and mechanical engineering. In 1996, when two of the largest pharmaceutical companies, Ciba and Sandoz, announced a merger that would create the second largest company in their sector, their individual stock prices soared 29% and 22%, respectively, and the Swiss index rose 5.1%, although most of the other stocks that are traded in the index hardly moved. Ciba and Sandoz play a key role in their country's market; in fact, their sum represents 25% of the Swiss *SMI* (Swiss Market Index); thus their price swings greatly influence the total index.

The European markets are very sensitive to changes in one business sector because many of the countries have a concentration of businesses in those sectors. In Italy, insurers represent a strong weighting; similarly, the utilities in Spain and banks in Greece play a similar role. As world business activity develops in one sector at a time, it has a different impact on each country, based on how important that sector weighs in the country's economy. We have already seen the results of these cycles when we analyzed the correlations and how they change over time.

Analysis of Relative Strength

As each market cycle of the world scenario is played out, there are rising and falling stars. At any time there are stocks in one market that are relatively stronger or weaker than other stocks, and there are also countries whose indices are stronger or weaker than those of other countries. If an investor could switch to the best performing markets at the right time, his or her capital would show spectacular growth. This is the goal of the professional portfolio managers who often take their work to extremes trying to maximize their returns. We will attempt only a simple version of their efforts and analyze the moments of strength and weakness. Our objective will be to find the most important rules for increasing the chances for profit while reducing the size and length of capital drawdowns.

The following is a review of the past relative strength and weakness of the most important world equity markets based on their stock indices. As a benchmark, we created a composite world stock index by weighting each of the principal country indices by that market's importance and capitalization. We called it simply the *world index*, weighted with the United States as 35%, the Far East (including Japan and the Pacific Rim) as 30%, and Europe as 35%. The index is not expressed in a single currency because each index within each sector must be quoted in their local currency.

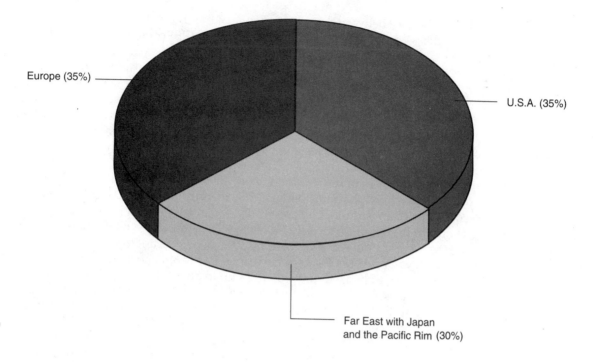

Europe (35%)

U.S.A. (35%)

Far East with Japan
and the Pacific Rim (30%)

How to Read the Relative
Strength Charts

The charts that we are going to discuss (Figures 3-10 through 3-14) will show an adjusted, or *normalized,* comparison between the market of each country (bold line) and the world index (thinner line). The oscillator shown at the bottom of each chart is a six-month relative strength indicator, calculated by subtracting the *rate of change* of one country's stock market index from the rate of change of the world index using the following steps:

1. Calculate the six-month *rate of change* (ROC) for a market:

    ROC (country index) = Today's country index value − country index value
    six months ago

2. Calculate the six-month rate of change for the world index:

    ROC (world index) = Today's world index value − world index value six
    months ago

3. Calculate the *relative strength* (RS):

    RS = ROC (country index) − ROC (world index)

If the difference between the rate of change of the country index and that of the world index is positive, then the relative strength (RS) of that market has been stronger than the average world performance; if RS is negative, the individual market has been relatively weaker than others. We have chosen to create a six-month oscillator because it is the minimum time frame in which fundamental changes can be seen.

Because this oscillator is calculated over the *past* six months, its readings give us information about today in terms of the past from which we must draw conclusions. Besides the positive or negative sign of the indicator, its up or down direction and its location on the chart give important information about what is happening to the price of the stock or index. The peaks and valleys of the RS indicator are particularly interesting because they identify points at which the speed of the current price direction *begins to slow*. Therefore relative strength not only shows direction, but the speed of the price movement. Traditionally, a relative strength of 20 means that prices are rising twice as fast as when it has an RS value of 10. Only when the RS value crosses the zero horizontal line, from above to below, can we say that prices have changed direction from up to down.

In our examples, a positive relative strength does not necessarily mean that the U.K. market, to be seen in Figure 3-11, was going up. Because this is a *relative* strength measurement, the country index may have gone *down*, but *less* than the average world market. We only know that its price was gaining over the world index and that "its relative strength was positive." If the U.K. index, the FTSE-100, was slower to rally than most other markets, we would say it was *relatively weak*, and RS would be negative.

The idea of relative strength is important; therefore, the following is a review of how the relative performance changed, during the decade from 1986 through 1995, for a few principal markets.

U.S. Relative Strength.   A look at Figure 3-10 quickly pinpoints the best "relative" periods, from 1986 to 1995, where Wall Street outperformed the other economies. There seems to be a cyclic tendency for the U.S. stock market to be weaker during the bullish phases and then stronger when a bearish period or a sharp correction occurs. The two drops in 1987 and 1991 are especially significant because they show a different pattern in which the U.S. market was the driving force in the decline of the world index.

This means that the U.S. market is usually leading the others, often anticipating and driving the periods of recovery throughout the rest of the world. From the center of Figure 3-10 to the far right, the U.S. market continues a steady rise while the world index falls away and then catches up at a faster rate. This periodic change of speed creates the appearance of a cycle in the relative strength index at the bottom of the chart. Because the U.S. economy exerts great influence over the policies of other nations, we find that other markets of the world are generally lagging the United States. When New York stops its rise, as it did at the beginning of 1990 and 1994, the world index shows a more prolonged decline; when the Dow resumes its climb, the world index catches up and becomes temporarily stronger. It seems that inertia causes the other markets to lag the United States.

Figure 3-10. The U.S. Dow Jones Industrial Average versus the world index, 1985–1995. The United States alternates between leading and lagging, often driving periods of recovery.

U.K. Relative Strength. The British market, as we assessed in former chapters, is among those most similar to the United States. All studies performed on historical data confirm this, as does the relative strength shown in Figure 3-11. In the first half of the chart, from 1985 through the beginning of 1991, the peaks, valleys, and general direction of the U.K. index is remarkably similar to the U.S. chart index. Looking only at the index value, the steady uptrend may appear very close to the Dow; however, the Financial Times Index tends to be more volatile than the Dow, which can be seen in the relative strength.

In 1987, for example, the difference between the six months rate of change of the Financial Times Index and that of the world index was +25%, which then turned to −25% after the crash. From 1991 through mid-1994 the RS index shows repeated swings from −10 to +15%, while the U.S. market had slower, more directional moves. In general, the peaks of the relative strength index for the Dow Jones Industrial Average are well below those of the U.K. index.

Japanese Relative Strength. The Japanese market has been very different from the others, as we discovered through the former chapters. The reasons for its low correlation with most world markets is clear if we look at Figure 3-12. Through 1989, the Tokyo stock index, the Nikkei, posted the strongest gains in the world, outrunning the world index by 30% by the end of 1989.

Contrasting with this strong gain, the relative strength index shows that the momentum of the market had been deteriorating since 1987. This is another way of saying that prices are rising at a slower and slower rate. For the Japanese, the U.S. crash represented only a minor uptrend correction, and the two years that followed were excellent. But those two years saw the relative strength oscillator start down, and in the early 1990s the RS pattern had turned negative.

While moving inside a wide range between the years 1993 and 1995, the Nikkei index alternated periods of relative strength and weakness. The amplitude of those relative movements was very high, far exceeding the 20 to 25% range of the U.K. FTSE-100, with extreme readings of +30 to −30%. This means that the six-month return of the Japanese market, at certain moments, was 30% better or worse than the world index.

German Relative Strength. In 1985 and 1986 many European markets, pushed by the mid-1980s euphoria, outperformed Wall Street. This group included Germany. The situation changed after the spring of 1986 when fears of inflation, to which the Germans are traditionally very sensitive for historical reasons, caused the Bundesbank to hold interest rates high rather than let them follow the declining world rates. That monetary policy caused the German stock market to turn sideways during the summer of 1986 and early 1987, while the New York and Tokyo markets, and the world index in general, collected new highs. The 1987 crash did the rest.

Figure 3-13 shows the early reversal in the relative strength oscillator, swinging from a premium of 30% over the world index at the beginning of 1986 to a low of −40% well ahead of the 1987 crash. Then, a reversal in the relative strength oscil-

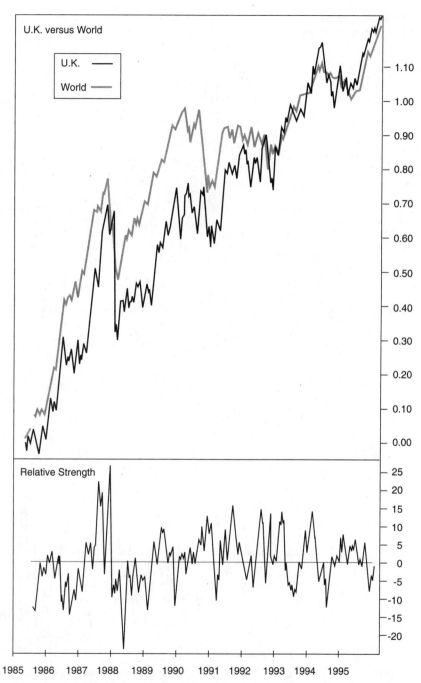

Figure 3-11. The U.K. FTSE-100 versus the world index, 1985–1995.
Similar to the United States, but more volatile.

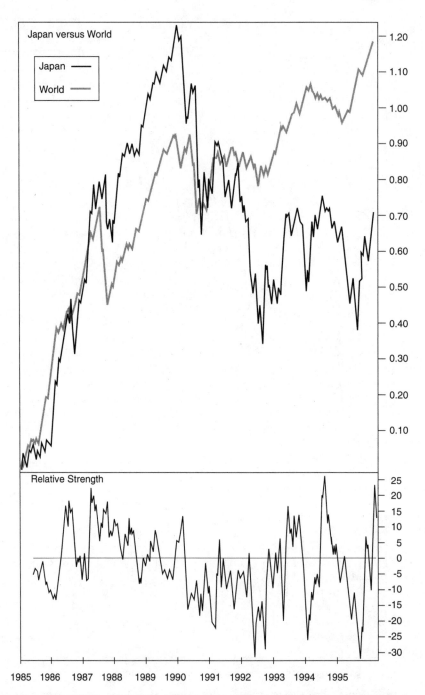

Figure 3-12. The Japanese Nikkei versus the world index, 1985–1995.
Very different performance from other markets, stronger in the 1980s and
weaker in the 1990s.

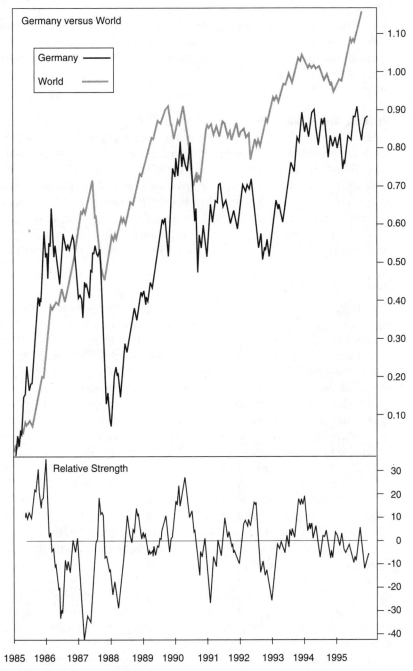

Figure 3-13. The German stock index (FAZ) versus the world index, 1985–1995. Changes in Europe are reflected in the alternating strength and weakness.

lator from early 1988 into 1990 coincided with the period when German stocks outpaced the other markets, almost doubling in two years. Although monetary policy caused interest rates to rise, the opening of Eastern Europe to business was an overwhelming driving force in the market and the new focus of politics in Europe. After that, the German market alternated strength and weakness. Its six-month returns varied from the world index by ±20%.

French Relative Strength. Paris also experienced a boom until May 1986 when, affected more by its strong economic neighbor Germany than by the more distant economies of the East or West, its market began to lose strength (see Figure 3-14). The similarity with Germany continued during the years ahead, and from 1988 to 1990 the French stocks, shown by the *CAC* (Cotation Assistée Continue) index, outperformed the world index. In 1994 and 1995 the market was clearly underperforming while Wall Street was collecting new highs. In fact, the European economies had many difficulties that created a sluggish economy while America continued its growth and successfully kept inflation under control.

Cyclic Lags among Three Blocs

The shifts of strength and weakness among the markets are evidence that there are lags in the price movements among the three blocs: America, Europe, and the Pacific Rim. We will continue to limit our example to this group because they represent most of the capitalization of world stocks. This helps to synthesize our description, but the concepts apply to any market, big or small. Figure 3-15 shows three individual markets together, the United States, Japan and Germany, as proxies for the three blocs from 1983 to 1995. Because it is difficult to distinguish the cyclic lags with the naked eye, we have summarized the major tops and bottoms of these markets in Table 3-6. Apart from a few cases in which a price shock caused the major bottoms to come at nearly the same time, there is usually a lag between the major tops or bottoms that lasted some months.

The way in which each market lags the other smooths out investment returns and helps to reduce drawdowns. This is a further confirmation of the benefits of diversification described in Chapter 2. You might see this more clearly in Figure 3-16, where only the tops and bottoms of hypothetical investments are used, in the manner of an old-fashioned "swing" chart, along with the equally weighted average shown as the bold, smoother line in the center. The results of the three investments would have been exactly the same, but if we had to place our own capital in one of these four choices, it is easy to guess which one it would be. The bold average line rises most consistently, and its decreases are much smoother than the others, yet it is composed of the three other series. Cyclic lags create a clear advantage for diversification.

The numbers speak for themselves. Despite the same final return of 250%, the standard deviations of the individual investments A, B, and C, were 21, 17, and 13%, respectively, while that of their average was only 9%. This would be an enviable improvement in the quality of the investment.

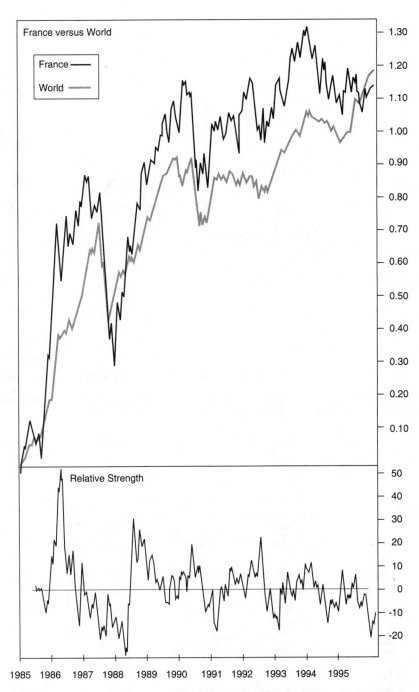

Figure 3-14. The French CAC-40 versus the world index, 1985–1995.
Affected by Germany, the French market represents the overall European underperformance during 1994 and 1995, seen more easily in the relative strength chart at the bottom.

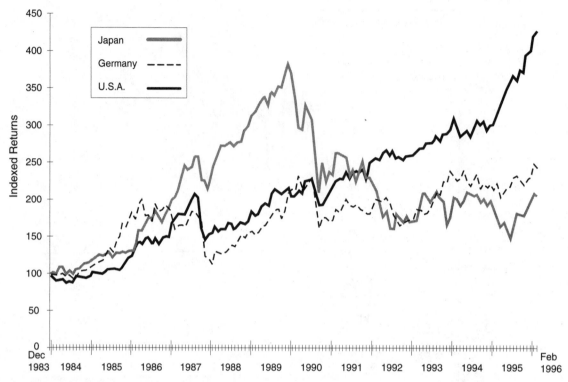

Figure 3-15. Comparing the lag patterns of three world index proxies, the United States, Japan, and Germany. Shifts in strength and weakness are very clear.

Table 3-6. Lags in Major Tops and Bottoms

	United States	Japan	Germany
Top	Dec. 83	May 84	Jan. 84
Bottom	Jun. 84	Jun. 84	Jul. 84
Top	Jul. 86	Sep. 86	Apr. 86
Bottom	Sep. 86	Oct. 86	Mar. 87
Top	Aug. 87	Oct. 87	Aug. 87
Bottom	Dec. 87	Jan. 88	Feb. 88
Top	Jul. 90	Dec. 89	Apr. 90
Bottom	Oct. 90	Sep. 90	Sep. 90
Top	Jul. 92	Mar. 91	May 92
Bottom	Oct. 92	Aug. 92	Oct. 92
Top	Jan. 94	Jun. 94	May 94
Bottom	Dec. 94	Jun. 95	May 95

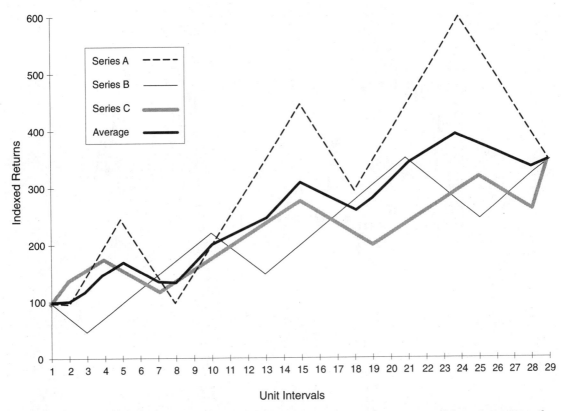

Figure 3-16. Simplified swing patterns. By looking at only the tops and bottoms of the index swings, the variation in patterns can be easily seen.

Relative Strength in Emerging Markets: Taiwan, Israel, and Mexico

If there are such differences among the biggest and most efficient markets, which usually react more or less uniformly to the global changes of the financial world, then we can expect even better results in the more volatile emerging markets. Those markets have wider swings because they are less liquid and the market participants are often acting on the same information, buying or selling at the same time. As a consequence we have sharp, fast trends.

Figure 3-17 is a chart of the Taiwanese index compared with the world index from mid-1989 to 1996. What is most impressive is the size of the relative swings compared to the major international economies, the United States, Germany, and Japan. The six-month rate of change, given by the relative strength oscillator, dropped 60% further in the 1990 bear market than the world index and was higher during the 1994 recovery by nearly the same percentage. It is interesting to note how this market avoided the drop experienced by most western markets in 1994, the result of increasing interest rates, and behaved in the opposite way, gaining in

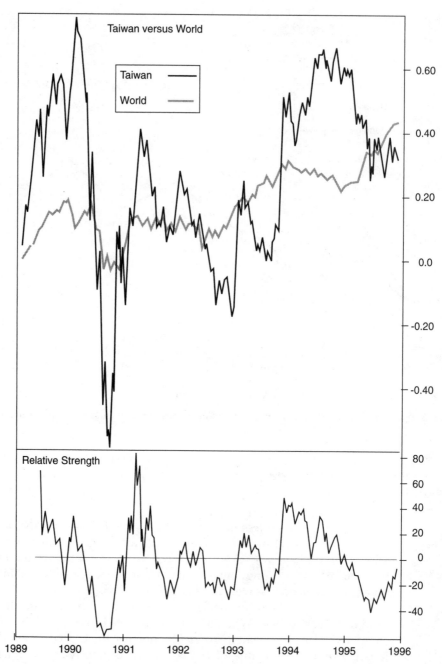

Figure 3-17. The Taiwanese index versus the world index, 1989–1996. There is much greater volatility than the major economies, as seen in the relative strength at the bottom.

relative strength. In the following year, 1995, when the western markets recovered, the Taiwan market did the opposite and underperformed the world index by more than 40%. This is a market that would be useful in a portfolio to improve hedging diversification.

Israel is a similar case. Figure 3-18 is a four-year example that shows, in addition to the usual periods of over- and underperformance compared to the world index, exceptionally unique cyclic lags. The Israeli market reached its peak in November 1993, two months ahead of the world index, and then began a bear market that sharply underperformed the world average, as an emerging market is likely to do. The bottom was reached in February 1995, this time lagging the world index by one month, and then started a six-month period of overperformance.

The third emerging market that we show is the Mexican index, seen in Figure 3-19. The relative strength (remember that it is the difference between the six-month price changes of the Mexican index and the world index) ranged from +50 to −40% and confirms the exceptionally wide swings of the emerging markets compared to the more developed international economies.

The Mexican market reached a top in September 1994 while most markets in the world were in a downtrend and then collapsed to find a bottom nearly coincidental with that of the international average. The 1995 recovery was relatively stronger, even in comparison to the higher volatility of other emerging markets.

Effects of Adding Emerging Markets to an International Stock Investment

The three emerging markets we just viewed, when compared to bigger and more efficient markets, are definitely more volatile. A glance at the performance of the world index and the three combined emerging markets, shown in Figure 3-20, is enough to see a marked difference in both volatility and direction for the two years 1993 and 1994. An average investment in Taiwan, Mexico, and Israel produced a return of 41%, equal to a compounded annualized rate of return of 18.7%. Offsetting that higher-than-normal return is a 6.5% standard deviation of monthly returns. Over the same period, the world index rose 21%, equal to a compounded return of 10.2% with a standard deviation of 3.1%. The volatility of the world index was less than half of our emerging market sample.

The emerging markets then have sharply higher risk in exchange for their increased profit potential. This example, which is far too small to be considered "robust," does give a good idea of the way emerging markets tend to react to global changes in stock prices. Sometimes they exaggerate the current move, and other times they are dominated by domestic issues.

Because of the high risk and the lack of liquidity in emerging markets, it is common for institutional investors to place only a small part of their funds into those markets. To decide how much is best, we will look at the effects of different weightings for a combination of primary markets, given by our world index, and emerging markets. Table 3-7 shows the results.

Figure 3-18. The Israeli index versus the world index, 1992–1995. There are extreme swings and obvious lags.

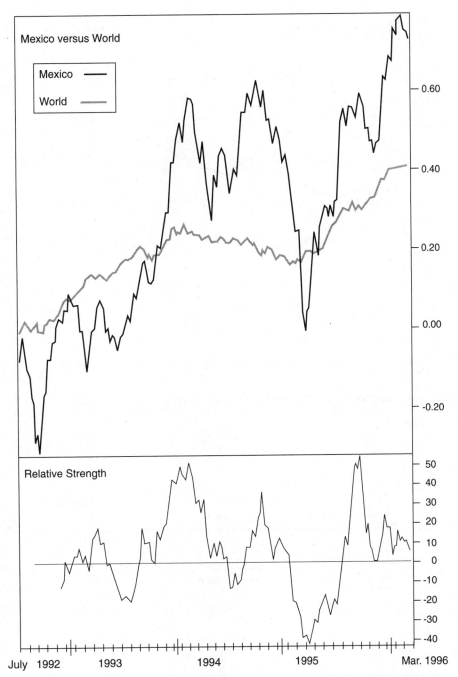

Figure 3-19. The Mexican index versus the world index, 1992–1995. Extremely wide swings in the relative strength are not surprising.

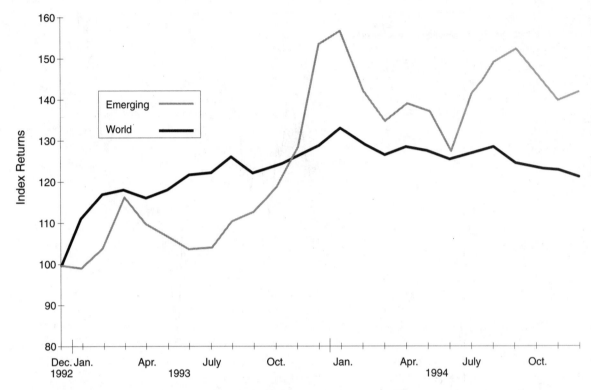

Figure 3-20. Performance of the world index and emerging markets, 1993–1994. The emerging markets (Taiwan, Mexico, and Israel), taken as an average, show greater returns but with much higher risk.

Table 3-7. Results of a Combined Portfolio of Emerging Markets with the World Index

Emerging markets weighting, %	Annual compounded rate of return	Standard deviation of monthly returns	Risk-adjusted ratio
0	10.1%	3.1%	3.23
5	10.6%	3.1%	3.42
10	11.0%	3.1%	3.58
20	11.9%	3.2%	3.78
30	12.8%	3.3%	3.82
50	14.5%	4.0%	3.62
100	18.7%	6.5%	2.87

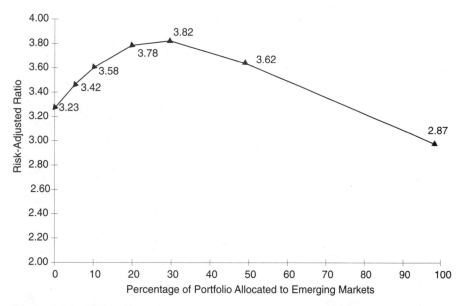

Figure 3-21. Risk-adjusted ratio. The ratio of returns to risk for varying percentage allocations of emerging market investments show that, when using more than 30%, the increased risk causes the total portfolio to decay.

The higher returns of the emerging markets will cause the total returns of the portfolio to increase as the emerging markets become a larger part of that portfolio. However, the faster increasing risk offsets the benefits as the percentage of emerging markets gets large. A quick look at the risk-adjusted ratio is an easy way to see that the results were only improved while the portion of investment in emerging markets remained no greater than 30% of the portfolio (see Figure 3-21). From a practical point of view, the portion of our investment that could be comfortably traded in emerging markets would be closer to 10%. The short observation period in this example and the hidden risk of unexpected changes in developing countries make a smaller investment allocation much more sensible.

These results are technically correct for this example, but they should be expected to change if we evaluate other emerging markets over different time periods. What is most important is the concept that emerging markets are very good for stock diversification because of their behavior, which is often different from that of more efficient, primary markets. This helps to increase returns and, to some extent, reduce volatility. Nevertheless, because those markets are much more volatile and uncertain, their investment weighting should be limited to a small portion of the total investment in order to keep the global investment volatility under control. Remember that even two or more completely unrelated markets will, from time to time, go in the same direction simply by chance. At those times the combined volatility would be very high.

4

How Dollar Bashing
Hurts and Helps

Years of Bull Markets in Foreign Currencies

A Tale of Two Friends

This is a story of two friends, the German Mr. Weiss, and the American, Mr. White. In 1985 Mr. Weiss, wishing to diversify his European-based investments, decided to put some money into U.S. real estate. At that time real estate prices continued to rise and Mr. Weiss wanted to participate in that uptrend. So he bought a small house in California at a price of 300,000 U.S. dollars. At that time, the dollar was in good shape in terms of its foreign exchange rate, so he paid 832,000 German marks for his house.

Within two years his investment had produced a good profit. In fact, he could sell the property for $400,000, a profit of 33%. Unfortunately, in the meantime, the dollar had significantly depreciated against the German mark. So, when he changed his $400,000 back into his home currency, he only got 728,000 marks. His 33% profit had turned into a 13% outright loss. It was even worse if you consider the lost interest on his money.

Mr. White was luckier. In July 1993 he decided to buy an apartment on the French Riviera. The cost was 2 million French francs, which was equal to 332,000 U.S. dollars at the current rate. Two years later he discovered, to his dismay, that the real estate crisis had also hit the famous Cote d'Azur and that his investment had devalued by 15% and was now worth only 1.7 million French francs. So he decided to take the loss because of rumors that prices would continue to drop. In the meanwhile, the French franc had increased its value against the U.S. dollar and when he exchanged the francs he had received from that losing investment, he got back $346,000 U.S. dollars. The profit of 4% was just enough to pay the brokerage commission, but Mr. White was still happy that he had avoided a loss thanks to an unexpected gift from the currency market.

The Importance of Currency in Foreign Investments

The significance of this story is the importance of currency fluctuations in foreign investments. We must remember that the foreign stock markets are denominated in their local currencies. When we analyze their revenues we assume that the results are in the original, or local, currency; nevertheless, we cannot forget that the foreign-exchange rate fluctuations can significantly change the investment's results.

It is one thing to analyze the performance of international markets and another to translate them into one single currency, for example, the U.S. dollar. The differences between the two are often astonishing.

We introduced this concept in Chapter 2, where the influence of currency shifts suggested that it was necessary to compare historic returns of a single market in both local currency and with all returns converted to a single currency, in our case, the U.S. dollar. While analyzing the effects of international diversification on stocks we concluded that a global strategy is better than a single market investment because it decreases the risk of volatility without depressing the reward expectations. As a matter of fact, a multimarket investment is not only dependent on equity prices but also on foreign exchange rates. If we want to correctly evaluate the results we must translate them into the investor's domestic currency or, for convenience here, into U.S. dollars.

When we buy foreign stocks we have a double risk—that of the market plus that of foreign exchange. In fact, an investment profit could be offset by a drop in the local currency rate (which is what happened to Mr. Weiss in our short story), or a loss could be recovered by the exchange rate (as in Mr. White's case). It is also possible that an investment can lose in two ways, once in the price of the stock and the other in the currency change. There is always a chance that any combination of profits and losses in the equity and currency will occur.

The largest stock markets in the world, in addition to the U.S., are denominated in very volatile currencies. Remember that all exchange rates must be quoted as one currency versus another, for example, there are 1.6 German marks to the U.S. dollar, or 1.9 Swiss francs to the British pound. They have all had impressive performances, both up and down, against the U.S. dollar. And, it is not difficult to find a 20% shift between the exchange rates of Japan and the main European markets such as Germany, France, and the United Kingdom.

Foreign Currencies Rise along with Equities

If we analyze, in dollars, the performance of an investment in foreign stocks for 20 years from 1975 to 1995, we will appreciate the benefits of the additional international choices because the U.S. dollar has experienced a prolonged bear market. The dollar-based international investor received a double profit, one from the foreign stock market plus one from the foreign currency.

You may be surprised at the change in the U.S. dollar, seen in Figures 4-1 and 4-2, based on the corresponding value of one dollar in Japanese yen and German marks, for the 25 years from 1971 to 1995. The charts clearly show the dollar's historic downtrend. As of 1995, after 25 years, the value of the dollar had decreased 50% against the German mark and 66% against the yen.

Therefore, a dollar-based investor who selected major foreign markets could have increased returns by an extra 80% from the German currency and 200% from

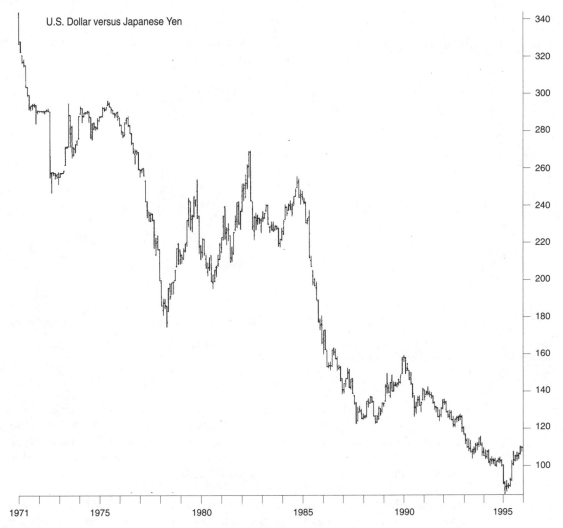

Figure 4-1. The U.S. dollar versus the Japanese yen, 1971–1995. There is a clear, historic downtrend.

Figure 4-2. The U.S. dollar versus the German mark, 1971–1995. While not as severe as the yen, the dollar has been steadily dropping against the mark.

the Japanese, over and above the appreciation of stocks. This means that the 355% increase of the Japanese Nikkei index translates into a 1250% in dollar value. German equities that grew 240% produced a 520% gain to the dollar-based investor. Figure 4-3 compares the same investment in German stocks, from 1981 to 1995, denominated in German marks and U.S. dollars.

Increased Profits and Risk.   We must not forget that the added advantage of a favorable change in the exchange rates can also turn out to be increased risk for

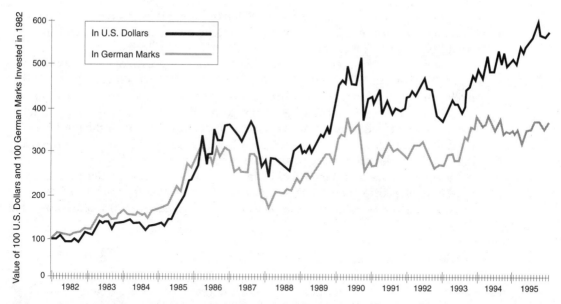

Figure 4-3. Performance of the German stock market in marks and U.S. dollars. By investing in the German market, returns would have doubled the gains in the market based on the loss in value of the dollar.

the investor. When the volatility of international stock markets is added to the volatility of foreign-exchange rates, the result is an opportunity for much greater profits with a similar increase in the amount of risk.

In fact, it is not uncommon to see double-digit fluctuations in currencies. Between 1975 and 1995, a period of high exchange-rate fluctuation, the range from low to high over a twelve-month period was 56% for the U.S. dollar versus the German mark (dollars per mark), 60% for the U.S. dollar versus the Japanese yen (dollars per yen), and 45% for the U.S. dollar versus the British pound (dollars per pounds sterling). Even the Canadian dollar, a currency strongly related to the United States because of close trade links, experienced several double-digit percent fluctuations against the dollar.

Stock and Currency Relationships

Looking a little deeper into the reasons for the changes and volatility will help to understand the amount of currency risk that can be expected. The most relevant questions are the following:

- Does the volatility of the dollar's value improve or worsen an investor's expectations about risk and return in the foreign equity markets?

- Is there any relationship between the trend of an equity market and that of its local currency versus the dollar?

The answers to those questions are crucial in order to understand whether there is a predictable pattern or simply random moves in currencies that affect return and volatility of equity investments.

To find the answers, we analyzed the three most representative equity indices for each year from 1975 to 1995, calculating the correlation coefficient between the twelve monthly returns and the corresponding change in the value of the dollar in the local currency of that market. If the correlation coefficient is near 1.0, then whenever the foreign equity market rises, the dollar rises; and, if the market falls, the dollar also falls. If the correlation coefficient is near −1.0, then the equities market and the dollar move in opposite directions.

Table 4-1 shows that there is no relationship or predictable pattern, because in most cases the correlation coefficient is close to zero, rather than near +1.0 or −1.0. Only 4 years out of 60 in the example (for three markets over 20 years), showed a

Table 4-1. Correlation of Non-U.S. Stock Movement versus the U.S. Dollar

Twelve monthly stock market returns for the years 1976 to 1995 are compared to the monthly changes in local currency versus the U.S. dollar. A correlation coefficient above +0.50 or below −0.50 show that there is a pattern of similar or opposite movements in the stock market and the U.S. dollar. These results are too variable and close to zero; therefore, there is no repeated pattern.

	German FAZ versus US$/DM	Japanese Nikkei versus US$/JY	British FTSE-100 versus US$/BP
1976	−0.05	−0.45	−0.63
1977	0.05	0.54	0.12
1978	−0.19	−0.08	−0.37
1979	−0.13	−0.04	−0.07
1980	−0.80	−0.24	−0.42
1981	0.23	−0.15	−0.21
1982	−0.35	−0.61	−0.50
1983	−0.48	−0.00	−0.04
1984	0.34	−0.64	0.23
1985	0.29	0.58	−0.11
1986	−0.06	−0.13	−0.45
1987	0.78	0.20	0.62
1988	−0.20	0.15	0.45
1989	−0.21	−0.29	−0.07
1990	−0.27	−0.42	−0.13
1991	0.09	−0.04	0.10
1992	0.66	−0.43	0.56
1993	0.32	−0.29	0.28
1994	0.03	0.01	−0.01
1995	0.57	0.55	0.17

significant negative correlation, below −0.50, which means that the equities of that country moved in a direction opposite to that of the dollar exchange rate. In this case both profits and losses are magnified when calculated in dollars. In eight cases where there was a positive correlation greater than 0.50, the volatility of stocks is smoothed by the opposite movement of the local currency. There were a total of 12 out of 60 cases in which the correlation was significantly positive or negative, showing that most of the time the stock patterns have little in common with those of currencies. Do not forget that a correlation value near zero, as described in Chapter 3, means that one market does not exhibit any pattern that depends upon the other.

A Weak Relationship

For certain traders in international markets, the fact that currency movements have little to do with stocks could be surprising. Many traders frequently justify the ups and downs of stocks by the influence of the dollar.

The benefits of a strong dollar for an export-oriented economy are clear to everybody: if the local currency weakens, it is easier to export abroad because product prices, once translated into dollars, are cheaper. In contrast, Japanese electronics, clothing, German cars, Italian furniture, and French wine have become noticeably more expensive in the United States. Even a multinational company that produces and sells its products around the world, such as the Swiss giants Nestlé or Ciba Geigy, will be hurt by a falling dollar when the earnings obtained worldwide are translated back into Swiss francs. It is true that during certain memorable periods the international markets were dollar dependent and that large currency price shocks saw a reaction in the stock market, but this is not the rule and cannot be relied upon.

In 1995, we witnessed a period when both Japanese and German markets were very sensitive to currency changes. Figure 4-4 shows a very similar pattern in the normalized chart of the Nikkei index and the U.S. dollar's exchange rate against the yen during 1995. The stocks of those already weak economies were bottoming out, and the effect of the U.S. dollar at that moment helped to encourage the recovery. In 1995, it was an issue of politics and trade between the United States and Japan. As long as the Japanese yen strengthened against the dollar, a condition not discouraged by the U.S. government, it would harm exports to the United States, its biggest trade partner. The strengthening of the dollar against the yen in mid-1995 was an optimistic sign for the Japanese markets, making the cost of their exports more reasonable to much of the world and indicating an unspoken policy change in the United States.

Table 4-1 shows that the correlations in 1995 between the U.S. and German markets and between the U.S. and Japanese markets were above 0.50, significant but not remarkably positive. This means that, while the overall pattern was similar, there were periods when they moved apart.

The effects of this can be seen in the volatility of investment returns. In 1995 the standard deviation of the monthly returns for the German equity market was 4.1% in the original currency, Deutschemarks, and only 3.5% in dollars, despite a volatile dollar per mark rate. In addition, German stocks produced a 12% gain in

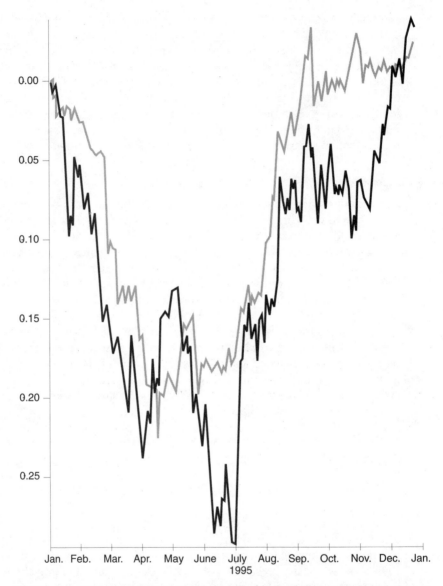

Figure 4-4. Japanese Nikkei (bold line) and U.S. dollars per Japanese yen exchange rate in 1995. Both values are normalized to allow comparison. This remarkably similar pattern, a high positive correlation, shows that during some periods the strength or weakness in the dollar can drive the stock market. This is not usually the case.

dollars and only 4% in marks. This is the classic example of helpful positive correlation where returns were improved and risk reduced.

Another example of meaningful correlation between stocks and currency was 1987, when the drop in German stock prices coincided with that of the dollar versus the mark as illustrated in Figure 4-5. In that situation the Federal Reserve Bank eased the monetary policy in order to avoid a financial collapse after the October crash. The dollar reacted badly to that painful situation.

Even with these clear examples, it is quite unusual for currency changes alone to influence equity prices. Normally, several other factors drive the markets and it is very difficult to say, before it occurs, which one will be the next driving force. Political developments, interest rates, inflation, consumer demand, and currencies are all interrelated and important to the market. Their individual impact depends on the current situation.

It is interesting that the rising dollar, which helped the German stock market to rise in 1995, caused the opposite effect in 1980. Figure 4-6 clearly shows their remarkably contrary moves throughout the year. The basis for this phenomenon was the high energy prices burdening the European economies. Germany was particularly sensitive to inflation, which was not yet under control. A rising dollar meant higher energy prices (which are always quoted in U.S. dollars) and imported inflation. Furthermore, the dollar's strength in the spring of 1980 was generated by a rise in short-term interest rates above 15%. High interest rates attract money away from other investments. It was clearly not a good environment for stocks.

These specific cases do not mean that we should try to find the underlying relationship between monetary policy and stock movement. While they are very clear in our examples, we have the benefit of hindsight. Experience shows that it is very difficult to identify the driving force in time to use it profitably. It is far safer to look at the long-term correlations and see that currency changes have little to do with equity markets apart from specific situations that usually do not last for long.

This Diversification Does Not Help

The immediate consequence of this assumption is that this type of diversification (the combination of foreign stocks plus the foreign currency) does not help to reduce volatility in most cases. Table 4-2 summarizes the standard deviations of monthly returns of three primary world equity markets, year by year, from 1975 to 1995, and compares them with the deviations given for the results of the same markets calculated in U.S. dollars.

For each of the three markets we examined, Japan, the United Kingdom, and Germany, there was a higher average deviation when we consider them in terms of U.S. dollars rather than in their original currency. This increase in volatility, obtained by adding a currency change to the investment in equities, is the net effect of the uncorrelated or random relationship between the stock and currency movements. When we analyzed the correlation coefficient among several equity markets in Chapter 3, we observed that in most cases they were correlated, yet we were able to reduce volatility through diversification. But if we add another element to our investment that is also volatile and whose movements are random with respect to our original investment, then we will always get additional volatility.

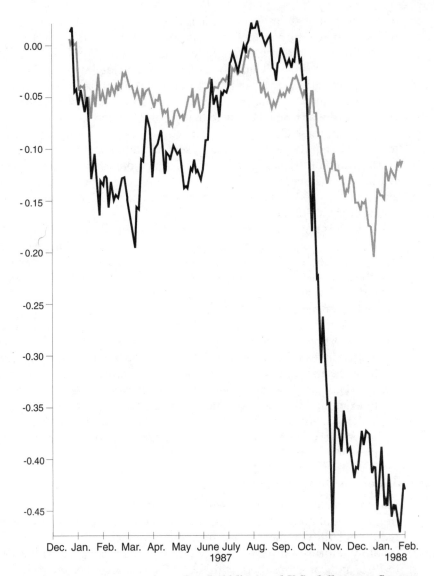

Figure 4-5. German stock market (bold line) and U.S. dollars per German mark exchange rate in 1987. The drop in stocks was immediately followed by a change in U.S. monetary policy intended to help the recovery. The result was a high positive correlation.

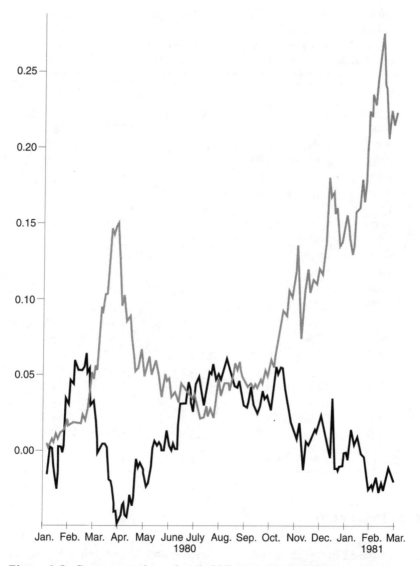

Figure 4-6. German stock market (bold line) and U.S. dollars per German mark exchange rate in 1980. A rise in the dollar against the mark caused a drop in German stocks, resulting in a high negative correlation.

Table 4-2. Standard Deviation of Monthly Returns of Three Primary Markets

A comparison of returns in local currency and in U.S. dollars shows that changes in the dollar increased overall risk.

	In local currency			In U.S. dollars		
	Japan	Germany	U.K.	Japan	Germany	U.K.
1976	4.6%	3.5%	7.7%	5.2%	3.8%	6.1%
1977	4.0%	2.6%	6.1%	3.8%	3.2%	6.2%
1978	2.1%	1.9%	3.6%	5.2%	5.3%	5.9%
1979	1.6%	2.4%	5.8%	3.5%	4.0%	6.5%
1980	2.0%	3.1%	5.6%	4.7%	6.5%	5.2%
1981	2.4%	3.5%	6.8%	4.9%	4.4%	7.4%
1982	3.7%	3.0%	3.2%	8.0%	4.8%	2.9%
1983	2.0%	5.2%	3.2%	3.1%	6.7%	4.2%
1984	4.9%	3.9%	5.4%	6.3%	4.1%	6.8%
1985	2.5%	4.6%	3.8%	3.0%	5.5%	6.0%
1986	5.5%	7.1%	4.8%	7.2%	8.5%	4.3%
1987	5.7%	8.1%	9.7%	6.4%	6.5%	11.0%
1988	3.8%	5.4%	3.7%	4.4%	6.5%	6.1%
1989	2.8%	4.5%	5.5%	4.9%	6.9%	6.5%
1990	11.3%	9.0%	5.5%	13.3%	10.2%	5.5%
1991	6.9%	3.9%	4.1%	7.3%	5.4%	6.1%
1992	7.2%	4.0%	5.4%	8.8%	3.9%	10.2%
1993	7.5%	3.9%	3.1%	8.6%	4.1%	4.7%
1994	5.8%	4.5%	4.9%	6.3%	4.6%	5.4%
1995	7.3%	4.0%	2.1%	6.1%	3.5%	2.9%
Average	4.7%	4.4%	5.0%	6.1%	5.4%	6.0%

A Change in Point of View

Sometimes our results improve, and sometimes they get worse. As a U.S. or dollar-based investor, the historic devaluation of the dollar significantly improved the returns of an investment in international markets, and in this case increased volatility is rewarded by higher returns. Therefore it is sometimes very useful to look at things from a different point of view. If currencies improved the results for a dollar-based investor, how did those same changes impact the revenues of an American portfolio held by a European investor?

The answer is shown in Table 4-3. The results of the Dow Jones Industrial Average given in German marks are compared with those same returns in U.S. dollars. The 495% profit that the investment in the 30 stocks of the Dow had produced in 20 years would have been reduced to 226% in German marks because of the weakness of the dollar through those years. This result is very similar to that

Table 4-3. Risk Expressed in Local Currency and U.S. Dollars

The standard deviation of returns in the Dow shows an increase when expressed in U.S. dollars, the result of prolonged weakness in the U.S. dollar added to stock market returns.

Year	Returns		Standard deviations	
	In U.S. dollars	In German marks	In U.S. dollars	In German marks
1976	16.8%	5.3%	4.79%	4.37%
1977	−17.3%	−26.5%	2.58%	2.89%
1978	−3.1%	−16.0%	5.06%	8.19%
1979	4.2%	−1.1%	4.19%	4.85%
1980	15.2%	31.7%	4.72%	3.51%
1981	−9.6%	2.5%	3.89%	5.56%
1982	19.8%	27.3%	4.37%	4.50%
1983	20.3%	38.0%	3.18%	2.91%
1984	−4.3%	10.7%	3.94%	5.49%
1985	28.1%	−0.9%	3.08%	5.06%
1986	25.1%	−1.5%	4.38%	6.56%
1987	3.6%	−15.3%	8.64%	9.68%
1988	8.4%	22.0%	4.38%	5.98%
1989	27.0%	21.6%	3.91%	6.74%
1990	−4.5%	−16.0%	5.24%	5.49%
1991	18.0%	20.2%	3.81%	5.98%
1992	7.2%	14.4%	2.51%	5.66%
1993	12.9%	21.1%	1.92%	3.56%
1994	2.1%	−8.9%	3.41%	3.67%
1995	33.5%	23.7%	2.54%	3.44%
Average	10.2%	7.6%	4.0%	5.2%
Total return	495%	226%		

of the German market during the same 20 years (239%), while the dollar revenue of the German market (519%) is very similar to the 495% of the Dow. It looks as if currencies played a Salomonic role.

Volatility Also Increases When Returns Decrease

Looking again at the Dow from the point of view of a German investor, we must emphasize that the revenue derived from the U.S. market, translated into German marks, was lower than that in the original currency because of the sharp devaluation of the dollar during those 20 years. Nevertheless, the standard deviation of monthly returns increased. This is further proof that the combination of the foreign currency and stock market returns created increased volatility but failed to produce that smoothing of choppiness that is the typical benefit of diversification.

The increased volatility in the returns of the European and Japanese markets, translated into U.S. dollars, could also be attributable to the higher revenues deriving from the strength in foreign currencies, but this is not the case for the opposite example. The U.S. market, translated into German marks, shows higher volatility despite lower returns.

Investor Risk Preference

Having identified this problem, an investor can hedge the currency portion of any foreign investment. By selling dollars equal to the amount invested in the U.S. stock market, a German investor is protected against changes in the U.S. dollar per German mark to the percentage extent of that hedge. A U.S. investor, buying stocks in Japan, can sell an equal amount of yen for the same protection. Therefore, rather than having to make a decision about both the stock direction and the currency direction, an investor can focus entirely on stocks simply by hedging the currency exposure, thereby also reducing the volatility. More aggressive investors can hedge 50% of the currency if they believe their own currency is likely to weaken or 100% to create a "currency-neutral" portfolio.

Hedging Currency Risk

The Risk of Foreign Exchange

Up until this point we have reviewed the importance of currencies to an investment in foreign stocks. Their swings can cause remarkable twists in the returns. The foreign currencies are often as volatile as stocks, and their relationship with the equity markets is unpredictable in most cases. The last decades of the twentieth century, as we analyzed in the last chapter, have been marked by a progressive deterioration of the U.S. dollar with respect to the European and Japanese currencies. This has resulted in an additional benefit for the dollar-based investors who bought international stocks. Currencies played a big role in their exceptional returns.

The global performance was very rewarding but the volatility of the foreign-exchange swings added an element of concern to the investment. If the equity markets, despite their erratic behavior, show a long-term rise in corporate wealth, the swings of exchange rates depend on monetary policies and macroeconomic variables. The trends of the exchange rates, often extended in magnitude and time, can develop in both directions, up or down.

It is true that the dollar has been very weak for many years but it should not be assumed that the downtrend will last forever. Even during those declining years we have witnessed large countertrend movements. The five years from 1980 to 1985 represent the most extreme example (see Figure 4-7) when the German mark lost half its value in terms of U.S. dollars, almost all the gain of the 1970s. A completely opposite movement developed afterward, followed by wide double-digit percentage swings. The Japanese yen also produced similar and even more

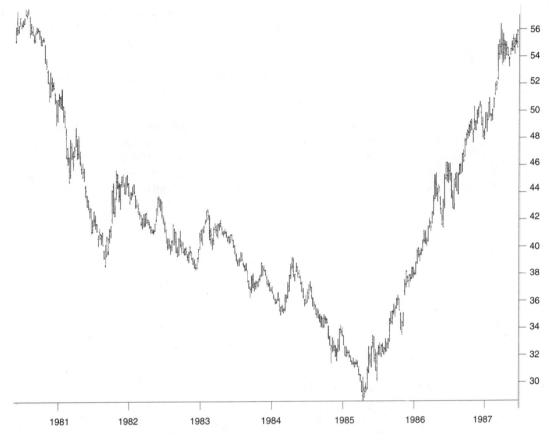

Figure 4-7. Dollar/mark (U.S. dollars per German mark) 1980–1987. The dollar has both the ability to be very strong and very weak.

extended moves in both directions. These two examples are enough to show the high risks of a systematic bet against the dollar.

From January 1980 to March 1985 the German stock index had increased 82%. During that time the Deutschemark had decreased by 48%. The result, in U.S. dollars, of an average investment in German equities was a loss of 6% in five years. Periods such as this are not uncommon and likely to be repeated; they show why a systematic exposure in foreign currencies is not considered prudent.

The Importance of Evaluating Currency Risk

We know that before investing we must evaluate the expected risk and return. This is a basic step in defining the size of our equity investment in relationship to our total investment portfolio. Once the amount of exposure is clear, our commitment depends on how much risk we are disposed to take, a trait called *investor risk preference.* The historical returns and volatility are the primary elements of that evaluation. If we invest in foreign equities we need the added analysis of the domestic currency. When we purchase foreign stocks we also purchase its currency, and this should be considered an investment by itself. As with every investment, this has both a risk and also an opportunity for reward and must be evaluated separately because it represents an investment decision that we must choose to accept or reject.

In fact, we could have a positive attitude towards a certain foreign stock market but not for its currency. For example, in 1989 the Japanese stock market was in very good shape. Its breakout to all-time highs in November 1988 was very promising. A purchase of the Japanese market when the Nikkei index was at about 29,000 points would produce a 30% gain before the end of 1989 (see Figure 4-8). Mean-

Figure 4-8. Nikkei investment example. A comparison between U.S. dollars per Japanese yen (top) and the Nikkei index from August 1988 to December 1989 shows a clear opposite trend. A weaker yen benefited the stock market but hurt an unhedged foreign investor.

while the Japanese yen had just reached historic highs too, around 83 U.S. dollars per 10,000 yen, but its subsequent behavior was not to be the same as the stock market. A bear market for the Japanese currency started near the end of 1988 and continued until April 1990. By that date the yen had decreased about 25% against the dollar. This means that most of the gain that could be achieved in stocks had been lost in the yen, whose negative pattern became even more evident after the spring of 1989. When the weakness of the Japanese currency became undeniable, even the unwary investors could still stop its damage by hedging the foreign currency.

Hedging to Avoid Risk

If we choose to avoid currency risk, and of course its associated profit potential, we must apply a hedging strategy. Of the numerous techniques available in the financial markets, we have selected a few examples to illustrate hedging. They deserve a more exhaustive description, and there is a profusion of complex litera-ture on this subject to which we would direct those readers who wish to know more. We will only try to show the possibilities, using the benefit of modern instruments and global markets, for facing the problems that stem from the unde-sired volatility of foreign currencies.

In concept, the hedging of currency risk is very simple. All you do is buy the for-eign stocks and sell the corresponding amount in foreign currency.

Because you do not want immediate delivery of the foreign currency that you sold, but want its protection while you own the foreign stocks, you will make a forward sale at a certain future expiration or delivery date. In other words, you put off the delivery of the currency while your capital is invested in stocks. To do this there is a premium to pay, which may appear to be a discount in your favor. It is the difference between the *spot* foreign-exchange rate that you can obtain for an immediate transaction (the *cash rate*) and the one applied for in a future delivery (the *forward rate*). This difference is mostly the result of the interest rate differential of the two currencies, with some anticipation added.

Let us suppose you are selling a foreign currency with an expiration, or deliv-ery date, of one year from now. You sell yen and buy dollars, but the yen is cur-rently yielding 2% for one year while the dollars pays 6% in the money market for the same maturity. You have two disadvantages. The "goods" you are selling are less profitable than those you are buying, and you have to wait one year before withdrawing the more profitable one. This second disadvantage is offset by a pre-mium of 4% in your favor. In this case, if you sell Japanese yen for delivery in one year, you will get a 4% more than the cash transaction.

If you want to sell Italian lire, which has a one-year yield of 9% compared to the 6% of the dollar, the opposite case applies. You sell the currency with a higher yield but you do not deliver it immediately; therefore, that purchase cannot bene-fit from its higher return right now. In this case you have to pay that 3% difference to the counterparty (the purchaser) in terms of a currency rate premium, but you benefit by delivering your lire one year later.

Of course you can end the trade whenever you want by making the opposite transaction at the same expiration with the prevailing currency rate. The following are two practical examples of how it works.

Examples of Currency Hedges

1. Forward Exchange Transaction.   In January 1988 we buy Japanese stocks with a value of 100,000 U.S. dollars. At that moment 100 yen are valued at 0.8257 U.S. dollars; therefore, our stock purchase is equal to 12,110,900 yen. In the meantime we want to sell yen with a one-year expiration. The forward rate is 0.8530, higher than the cash rate because the interest rate differential is in our favor. Our forward exchange transaction nets us 103,306 U.S. dollars at the expiration of January 1989.

By September 1988 our Japanese stocks had risen the pleasing amount of 25% and we decide to sell them, receiving 15,138,000 yen when they are cashed in. When we translate those yen into dollars, the exchange rate is 0.7350 per 100 so we get only 111,264 U.S. dollars. The 25% gain is reduced to 11% because of the Japanese yen devaluation. But we still have a forward foreign-exchange transaction outstanding. We had sold 12,110,900 yen and bought 103,306 U.S. dollars with a January 1989 forward delivery. Therefore, we are going to buy the original 100,000 U.S. dollars worth of yen, maturity January 1989, at the current rate of 0.7430 U.S. dollars per 100 yen and pay only $89,983. Then, in addition to $11,264 we will get $13,323 for our forward currency transaction. This amount, added to the net profit from stocks, means a gain of 24,587 U.S. dollars ($11,264 from stocks plus $13,323 from the currency hedging). The net benefit, excluding transaction costs, has been 24.6%, virtually the same as the gain of Japanese stocks without the currency concerns.

If we had decided not to sell our Japanese shares before the expiration of the foreign-exchange transaction in January 1989, we could roll the foreign-exchange transaction forward to a new expiration date for a small cost. If the yen had gone up instead of down, we still had our investment in Japanese stocks to balance the foreign-exchange position. In that case we would not have benefited from the currency rise but only from the stock performance.

This procedure can be done with the same bank agent or stockbroker that we used to trade and deposit the stocks. Those securities will be used as a guarantee with the financial institution to cover the financing and currency risk of the transaction.

2. Options on Currencies.   Another way to hedge is to buy currency options. This choice is very familiar to portfolio managers. An option is the right to buy or sell a specific financial asset at a certain price within a preset expiration date. These options can be used as a speculative tool as well; however, their employment as a hedging tool is one of their more interesting aspects. Just as with the well-known options on stocks, modern financial markets allow the trading of options on almost every tradable asset. It is particularly easy to trade options on the most liquid currencies.

Going back to the example above, we could have bought *put* options on the yen, the right to *sell* a certain amount of yen with a specific expiration date, at a certain price called the *strike price*. In our example the strike price could be 0.8250, corresponding the value of the dollar per yen at that moment (an option *at the money*). The price of the option in such a case represents the premium we are willing to pay for it. The option price is the maximum amount we will risk from a loss in the transaction. If the yen went up we will lose all the money we spent for the option, but we will have gained on the amount of yen invested in stocks. In the case of a drop in the yen, which happened in this example, we could sell the put option in the same way we would have closed out our forward currency trade and take a profit that offset the currency loss in the equity investment. With an option, however, the premium paid is not recovered if held to expiration and continuously declines in value based on *time decay*. It is the cost of allowing *unlimited* currency profit for limited risk.

An option strategy is a little more sophisticated than a forward cash transaction and requires that we compare the premium that we are going to pay with the amount we want to protect. This technique, nevertheless, contains the highly desirable advantage that we are protected from a drop in the foreign currency, but if this does not happen, we are likely to benefit from nearly its entire rise, less the amount we paid for the option, which is always lost.

As an example of how this could work, we buy German stocks worth 100,000 U.S. dollars. At that moment 100 Deutschemarks are worth 66 U.S. dollars (a rate of 0.6600 as quoted on the Chicago Mercantile Exchange International Monetary Market); therefore, we buy put options with a one-year expiration and a strike price of 66 at a premium of 2.5. We pay a total of $3787 ($100,000 divided by $66, then multiplied by 2.5) to hedge a US$100,000 investment.

After one year the Deutschemark has risen to 77, a gain of 16.6%; therefore, our put option will be worthless. Fortunately, we still have the 16.6% gain, minus the 3.2% that we lost by purchasing the put option. This results in a 12.8% gain and the satisfying thought that if we had sold Deutschemarks using a forward transaction, we would not have had any profit at all.

If the situation had been different, and the German mark had fallen to 55 after one year, then the value of the option at the expiration would have been 11 U.S. dollars. We lost the premium anyway, which goes to zero by the expiration, and we netted a gain of $8.50 instead of a loss of $11 on the currency move. By coincidence, when we translate everything into U.S. dollars, we gained 16.6% in stocks, lost 11/66 points in the currency transaction, equal to 16.6%, and lost 3.2% on the option; in total, we suffered a 3.2% loss instead of breaking even on the entire hedged stock investment.

Had the currency remained unchanged from the original hedging level, we would have netted the same as if the German mark had appreciated, a 12.8% gain.

Using Futures Contracts on Currencies

While the use of futures contracts is another sophisticated way to hedge, it is a much easier process for the smaller investor and one that is readily accessible to any institution. Futures contracts on currencies are traded on principal future exchanges, with the greatest liquidity found on the International Monetary Market (IMM) of the Chicago Mercantile Exchange. The most actively traded are the U.S. dollar–denominated Canadian dollar, Australian dollar, German mark, Japanese yen, Swiss franc, and British pound, but recent additions of cross rates (currencies not denominated in U.S. dollars such as the German mark per Swiss franc) and emerging market currencies, such as the Brazilian real and the Mexican peso, show increasing investor interest.

By far, most institutional trading of currencies takes place in the Interbank market, a network of major bank dealing rooms. After establishing credit, a professional investment manager, corporation, or other commercial institution can call the trading desk of any large bank to get quotes and perform transactions. In most cases, a purchase of currency in the Interbank market can be transferred to an equivalent futures position (an *exchange for physicals*) for a small cost and then conveniently offset on the futures exchange. This effectively creates a 24-hour market for everyone.

This hedging technique is similar in concept to a forward transaction. Each *contract* represents a certain amount of foreign currency, for example 125 million yen, 125,000 Swiss francs, or 125,000 German marks. They are traded at fixed expirations, most commonly deliverable every three months, in March, June, September, and December, corresponding to other financial markets. You can buy long (enter a new long transaction) or sell short (enter a new short sale transaction) the futures contract with equal ease.

When you initiate a sale in a futures contract, you then hold a short position, requiring either delivery or offsetting by the expiration date. A short position has unlimited risk if the foreign currency goes up, but that risk provides a hedge and protects the currency investment that is an integral part of a long position in stocks.

You can close your futures trade whenever you want. A deposit called the *margin* is required by the futures broker. This is not the same as the margin available for a stock position, but simply a "good-faith" deposit that would increase along with an eventual loss. You are always liable for the full amount of the changing currency value if it is not in your favor. New margin agreements between exchanges may make this financially easier for hedgers by recognizing that there is an offsetting transaction that compensates for the currency losses.

One limitation of using futures is the fixed amount of currency represented by each contract. In fact, if the investment to be protected is stock valued at 180,000 German marks, you can only hedge by selling one (125,000) or two (250,000) futures contracts, neither of which gives you the proper level of protection. The use of futures contracts is more appropriate for those smaller asset managers who need immediate access to very liquid and efficient markets and for investors who can work with positions that are not perfectly hedged.

There is no "best" method for hedging. It depends on the investment philosophy and risk exposition of the individual portfolio manager or investor. It also depends on the frequency of his or her intervention in the market and the size of the investment to be hedged. Each portfolio and investment philosophy requires a suitable foreign currency hedging strategy.

How to Profit from Periods of Strength in Foreign Currencies

A Third Alternative

Is there a better way to use foreign currencies than by hedging them systematically within the international equity investment, removing all the risks and at the same time eliminating the possible profits? A third alternative may be best, even highly desirable for most investors. It is simply a plan to hedge the risk of foreign currencies when the ones in which you are invested are weak and the dollar is strong. This might also be thought of in the opposite sense, letting profits run in the invested currency when the dollar is weak. If successful, this would be the optimal solution to our foreign-exchange problems.

Follow the Trend

The concept of *following the trend* is a fundamentally sound building block for most trading programs. It seems so simple and yet we sometimes discard the idea as impossible. Because it has been adopted by many institutions into their trading practices, we might think that there is no room for us. But neither is true. Currency changes are driven by government policy or sometimes lack of policy. Changes in foreign-exchange rates can be prolonged and large, with ample opportunity to allow nearly everyone interested to participate.

Nobody, of course, is able to forecast the changes in currency trends just at the time they occur. Nor can we be correct all the time. Instead, we will be more practical and propose the same trend-following techniques upon which many of the successful trading and allocation systems are based. The approach is to take advantage of the trend once it has started, and assume that it will persist until an opposite trend, or contrary signal, takes place. The aim is to take the maximum advantage of the trends without forgetting that, using this technique or any other indicator, we will be always lagging the actual market turns. But when a major trend develops, the benefits will far outweigh the effort and inconsistencies of the trials.

We are therefore adding a new element to our global analysis, the ability to take advantage of opportunities offered by the market, whether in currencies or equities, rather than passively accepting the risks given by the prices swings of the market.

These techniques, which will be discussed only generally here, will be reviewed more extensively in Chapter 5, with examples using the equity markets. The intention is not to find the "best" trading methods but to show only the opportunities for improving an investment strategy and a way of assessing the expectations for success. First, we will look at the benefits that can be derived from applying certain methods to foreign exchange in order to increase the investment results in international equities.

Currency Swings Offer Opportunities and Not Only Risk

The sharp, extended trends of exchange rates offer unique opportunities for those trying to catch them, not just within the brief periods of frantic trading activity but rather in a medium-term perspective. Figure 4-9 is a monthly chart of the U.S. Dollar Index from 1977 to 1996. This is a trade-weighted index of the dollar value versus the foreign currencies. The most actively traded currencies, which are also the most representative of the world economy, weigh more heavily in the Index than those representing less important financial interests. A look at the long-term chart helps to clarify the way the dollar develops its trends and the frequency and

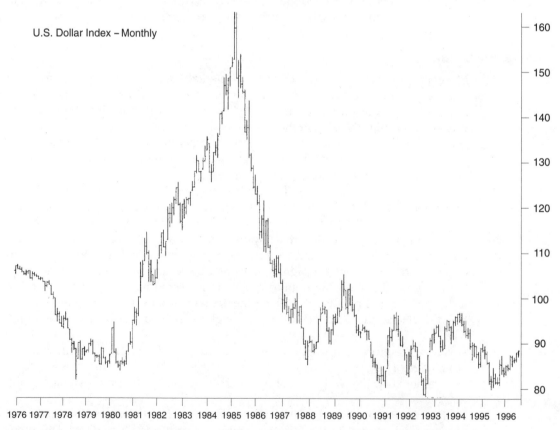

Figure 4-9. Major currency trends in the U.S. Dollar Index from 1977 through June 1996. Very large swings offer hedging opportunity.

size of those moves, which is even more relevant for our purposes. Periods of only a few years in length were enough for the dollar to double in value or decline by one half. It is well worth the effort to somehow try to manage such extended trends as part of the investment process. The method we will use is not that of a market guru but a simple a medium-term trend-following technique.

A Simple Technique

One of the most reliable, simplest, and oldest of the trend-following methods, used by many technicians, is the *price channel breakout rule*. To apply this technique, you buy when the weekly closing price is above the highest price recorded over the past N weeks (for example, 26 weeks for a six-month period) and sell when the closing price moves below the lowest level of the same N-week period. We will use a period of ten weeks in order to create a medium-term analysis. This is not designed for the fast reactions of a currency trader, but it is better for an equity investor.

This method has some advantages that are not shared by most trend indicators:

- It reacts quickly to sharp price changes within its time period. This removes some of the delay common to many other methods.

- It holds onto a position longer, because prices must break out in the opposite direction before the current trend is rejected. This prevents the flip-flopping familiar to traders who use more traditional moving averages.

We tested this method by defining the following trading rule:

Hedge the currency of your foreign stock investment when its price moves above the 10-week high, "unhedge" (*lift the hedge*) when the currency price moves below the 10-week low.

This is based on a foreign-exchange quote that shows a weakening foreign currency when the price rises, such as the mark gaining over the dollar for a U.S. investor. The number of marks per dollar is the typical form of quote on the Interbank market (while Chicago's IMM quotes dollars per mark).

The way the method works is illustrated in Figure 4-10, which shows the German mark from 1980 to 1993. The straight dark line represents the periods during which the German mark is hedged based on the 10-week breakout. In fact, this corresponds to the downtrends. The unhedged periods are represented by the absence of a dark line, which are intended to be most of the uptrends.

To better understand the chart, note that if the dark line angles downward it means that the hedging decision was right. If it points upward, then the signal given by the method was wrong because we covered our currency short sale at a higher price. In general, the steeper the angle of the dark line, the higher the return from the trade or the larger the loss.

Table 4-4 gives the results of applying this hedging method to the German mark according to the signals produced using a 10-week breakout period. In this analysis of a test on historical data, called *backtesting*, there were 20 hedging transactions

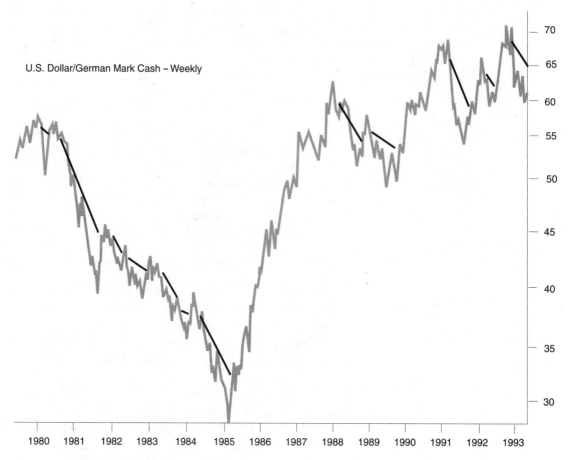

Figure 4-10. Trends identified for U.S. dollars per German mark. The dark line segments indicate the downward trends in the mark that were hedged using a 10-week breakout method.

in about 20 years with an average profit for all trades of 5.5% and about 60% profitable decisions. The years from 1980 through 1984 produced a series of bad decisions because in that period the dollar was very strong; all the signals to remove the hedge on the German mark were false because all the 10-week breakouts in that period were only upside corrections within a major downtrend.

If we consider that the total of the negative trades in the backtest is −19.2% during the period when the German currency decreased more than 50%, we can confirm that this tactical method produced satisfactory hedging results. Note that this simple test does not include commissions and slippage. The complete performance summary is not shown, despite the positive results of backtesting, because this system is not intended to be a stand-alone profit strategy but an integrated support system within an equity investment.

Table 4-4. Results of Backtesting: Removing the Hedge in the German Mark According to the 10-Week Breakout System

Unhedge		Hedge		
Date	Price	Date	Price	Profit or loss
01/30/76	38.62	05/21/76	38.71	0.23%
07/30/76	39.32	01/28/77	41.14	4.61%
04/08/77	41.95	05/12/78	47.35	12.88%
07/07/78	48.59	06/04/79	52.83	8.72%
06/22/79	53.91	02/22/80	56.82	5.40%
05/23/80	56.40	08/22/80	55.52	−1.55%
09/18/81	44.33	01/15/82	43.22	−2.51%
04/30/82	42.90	06/18/82	40.52	−5.55%
12/03/82	41.10	05/20/83	40.19	−2.21%
10/07/83	38.97	11/18/83	36.95	−5.17%
02/17/84	37.26	04/05/84	36.46	−2.15%
03/29/85	32.67	07/17/87	53.65	64.22%
08/28/87	55.19	05/02/88	58.72	6.40%
10/14/88	55.37	06/01/89	55.04	−0.61%
10/20/89	53.85	08/03/91	63.69	18.28%
09/13/91	59.17	02/21/92	60.33	0.25%
05/15/92	62.11	10/30/92	64.89	4.48%
09/03/93	61.65	11/19/93	58.28	−5.48%
03/11/94	59.38	12/02/94	63.29	6.58%
02/17/95	67.52	11/08/95	69.40	2.78%
Average trade				5.48%
Number of trades				20
Fraction of profitable trades of total				60%

To see that this is not an odd situation that works for just the U.S. dollar against the German mark, Table 4-5 shows the same backtesting for the Japanese yen and Figure 4-11 is the corresponding price chart with each hedged trend shown. Figures 4-12 and 4-13 give the pattern of trades for the British pound and Swiss franc, denominated in U.S. dollars. These examples give the comfortable feeling that the investor can be fully invested when the currencies are strong and well hedged when they are weak. The lag in the decisions and the wrong signals are well balanced by the big trends that have been correctly identified.

A Big Improvement in Foreign Equity Investment Returns

To see the impact of this currency hedging method on a global investment in equities, we must analyze the results of a test on historical data, called backtesting. To

Table 4-5. Results of Backtesting: Removing the Hedge in the Japanese Yen According to the 10-Week Breakout System

Unhedge		Hedge		
Date	Price	Date	Price	Profit or loss
02/08/76	33.26	06/04/76	33.30	0.12%
07/02/76	33.68	10/22/76	34.05	1.10%
01/21/77	34.45	11/17/78	51.04	48.16%
05/02/80	41.82	04/03/81	46.90	12.15%
09/18/81	44.18	01/29/82	43.82	−0.81%
11/26/82	40.04	06/10/83	41.32	3.20%
09/30/83	42.49	05/18/84	42.88	0.92%
03/29/85	39.90	10/24/86	61.80	54.89%
01/16/87	65.25	06/26/87	68.30	4.67%
08/28/87	70.44	06/24/88	76.68	8.86%
10/14/88	78.98	01/13/89	78.52	−0.58%
05/25/90	66.80	12/21/90	73.80	10.48%
02/08/91	78.25	03/15/91	72.57	−7.26%
09/13/91	74.48	02/28/92	77.19	3.64%
05/22/92	77.33	12/04/92	80.00	3.45%
02/12/93	82.85	10/15/93	93.45	12.79%
02/18/94	95.60	01/06/95	99.01	3.57%
02/17/95	102.77	07/14/95	113.83	10.76%
Average trade				9.45%
Number of trades				18
Profitable trades as % of total				83

do that we compared the yearly returns from 1976 to 1995 for two principal foreign indices, the German FAZ and the Japanese Nikkei, both with all currency hedges (and removal of hedges) based on the full currency commitment of 100%. We then added the yearly returns of our currency hedging strategy using the 10-week breakout method to the returns of the foreign index (as though it were an entirely unhedged investment), translated into dollars.

The results speak for themselves. Table 4-6 is a summary of the simulations of both the German and Japanese markets. The improvement produced by this simple trend-following method on global results is startling. An increase in volatility of returns, as measured by the standard deviation, is more than offset by the higher compounded rate of return; therefore, the ratio between the two, the risk-adjusted ratio, improves significantly.

The improvement is even more evident by plotting the results. A comparison of the three methods (100% hedged, 100% unhedged, and using the trend system) is

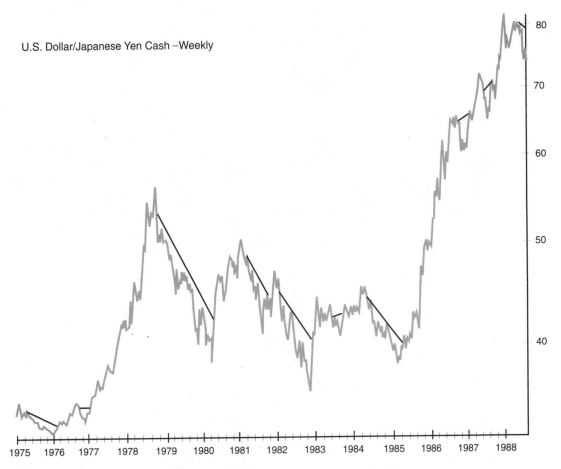

U.S. Dollar/Japanese Yen Cash –Weekly

Figure 4-11. Trends in U.S. dollars per Japanese yen.

shown by Figure 4-14 for the German market and in Figure 4-15 for the Japanese Nikkei. In both cases the systematic hedging and unhedging far improves both passive approaches.

The Trend-Following Method and Diversification

It is also interesting to analyze the impact of adopting of such a method for trading an international portfolio. In previous chapters we have already evaluated the positive effect of diversification on both returns and volatility. If we had distributed our available investment capital one third in the United States, one third in Japan, and one third in Germany and if we had used the 10-week breakout system to hedge and unhedge the Japanese yen and German marks corresponding to the

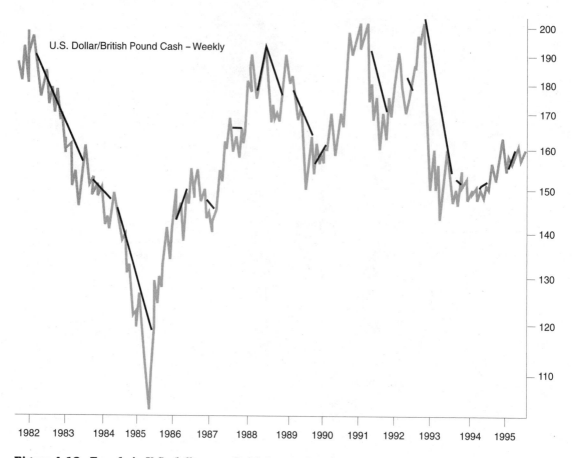

U.S. Dollar/British Pound Cash – Weekly

Figure 4-12. Trends in U.S. dollars per British pound.

stock investments of those countries, then the results would have been even better. The summary, similar to the previous ones, is shown in Table 4-7.

The currency hedging strategy resulted in a 16% annual compounded rate of return over 20 years and a risk-adjusted ratio of 0.72. Both values are a substantial improvement over either of the passive methods. A look back to Chapter 2 will help to remind us that, for a buy-and-hold simulation, this ratio showed approximately 0.50 as the best figures and only through a portfolio of international diversification.

Figure 4-16 is a chart that gives the result of $100 invested equally in those three markets using the three strategies of hedged, unhedged, and systematic hedging.

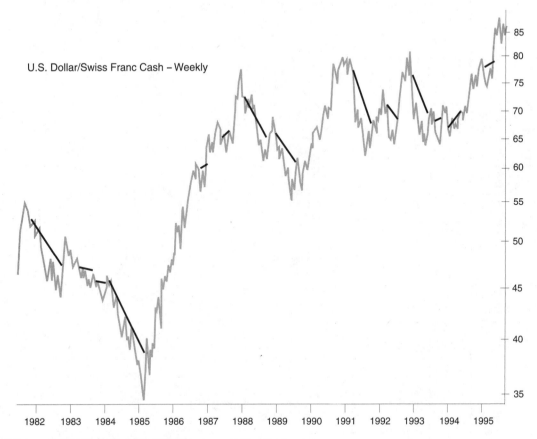

U.S. Dollar/Swiss Franc Cash – Weekly

Figure 4-13. Trends in U.S. dollars per Swiss franc.

Conclusion

The method we have shown for deciding how to profit from upwards trends in currencies and when to hedge their weakness is just one among thousands of systems that could be created for this goal. We do not want to exaggerate the quality or success of this method. The 10-week breakout system is too slow for a currency trader, and it is too simple for a sophisticated risk control strategy. It may have long periods in the future when it will be consistently wrong in signaling the direction of the trend. We just wanted to show the opportunities that are possible using a simple trend-following method for hedging the risk of foreign currencies and to try, using that example, to illustrate the importance and size of currency trends. The analysis given in this chapter shows that this is possible.

Table 4-6. Comparison of Integrated Test Results of Hedged and Unhedged Currency Returns for the German FAZ and the Japanese Nikkei

1: Returns in the original currency; 2: dollar translation of yearly returns; 3: yearly returns of "ten-week breakout" hedging system; 4: sum of 2 and 3, the yearly returns in U.S. dollars plus returns of the hedging system.

	Yearly returns of German FAZ index					Yearly returns of Japanese Nikkei index			
Year	1	2	3	4	Year	1	2	3	4
1976	-7.7%	2.5%	1.0%	3.5%	1976	14.4%	19.1%	1.2%	20.4%
1977	8.4%	21.8%	10.6%	32.4%	1977	-2.4%	18.6%	21.0%	39.6%
1978	6.9%	23.3%	12.1%	35.4%	1978	23.4%	53.1%	22.5%	75.5%
1979	-11.6%	-7.0%	3.9%	-3.1%	1979	9.5%	-11.5%	0.0%	-11.5%
1980	-2.1%	-14.4%	-3.5%	-17.9%	1980	7.5%	27.2%	15.3%	42.5%
1981	-0.7%	-12.2%	0.7%	-11.5%	1981	8.8%	0.5%	-0.9%	-0.4%
1982	14.4%	7.7%	-6.5%	1.2%	1982	4.4%	-2.3%	3.8%	1.5%
1983	39.1%	21.3%	-9.6%	11.7%	1983	23.4%	25.0%	-1.4%	23.6%
1984	8.3%	-6.4%	-2.2%	-8.6%	1984	16.7%	7.4%	0.9%	8.4%
1985	64.3%	112.8%	25.3%	138.1%	1985	13.3%	42.4%	24.1%	66.5%
1986	8.0%	37.3%	27.0%	64.3%	1986	43.9%	82.0%	24.8%	106.8%
1987	-37.1%	-23.1%	18.4%	-4.7%	1987	14.6%	49.6%	17.5%	67.1%
1988	29.3%	14.7%	-5.6%	9.1%	1988	39.4%	35.1%	10.3%	45.4%
1989	34.7%	41.1%	7.0%	48.2%	1989	29.5%	12.6%	-2.0%	10.6%
1990	-18.6%	-7.7%	13.6%	5.9%	1990	-38.7%	-35.1%	10.5%	-24.6%
1991	6.2%	4.1%	6.2%	10.3%	1991	-3.6%	4.7%	-0.7%	4.1%
1992	-5.8%	-11.6%	-3.9%	-15.6%	1992	-26.4%	-26.3%	0.7%	-25.6%
1993	40.6%	30.9%	-5.5%	25.4%	1993	2.9%	15.0%	12.8%	27.8%
1994	-7.4%	3.9%	6.6%	10.5%	1994	13.2%	26.8%	3.6%	30.4%
1995	4.0%	11.9%	2.8%	14.7%	1995	0.7%	-2.8%	10.8%	8.0%
20-year return	239.30%	517.30%		1175.40%		355.8%	1245.9%		3895.3%
Compounded rate of return	6.3%	9.5%		13.6%		7.9%	13.9%		21.5%
Standard deviation of returns	23.4%	29.7%		35.4%		19.3%	27.7%		34.4%
Average yearly return	8.7%	12.5%		17.5%		9.7%	17.1%		25.8%
Risk-adjusted ratio	0.27	0.32		0.38		0.41	0.50		0.62

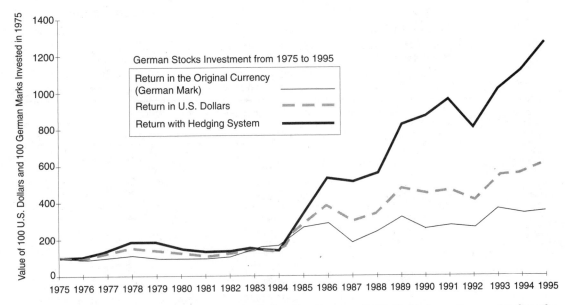

Figure 4-14. Comparison of hedging methods for the German FAZ. Hedged results are significantly better.

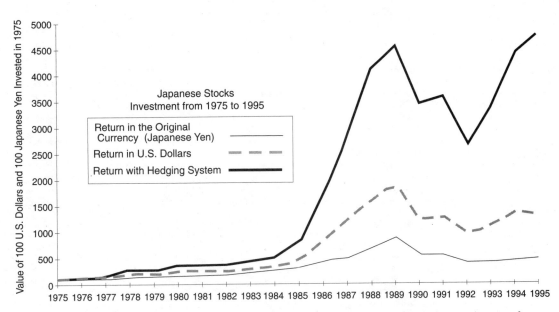

Figure 4-15. Comparison of hedging methods for the Japanese Nikkei. Although it appears much more volatile, hedged returns are far better than other choices and have a higher risk-adjusted ratio.

Table 4-7. Comparison of Hedging Methods Applied to a Simple
International Portfolio

The currency of each non-U.S. dollar market is hedged and unhedged
using the 10-week breakout method applied to each market individually.
1: returns in the original currencies; 2: dollar translation of yearly
returns; 3: yearly returns using the "ten-week breakout" hedging system.

	Yearly % returns of an international stocks portfolio		
Year	1	2	3
1976	7.9%	12.8%	13.6%
1977	−3.8%	7.7%	18.2%
1978	9.0%	24.4%	35.9%
1979	0.7%	−4.7%	−3.5%
1980	6.9%	9.3%	13.3%
1981	−0.5%	−7.1%	−7.1%
1982	12.8%	8.3%	7.5%
1983	27.6%	22.2%	18.5%
1984	6.9%	−1.1%	−1.5%
1985	35.3%	61.1%	77.6%
1986	25.7%	48.1%	65.4%
1987	−7.4%	9.0%	20.9%
1988	26.8%	20.6%	22.1%
1989	30.4%	26.9%	28.6%
1990	−20.6%	−15.8%	−7.7%
1991	6.8%	8.9%	10.8%
1992	−8.6%	−10.5%	−11.6%
1993	19.1%	19.9%	22.3%
1994	2.6%	11.0%	14.3%
1995	12.7%	14.2%	18.7%
20-year return	418.7%	850.4%	1845.6%
Compounded rate of return	8.6%	11.9%	16.0%
Standard deviation of returns	14.6%	18.4%	22.4%
Average yearly return	9.5%	13.3%	17.8%
Risk-adjusted ratio	0.59	0.65	0.72

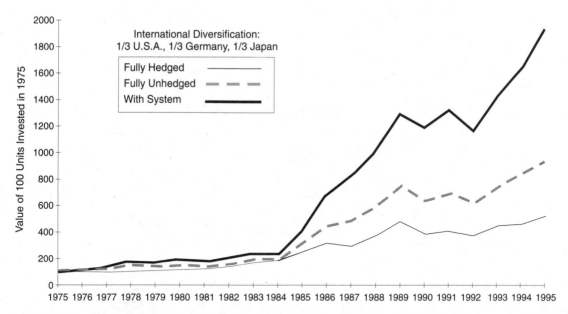

Figure 4-16. Comparison of hedging methods for an international portfolio. Results are even better when diversification is added.

It is also best to always fall back on the big picture. Small trends in currencies are caused by minor events, while major trends are the result of economic policy or perceived policy. The large price changes do not come often, but they should not be missed. There is no amount of institutional and commercial trading that can eliminate those opportunities because they are big enough to absorb any amount of participation. Nor is it necessary to apply sophisticated mathematical formulas to identify when they occur. A simple trend-following method will do nicely. You might set your hedge a little later, but you will still benefit in the end.

5

How to Diversify

Foreign Stocks Traded on Wall Street

There are several ways to set up an investment in international stocks. In theory, the simplest one is the direct purchase of foreign equities at their domestic exchanges; that is, in the country of origin. The investor adopting this solution should have reliable international stockbrokers or bank agents who can execute the transactions properly, despite the distances and time lags between the markets being traded. They must keep the foreign currency accounts, have the custodial responsibility to take care of dividends and splits, and be able to resolve any technical problem that could arise from the ownership of a foreign security.

Yet some institutions specialize in certain markets, and some in others; therefore it is often necessary to work with several representatives in order to keep an investment truly diversified. Furthermore, if we want to expand to emerging markets of far less financially developed countries, we will need to face such basic problems as liquidity and even the regulatory obstacles to trading in those markets. These countries may require that your account be serviced by a few approved institutions that in most cases apply huge transaction fees.

American Depositary Receipts: A Good Alternative*

To bypass most of the problems caused by directly accessing a stock in a foreign market, we can choose among several hundred big or small foreign stocks traded in the United States in the form of American depositary receipts (ADRs), defined as follows. A U.S. bank (the depositary) issues a certain number of negotiable cer-

*See *The McGraw-Hill Handbook of American Depositary Receipts* by Richard J. Coyle (McGraw-Hill, New York, 1995), which extensively covers all the related topics and the legal aspects.

tificates representing foreign stocks. The original stocks are owned by the bank and are located in the foreign country where the issuer is incorporated.

The ADRs are issued in the United States and are evidence of the depositary's ownership. They are traded in U.S. dollars, no matter what the country of origin. Dividends are paid in dollars. They trade, clear, and settle in the same way as domestic issues.

Each ADR represents a multiple or a fraction of the original foreign security. The ratio is often one ADR for ten foreign stocks if the foreign shares are very low, but it may change depending on the price of the deposited foreign security. In fact, the ADRs' prices tend to stay within the usual price range at which the American stocks are traded.

Because of the desire to make this market easily accessible to every kind of investor in the United States, it is not unusual to see a stock split in a high-priced ADR for which there is no corresponding split in the original foreign stock.

History of the ADRs

The first American depositary receipt was issued in 1927 by the Guaranty Trust Company. Consider how time differences between markets, delays in the delivery of stocks from one continent to another, and transmission of trading orders would have been a problem in those years when telecommunication and transportation, compared to those of today, were rough, slow, and very expensive. The ADR was a revolutionary idea that opened the door to investing in foreign securities from America.

During the late 1920s, 18 ADRs were issued, among them some well-known British companies, such as BAT Industries (British-American Tobacco) and Courtaulds, and The General Electric Co., which remain blue chip-companies today on both sides of the Atlantic.

At that time all ADRs were "unsponsored" issues. We must distinguish between two kinds of ADRs, *sponsored* and *unsponsored.* The unsponsored ADRs are created by one depositary; the only document consists of the shares issued by that depositary. In this way other depositaries can clone the unsponsored ADR facility and create duplicates.

The sponsored ADR facilities are, instead, exclusive to one depositary. This is the most common practice today. Foreign issuers prefer sponsored ADR facilities in order to keep better control of their securities traded in the U.S. market. While most ADRs were unsponsored in the past, this kind of issue is now becoming obsolete. In 1983 only 7% of the 585 depositary receipt programs were sponsored. The sponsored programs comprised 53% in 1992, while the total number of ADRs increased by about 80% during those ten years.

The great depression that followed the market crash of 1929 interrupted the creation of new ADRs. In an unfriendly financial environment also characterized by new restrictive laws for issues introduced after the creation of the Securities and Exchange Commission and the subsequent world war, there were no new ADRs until the Dutch conglomerate Unilever appeared in 1955.

It was not until the 1980s that an exponential increase in new ADR issues began, continuing into the 1990s. There were 700 ADRs listed in 1986, 836 in 1990, and more than 1000 listed in 1995. Most of the trading activity, nevertheless, occurs among approximately 200 of the best known issues.

A list of 49 ADRs that represents the most important companies and business sectors in the world is shown in Table 5-1. These stocks are the components of the American Stock Exchange (AMEX) International Index, which is an exclusively ADR equity index traded at the American Exchange. The issues are also among the most liquid in the market. In 1990 the ADRs represented 3.8% of all the shares traded on the New York Stock Exchange (NYSE), the AMEX, and the NASDAQ indices combined. In 1993 they accounted for 6.3%. Their annual dollar volume increased from $75 billion in 1990 to $200 billion in 1993.

This evolution reflects the growing interest in foreign stocks within the trend toward investment globalization. From 1988 to 1995 the volume of ADRs traded has grown an average of 33% compared to a 13% growth for the U.S. stocks.

At the end of 1994 the U.S. investors held about 0.4% of the total world capitalization, with foreign stocks representing 5% of their portfolios. Pension funds and the institutional investors in general are increasing their targets for the foreign equity stake in their portfolios. Such an allocation could reasonably reach 20% to 25% by the early twenty-first century. This indicates that the need for diversification is growing fast. It is pushed along even further by the exceptional performance of U.S. stocks in the mid-1990s, which has encouraged private and institutional investors to ease out of their current holdings, bank the profits, and choose a smaller investment in other cheaper and lagging markets. This is an excellent environment for new ADR programs.

The Advantages of Investing in ADRs

The reasons why it is more advantageous for the American investor to trade ADRs instead of foreign domestic certificates are easy to understand. An overseas trade could readily involve many counterparties. Besides the actual stock market transaction, an equity trade implies a series of procedures that are time consuming and expensive if made with different countries. The most common problems are settlement difficulties and delays. Nonstandardized transferring and clearing procedures create inconveniences.

The use of ADRs avoids those problems. The handling of all securities follows the same format, and all the clearing procedures conform to U.S. standards. Investors, from a procedural point of view, feel as comfortable as if they had traded in the domestic market.

Costs are also lower. The higher commissions often charged by foreign counterparties are avoided as are the safekeeping fees of a custodian located abroad. The ownership rights of the shareholder are guaranteed by the fact that the ADRs are registered in the United States and transactions are recorded in America.

Trading in ADRs avoids the problems of receiving shareholder dividends in foreign currencies and converting them into dollars. Even if specialized brokers took

Table 5-1. The AMEX International Index, Comprised of the 49 Most Representative Foreign Companies Traded in New York

Company	Business sector	Country	Ticker symbol	Index weighting, %
Toyota Motor	Auto, trucks	Japan	TOYOY	8.74
Royal Dutch Petroleum	Oil, gas	Netherlands	RD	8.11
Bank of Tokyo	Banks, financial	Japan	MBK	6.74
British Petroleum	Oil, gas	United Kingdom	BP	4.84
Glaxo Wellcome	Pharmaceutical	United Kingdom	GLX	3.91
Matsushita Electronics	Electronics	Japan	MC	3.63
Hitachi	Electrical equipment	Japan	HIT	3.06
Broken Hill	Metals, diversified	Australia	BHP	2.88
Daimler Benz	Auto, trucks	Germany	DAI	2.81
BAT Industries	Tobacco	United Kingdom	BTI	2.52
Sony	Electronics	Japan	SNE	2.39
Honda	Auto, trucks	Japan	HMC	2.37
Unilever	Food processing	Netherlands	UN	2.21
Ericsson	Telecom. equipment	Sweden	ERICY	2.17
LVMH	Wine, spirits	France	LVMHY	2.15
Nissan	Auto, trucks	Japan	NSANY	2.06
Hong Kong Telecom	Utilities, telecom.	Hong Kong	HKT	2.05
Tokio Marine	Insurance	Japan	TKIOY	2.01
Barclays	Banks, financial	United Kingdom	BCS	1.99
Reuters	Publishing	United Kingdom	RTRSY	1.94
Elf Aquitaine	Oil, gas	France	ELF	1.89
NEC	Computers	Japan	NIPNY	1.74
National Westminster	Banks, financial	United Kingdom	NW	1.69
Telefonica de Espana	Utilities, telecom.	Spain	TEF	1.67
Total	Oil, gas	France	TOT	1.65
Endesa	Utilities, electric	Spain	ELE	1.63
News Corp.	Publishing	Australia	NWS	1.60
Fuji Photo	Electronics	Japan	FUJIY	1.58
Hanson	Holding, diversified	United Kingdom	HAN	1.52
Canon, Inc.	Office equipment	Japan	CANNY	1.51
Smithkline Beecham	Pharmaceutical	United Kingdom	SBH	1.49
Kyocera	Electronics	Japan	KYO	1.30
National Australian	Banks, financial	Australia	NAB	1.27
Philips Electronics	Electronics	Netherlands	PHG	1.19
Norsk Hydro	Chemicals	Norway	NHY	1.09
Volvo	Auto, trucks	Sweden	VOLVY	0.98
Imperial Chemical	Chemicals	United Kingdom	ICI	0.96
Fiat Spa	Auto, trucks	Italy	FIA	0.93
TDK Corp.	Electronics	Japan	TDK	0.76
Telecom New Zealand	Telecommunications	New Zealand	NZT	0.76
Rank Organisation	Entertainment	United Kingdom	RANKY	0.70
ASEA AB	Machine, diversified	Sweden	ASEAY	0.69
NOVO Nordisk	Medical biotechnology	Norway	NVO	0.53
Electrolux	Home appliances	Sweden	ELUXY	0.39
Montedison	Chemicals	Italy	MNT	0.33
Elan Corp.	Pharmaceutical	Ireland	ELN	0.24
Fila Holding	Shoes, leather	Italy	FLH	0.24
Pacific Dunlop	Misc. Manufacturing	Australia	PDLPY	0.23
Benetton	Textiles	Italy	BNG	0.22

care of this to avoid inconveniences, it would require time to process the transactions, causing delays in payment and added expenses that could dramatically reduce the amount of the dividend payment. For the ADR holder, the depositary takes care of the whole procedure and promptly sends, in dollars, the entire dividend amount.

The information on the reporting of foreign stocks is often delayed and fragmented. In the case of ADRs, it is much easier to get this information from an American broker. The investors receive all the reports in English through the depositaries, including all the news regarding special events.

For all this convenience and comfort there are some disadvantages. At first, it seems a benefit that these foreign stocks are trading during the same hours as other U.S. stocks, from 9:30 a.m. to 3 p.m. on the New York Stock Exchange. This allows the execution prices to be easily monitored and controlled. But for Asian securities, these trades are made when those markets are closed, and for European shares there is only a small overlap where European trading stops shortly after U.S. trading begins.

These time and location differences cause lower price volatility and less volume, or liquidity. By the time the U.S. market begins trading Asian shares, all the business and economic news from that region is in the market already. The Japanese or Chinese governments are not going to release their balance of trade figures, and Toyota Motors of Japan or Hong Kong Telecom will not post their quarterly dividends at midnight, when the New York Stock Exchange is trading. Therefore, those ADRs tend to be less volatile than either a typical U.S. stock or the same security as the ADR trading in its own country. A short-term price change that might occur on the U.S. market is limited to the action of those traders who are trying to interpret how a global news or economic event would immediately affect a foreign stock.

It is not surprising that the volume of trading on the ADR in New York is less than the same stock traded in its own country. The main components of the demand for a stock always originate at the company's primary location and major business center. Individual investors are more likely to understand and invest in companies operating in their own countries; however, institutional investing is much more flexible and is moving large portions of its portfolios into foreign holdings. An institution will trade at any place and time that will allow it to fulfill its objectives.

Unusual Global Effects. The stock market crash of 1987 is still a good example of global trading. On October 19, the Dutch stock Philips Electronics recorded a loss of about 12% in Amsterdam, where the market closes its session during the early NYSE trading hours. The local trading hours of 9:30 a.m. to 4:30 p.m. mean that the Amsterdam exchange, a six-hour time change from New York, closes one hour after the New York Stock Exchange opens. The ADR continued to be traded on Wall Street after the close of the Amsterdam market and followed the dramatic plunge of all stocks, extending the loss to 24% by 4 p.m., the close of trading on the New York Stock Exchange. An additional 10% loss was recorded in Amsterdam the day after. In this case the ADR had anticipated the domestic stock price behavior because the main cause of the slide was the events occurring abroad.

Currency Shifts.   The other imponderable factor that could affect the daily volatility of an ADR is the corresponding foreign currency exchange rate. The change in value of a currency is the result of global currency trading that weighs the relative effects of interest rate policy and inflation on importing and exporting for each country. Since the ADR's price is traded in U.S. dollars, it must be translated each day according to the current exchange rate of the originating country. In fact, because currency prices are quoted in the Interbank market continuously and can change quickly, the price of the ADR can be changing throughout its trading in New York, entirely based on currency changes.

The following is a comparison between the daily average intraday volatility of five foreign blue-chip stocks and the corresponding ADRs in 1995:

Company	Daily average (% volatility)		
	Domestic share	ADR	$/Currency
Sony Corp. (Japan)	2.2	1.1	1.25
Unilever Plc. (U.K.)	1.5	0.7	0.86
Daimler (Germany)	1.1	0.8	1.19
Fiat (Italy)	2.1	1.2	1.07
Elf (France)	1.9	1.3	1.02

The average intraday volatility of the five stocks of this example is about 1.7 times that of the corresponding ADRs. This shows that global influences and currency changes are not enough to raise the volatility in the ADR by very much after normal business hours. A lower volatility means less surprises in the execution price; you can expect to buy or sell the ADR shares reasonably close to the last closing price of the stock in the country of origin.

Do ADRs Really Reflect the Underlying Foreign Stocks?

It is safest never to assume too much without verification. Before relying on the ADR, we should see how close those prices are to the underlying foreign stock. Perhaps large swings in currency exchange rates and global events cause the price of the ADR to be far different from its foreign shares, and the ADR has taken on a life of its own.

Table 5-2 shows an example of four foreign blue-chip companies: LVMH (France), previously named Louis Vuitton Moët Hennessy, Philips Electronics (the Netherlands), Toyota Motors (Japan), and British Gas (United Kingdom). For each company there are two columns: the first one reports the monthly returns of the stock traded in the country of origin, translated into U.S. dollars; the second col-

Table 5-2. Comparison of Returns of Domestic Shares versus ADRs

Date	LVMH Domestic	LVMH ADR	Philips Electronic Domestic	Philips Electronic ADR	Toyota Motors Domestic	Toyota Motors ADR	British Gas Domestic	British Gas ADR
Feb. 1992	1.0%	1.1%	13.0%	13.6%	−3.2%	−3.1%	0.40%	−2.73%
Mar. 1992	−4.3%	−3.8%	−0.6%	0.0%	−7.8%	−9.0%	−3.62%	−1.97%
Apr. 1992	−2.1%	−0.8%	3.6%	3.8%	7.9%	8.7%	5.93%	8.31%
May 1992	−3.9%	−7.3%	4.8%	3.6%	5.1%	5.9%	3.10%	0.26%
Jun. 1992	1.8%	3.8%	−17.8%	−17.5%	−2.7%	−3.3%	−1.58%	−2.11%
Jul. 1992	−5.8%	−4.4%	−17.9%	−17.7%	−3.3%	−2.5%	−1.27%	−0.81%
Aug. 1992	6.1%	4.1%	5.0%	5.2%	6.3%	5.6%	4.08%	3.26%
Sep. 1992	3.8%	2.3%	−5.7%	−7.4%	−1.6%	−0.5%	−8.93%	−7.89%
Oct. 1992	−13.2%	−12.5%	−24.3%	−22.1%	−2.2%	−3.3%	−3.46%	−0.00%
Nov. 1992	0.7%	−0.4%	4.3%	3.4%	0.6%	−0.3%	0.14%	−3.71%
Dec. 1992	−3.1%	−2.4%	−4.1%	−5.5%	3.9%	3.9%	4.51%	3.86%
Jan. 1993	−14.0%	−12.9%	20.4%	19.8%	−4.3%	−4.7%	−4.21%	−2.29%
Feb. 1993	3.0%	1.3%	−9.7%	−7.8%	1.1%	1.1%	0.34%	−0.88%
Mar. 1993	15.5%	15.5%	17.6%	16.8%	15.9%	14.9%	12.23%	11.80%
Apr. 1993	1.2%	1.6%	0.0%	7.2%	19.9%	19.6%	0.75%	0.79%
May 1993	−2.9%	−2.3%	11.0%	3.4%	−3.6%	−2.6%	−5.52%	−4.19%
Jun. 1993	0.9%	2.4%	3.3%	2.4%	−5.7%	−6.7%	−0.99%	−1.64%
Jul. 1993	1.8%	0.7%	0.5%	0.8%	8.7%	9.4%	2.63%	3.06%
Aug. 1993	7.0%	7.8%	23.0%	23.6%	2.4%	3.4%	7.33%	7.55%
Sep. 1993	−10.4%	−10.3%	4.0%	3.8%	1.2%	1.0%	−0.24%	−0.25%
Oct. 1993	−4.8%	−4.3%	2.3%	2.5%	6.2%	6.4%	4.37%	7.54%
Nov. 1993	−1.3%	−2.0%	−6.4%	−6.6%	−13.1%	−19.0%	−5.54%	−7.71%
Dec, 1993	2.1%	2.6%	6.1%	5.8%	7.1%	14.6%	3.93%	4.30%
Jan. 1994	6.6%	6.5%	21.9%	22.4%	12.9%	11.8%	5.58%	4.37%
Feb. 1994	1.9%	0.9%	−1.8%	−2.0%	7.6%	7.7%	−9.80%	−9.30%
Mar. 1994	8.0%	7.0%	10.5%	9.1%	−2.3%	−0.8%	−6.38%	−7.95%
Apr. 1994	10.3%	11.9%	7.4%	7.9%	2.3%	1.8%	−3.39%	−2.51%
May 1994	−6.1%	−6.8%	−5.1%	−3.9%	4.8%	2.9%	−8.24%	−6.85%
Jun. 1994	−0.1%	0.4%	3.9%	2.7%	9.5%	11.5%	3.73%	1.84%
Jul. 1994	14.8%	14.7%	6.2%	7.4%	−4.5%	−5.7%	0.00%	1.20%
Aug. 1994	2.5%	4.3%	5.8%	5.7%	0.9%	1.9%	12.77%	10.42%
Sep. 1994	0.1%	0.4%	−5.8%	−6.9%	−4.7%	−5.2%	0.77%	0.81%
Oct. 1994	−2.1%	−3.0%	8.4%	7.8%	6.4%	7.5%	1.59%	1.34%
Nov. 1994	−0.8%	−0.4%	−8.6%	−7.6%	−2.6%	−3.0%	1.23%	1.85%
Dec. 1994	−1.3%	−1.9%	−2.1%	−2.9%	−1.5%	−1.3%	1.68%	1.04%
Jan. 1995	0.3%	1.2%	6.3%	7.2%	−8.1%	−9.4%	−2.38%	−1.54%
Feb. 1995	0.7%	0.8%	4.9%	4.4%	−6.8%	−5.7%	−4.03%	−4.17%
Mar. 1995	23.2%	22.2%	3.2%	3.8%	10.8%	13.6%	1.06%	1.63%
Apr. 1995	−3.4%	−3.2%	12.0%	12.8%	1.9%	−0.7%	4.58%	4.28%
May 1995	−0.2%	0.3%	4.2%	4.2%	−4.0%	−4.4%	−1.29%	−0.51%
Jun. 1995	−4.8%	−4.9%	6.6%	6.5%	2.3%	3.6%	−4.08%	−5.15%
Jul. 1995	7.4%	4.1%	14.4%	15.2%	4.7%	3.6%	0.99%	1.63%
Total return	29.8%	28.3%	177.1%	181.4%	80.0%	78.3%	3.80%	2.20%
Correlation *		0.99		0.98		0.97		0.95

*Correlation between domestic stock returns in U.S. dollars and ADR returns.

umn shows the monthly returns of the corresponding ADR. At the bottom of each column is the total return from January 1992 to July 1995.

The correlation coefficient, based on the monthly returns of each domestic stock and ADR pair is very close to 1, reflecting the strict, nearly identical relationship between the two price series. The little differences that occur sometimes are caused by the time lag between the New York market close and the foreign market close. The fluctuations in currency markets that occur in the middle are partly responsible for those differences; nevertheless, they do not change the overall pattern of the results.

A Few Words about Securities Law

The U.S. securities laws require very extensive disclosure from the foreign companies wishing to access the American capital markets by being listed on a U.S. exchange. Both the initial offering of securities to the public and the subsequent trading are strictly regulated. This is an additional guarantee for the investors. In fact, the Securities Act of 1933 makes it illegal to sell securities to the public if they have not been registered with the SEC, the Securities and Exchange Commission.

One of the requirements of the foreign company wishing to use the ADR market is to reconcile its accounts according the U.S. *generally accepted accounting principles* (GAAP). They must also disclose the information required by the SEC under the Securities Act, such as share ownership, financial reports, and insider trading.

Many foreign issuers find it attractive to offer their securities in the U.S. market because of its enormous depth, the low costs of equity financing on an international scale, and the logical relationship between an equity base in the United States and the extension of their business operations to America. Nevertheless, all of the government regulations and procedures sometimes discourage the issuers. U.S. requirements are often stricter and more complex than those foreign issuers are used to fulfilling in their home country.

These hurdles are the reason why the depositary receipts do not yet fully represent all foreign stocks and why many important European and Japanese firms are not part of the ADR family as they should be. Even though many important foreign blue-chip companies are still absent from the list of the available ADRs, we can still say that the choice is very good for investors wishing to build a portfolio of diversified overseas stocks, as we are going to show in the next sections.

Considerations about the Foreign
Stock Valuation

American depositary receipts are sold in dollars in the United States and are subject to trading and custody rules. Yet their nature as foreign stocks must not be forgotten, and they should not be analyzed in the same manner as U.S. stocks. Usually, it is hard to compare values of the equities of one country to those of another because of different market influences such as interest rates, earnings scale, inflation, and other economic and political factors.

The same valuation standards used for the American stocks are often inappropriate. The underlying value of foreign stocks, even if also traded in the United States, usually originated in the foreign country where most of their capitalization resides. A smaller part is traded abroad with the few exceptions of multinational companies, such as Unilever, Smithkline Beecham, or Royal Dutch Shell, whose stocks are priced simultaneously in several markets with large, almost equal volume.

Investors in international stocks must be particularly wary not to use the same evaluation methods that apply to the U.S. stocks in terms of the familiar price to earning ratios. The example of the Japanese stocks is symptomatic. In the 1980s, especially when compared to 1990, the end of the decade, Japanese equities traded at exaggerated price to earning ratios. Some analysts asserted that other valuation methods had to be used for Japanese stocks. As a matter of fact, the market continued to collect record after record during several years despite its unrealistic equity prices. It was only at the end of the last decade that the investor realized that the market was too expensive. One of the strongest market rallies in history turned into a long and exhausting bear market.

It is the replay of the same old story that has little to do with the corporate balance sheets. Nevertheless, a diversified investment in U.S. and Japanese stocks, as we already stated and analyzed in Chapter 3, had been a successful choice that significantly improved investment results in terms of risk compared to reward, despite all the extremely sharp market swings.

In the big picture, foreign stocks should be used in an equity portfolio for the purpose of diversification and to improve the quality of the investment results. The analysis of foreign stocks must take into consideration the reality of their domestic markets.

A Useful Tool Worldwide

The value of the depositary receipts as a vehicle to build an international equity portfolio is not recognized only by Americans. Global portfolio managers worldwide find ADRs a worthy alternative to the direct purchasing of foreign stocks in their country of origin. Take the example of fund managers who, no matter in which country they are based, need to implement a world stock strategy that includes U.S. equities. If all the securities they are going to trade are listed on Wall Street, they can benefit from all the advantages we have discussed by using only one currency and one counterparty, especially avoiding the waste of time and money generated by the need for several custodians. The task of keeping multiple currency accounts and processing cash dividends from different countries subjected to different fiscal rules would require a more expensive and less flexible administrative structure.

If we decide to sell a German stock and replace it with a Spanish one, then we need to change the marks we obtain from the sale into the pesetas needed for the purchase. Perhaps the settlement dates for the two trades are not the same because of different market rules. If we use ADRs instead we will avoid all those problems. The same benefits that work for Americans are also an advantage for all world investors as well.

Limitations.   The main drawback of using ADRs is the limited listings represented by this market. If it is necessary to choose from a much broader list of stocks in a specific foreign market, then the direct access is irreplaceable. ADRs traded on Wall Street do not represent any one foreign market sufficiently to allow extensive choice. Large, specialized institutions, whose business is to manage specific international funds, will go directly to the foreign markets. Their size and structure impose this choice.

The use of ADRs is therefore more suitable for the smaller fund managers and private investors wishing to invest abroad who can benefit from all the advantages of international diversification while avoiding the difficulties of overseas trading and who are not bothered by choosing a substantial company from a shorter list.

Currency Risk

Since an ADR is traded in U.S. dollars, its value is the translation from the original currency price of the foreign stock. Price changes in that foreign currency significantly influence the ADR's value, especially if the currency is as volatile as the European or the Japanese ones. This volatility is an additional risk factor in the investment that should be considered and treated seriously.

If an investor in foreign equities does not want to take the currency risk, that risk can be hedged in one of the ways we described in Chapter 3. Any amount invested in ADRs representing stocks of a certain country that need protection from currency swings can be hedged by selling the corresponding dollar amount of the underlying currency using a cash forward exchange transaction, using futures, or buying a put option. If no hedging strategy is used, then the currency fluctuation will influence the result of the investment together with the equity price swings.

By selling the foreign currency (vis-à-vis the U.S. dollar) the buyer of ADRs is protected from a decline in that currency, with respect to the U.S. dollar, which would force down the price of the shares. At the same time, if the price of the foreign currency gained against the dollar, you would not benefit. By buying a put option in the same currency, you pay a premium for protection against the decline in the foreign currency but have an opportunity to profit from its rise.

Figure 5-1 shows a normalized comparison between the Japanese stock Toyota and its ADR from 1990 to 1995 by setting their values to 100 on January 1, 1990. A quick glance is enough to state that the performance of the value of the stock in U.S. dollars has been much more rewarding than the investment denominated in Japanese yen. This has been possible because of the dollar's 30% depreciation against the yen in recent years. In fact, over the six-year period the ADR gained a good 47% while the stock traded in yen decreased about 3%.

In this case a fully hedged ADR, protecting the investor from a drop in the yen, would have proved to be quite disappointing, because all the revenue of the ADR

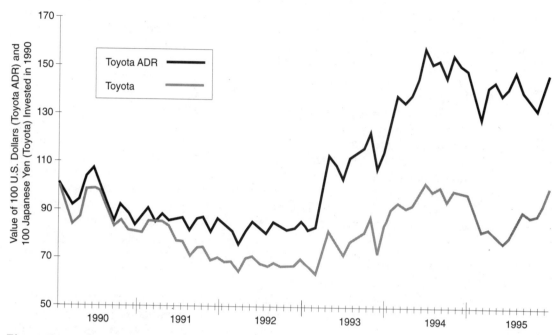

Figure 5-1. Comparison of Toyota shares traded in Japan (in yen) with its ADR (in U.S. dollars). Trading in U.S. dollars has been an advantage.

was generated by the gain in the value of the yen. A particular trading strategy for the currency itself could be the best solution, and examples of this can be found in Chapter 3.

This opportunity to either hedge or not hedge is an important benefit to trading ADRs. If you do not want the exposure of currency swings but are only looking for portfolio diversification based on independent equity movements, then a fully hedged position is the solution. On the other hand, diversification can be enhanced by only partially hedging the currency. You then hold a truly international portfolio, where your investment takes on a world value. If the economy of the Far East is strong, you gain in all those shares traded in that time zone. If the price of an imported Japanese car rises, so does your portfolio. However, if the U.S. dollar is stronger, your ADR will lose relative value, but imports will be cheaper. Overall, your portfolio represents both domestic and international trade and protects you from inflation in the true sense at a time when products are manufactured everywhere in the world.

Results of an ADR Portfolio
Compared to U.S. Stocks

What results can be expected when investing in ADRs rather than in U.S. stocks? Because ADRs are a substitute for investments abroad, the answer could be found in Chapter 3, where we analyzed in some depth the results of international diversification through the history and market behavior of foreign stock indices.

Yet an index is a collection or basket of stocks, and if we want to duplicate those same returns we should buy the same equities that compose the index. We know with the ADRs available, even if their number is rapidly increasing, it can be difficult to find certain representative blue-chip companies of many foreign markets. In other words, it is not always possible to replicate the foreign stock index that we want to use through the ADRs. If the British, Japanese, and Dutch stocks are represented by well-known blue-chip companies such as Toyota, Sony, British Telecom, and Unilever, there are other important markets, such as Germany, that do not have the best sample of stocks as ADRs.

ADRs, nevertheless, even if they do not perfectly represent the foreign indices as the Nikkei or the FTSE-100, contain so many possibilities of investment and choice that it is very likely that we can find satisfactory diversification.

Do the ADRs Give the Same Results as Foreign Indices?

Having argued that it is more practical to use ADRs than to try to trade directly in another country, we need to show that convenience can also be profitable. The aim of this section is to analyze the possibilities that ADRs offer in order to obtain the same benefits of diversification represented by the full country index discussed in Chapter 3.

To accomplish this we compared the returns of the international market indices to those of two indices of ADRs. The AMEX International Index, containing 49 foreign blue-chip companies, can be found in detail, with its components and respective weightings, in Table 5-1 on page 136. The other is the NASDAQ ADR Index comprised of 101 items; many of them are small capitalization stocks with an added representation of emerging markets.

The stocks in the AMEX International Index can be grouped to show the percentage weighting by country (see Table 5-3). Because the AMEX International Index is a capitalization-weighted index, stocks such as Japanese Toyota or European Royal Dutch are weighted more than 8% in the basket, while other important car makers, such as Volvo or Fiat, are weighted less than 1%. The index is globally well distributed by country, excluding the United States, of course. Japanese stocks represent about 38%, European stocks 53%, Pacific Rim stocks 7%, and Hong Kong stocks 2%. However, this basket also has shortcomings: it does not correctly represent Germany, where the only company present in the index is Daimler Benz, and the French companies LVMH, Elf, and Total are certainly not a reasonable facsimile of the CAC index of French stocks.

Fortunately, we are not forced to use this index in order to get a portfolio of diversified ADRs in our investment, and there are many other individual equities available instead. This index does point out that there are ADR issues lacking and definite limitations for the investor who wants to follow the same performance patterns as the main foreign indices.

Table 5-3. Components and Weighting of the
AMEX International Index

Component	Weighting, %
Japan	37.90
United Kingdom	21.55
Netherlands	11.52
Australia	5.99
France	5.69
Sweden	4.22
Spain	3.30
Germany	2.81
Hong Kong	2.05
Italy	1.71
Norway	1.62
New Zealand	0.76
Ireland	0.24

To evaluate whether our available basket satisfies the expectations of international diversification, we have compared its past performance to a benchmark diversification of foreign indices translated into U.S. dollars. For this example, we used the following composition as a good proxy of market distribution by importance: Japan 40%, Great Britain 20%, Germany 12%, France 10%, Netherlands 5%, Italy 4%, Spain 4%, and Australia 5%.

Figure 5-2 is a chart that compares our index basket to the AMEX International Index from 1989 to 1995. There is no mistaking the similarities of the two returns seen in the figure and shown in Table 5-4, and despite the structural differences between the two portfolios and the variances in some years, we can say that the similarity between the two is quite good. The correlation coefficient, considered a strong indicator of common movement in the monthly returns of the two series, is 0.86. While not perfect, it can be viewed as very good. The compounded rate of return for the basket of indices was 5.39%, compared to a 6.40% return for the AMEX International Index. Also, the standard deviation of yearly returns is similar (17% versus 14%).

The other index of ADRs, the NASDAQ ADR Index, is very different from the AMEX International Index because it is comprised of many smaller stocks, including companies in Latin American and other emerging markets. These shares greatly impact the index pattern, offsetting some of the more substantial firms, such as Sweden's Ericsson and the British Reuters, which are weighted a good 35% of that index.

The returns of the NASDAQ ADR Index have been much higher than the AMEX index from 1989 to 1995, because these smaller foreign stocks outperformed the blue-chip companies and because there are fewer Japanese stocks in the index, which, as we well know, have been very weak since the early 1990s.

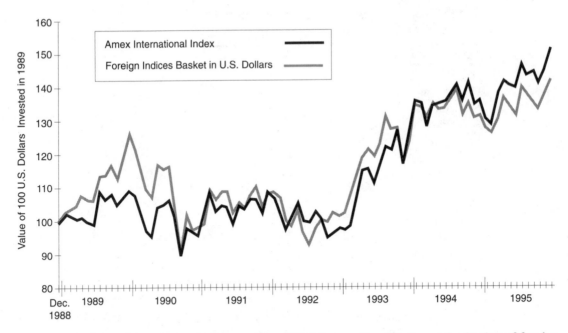

Figure 5-2. Comparison of returns between the AMEX International Index and a basket of foreign indices converted into U.S. dollars. There is no mistaking the similarities.

Not All ADRs Look the Same

A comparison of the two ADR indices is shown in Figure 5-3. The better performance of the NASDAQ index is evident. In fact, its return of 79% from May 1989 to the end of 1995 was nearly double the 40% of the more conservative AMEX International Index during the same period. The standard deviation of yearly returns was higher for the NASDAQ index, as would be expected, but not proportionately as high as the increase in returns, and confirmed by a higher risk-adjusted ratio. These values appear in Table 5-5. Even with the very different mix for the NASDAQ index, we can see that its performance pattern is much closer to the other ADR index than to the Dow.

Up to now we have assessed the performance of two ADR indices that give a representative but somewhat distorted portfolio of the foreign stock markets. They do not, however, give an investor much of a choice in creating a personalized selection of foreign stocks. Most of this problem can be attributed to the way in which these indices have been constructed. We find that there is excessive use of certain stocks or markets to the detriment of others that are totally absent or underweighted. We should not be obligated to accept a portfolio of foreign stocks that were designed for some purpose other than our own investment portfolio.

Table 5-4. Comparison of Returns between the AMEX International Index and a Basket of Foreign Indices Translated into U.S. Dollars

A represents the foreign index basket in U.S. dollars, B the AMEX International Index.

	Yearly returns				
	Year-end	A	B	A	B
	1988	100.0	100.0		
	1989	127.6	110.3	27.6%	10.3%
	1990	98.5	96.1	−22.8%	−12.8%
	1991	108.7	109.4	10.4%	13.8%
	1992	101.8	98.1	−6.3%	−10.3%
	1993	124.9	124.5	22.7%	26.9%
	1994	132.9	137.4	6.4%	10.3%
	1995	144.5	154.4	8.7%	12.4%
Seven-year return		44.5%	54.4%		
Compounded rate of return		5.39%	6.40%		
Average yearly return		6.7%	7.2%		
Standard deviation of returns		17.1%	14.0%		
Risk-adjusted ratio		0.32	0.46		
Correlation index*		0.86			

Basket composition of A

Japan	40%
Great Britain	20%
Germany	12%
France	10%
Netherlands	5%
Italy	4%
Spain	4%
Australia	5%

*On monthly returns.

Finding a More Impartial Benchmark

For this reason we built our own index of 60 ADRs, including 15 Japanese, 35 European, 6 Australian, 2 South African, and 2 Far Eastern stocks. Each equity is given the equal weight of 1.66% ($\frac{1}{60}$) in the index. The list of stocks is given in Table 5-6, together with the annual returns of this basket for the six years from the end of 1989 to the end of 1995.

The results of our basket fall somewhat in the middle of the two ADR indices, the AMEX and the NASDAQ. This means we can construct any number of portfolios and get a reasonably realistic view of how the ADR market can be used. Figure 5-4 shows an annual performance comparison of these three investments, the AMEX International Index, the NASDAQ ADR Index, and our basket of 60 ADRs, which falls in the middle.

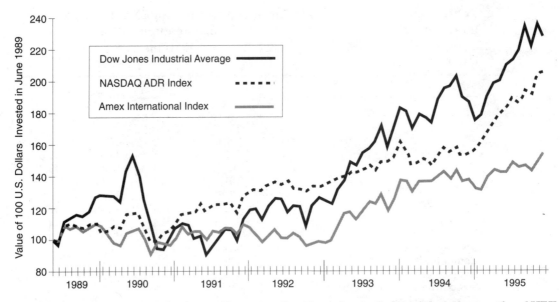

Figure 5-3. Comparison of returns between the Dow Jones Industrial Average, the AMEX International Index, and the NASDAQ ADR Index. Although the NASDAQ had greater volatility, the two ADR indices had related patterns.

Table 5-5. Comparison of Returns among the Dow Jones Industrial Average, The AMEX International Index, and the NASDAQ ADR Index

				Yearly returns		
Year-end	AMEX Intl.	NASDAQ ADR	Dow Jones	AMEX Intl.	NASDAQ ADR	Dow Jones
1989	100.00	100.00	100.00			
1990	87.27	78.84	95.50	−12.7%	−21.2%	−4.5%
1991	99.34	88.32	112.65	13.8%	12.0%	18.0%
1992	89.09	98.85	119.90	−10.3%	11.9%	6.4%
1993	113.03	135.14	136.35	26.9%	36.7%	13.7%
1994	124.70	146.86	139.27	10.3%	8.7%	2.1%
1995	140.15	179.16	185.86	12.4%	22.0%	33.4%
Six-year return	40.1%	79.2%	85.9%			
Compounded rate of return	5.8%	10.2%	10.9%			
Average yearly return	10.6%	18.3%	14.7%			
Standard deviation of returns	15.3%	19.1%	13.4%			
Risk-adjusted ratio	0.38	0.53	0.81			

Table 5-6. Selection of 60 International Blue-Chip ADRs

Ticker Symbol	Company	Country
BHP	Broken Hill	Australia
FAI	FAI	Australia
NAB	Nat. Bank Australia	Australia
NWS	News Corp.	Australia
PDLPY	Pacific Dunlop	Australia
SPPTY	South Pacific Petroleum	Australia
LVMHY	LVMH	France
TCSFY	Thomson	France
HKT	Hong Kong Tel.	Hong Kong
BNG	Benetton	Italy
FIA	Fiat	Italy
MNT	Montedison	Italy
TOYOY	Toyota	Japan
HIT	Hitachi	Japan
SNE	Sony	Japan
HMC	Honda	Japan
NSANY	Nissan	Japan
NIPNY	NEC	Japan
FUJIY	Fuji Photo	Japan
CANNY	Canon, Inc.	Japan
TDK	TDK	Japan
KNBWY	Kirin Brewery	Japan
MITSY	Mitsui & Co.	Japan
TKIOY	Tokio Marine	Japan
KUB	Kubota	Japan
IYCOY	Ito Yokado	Japan
KYO	Kyocera	Japan
AKZOY	Akzo Nobel	Netherlands
KLM	KLM	Netherlands
PHG	Philips Electronics	Netherlands
RD	Royal Dutch Petroleum	Netherlands
UN	Unilever	Netherlands
PHI	Philippine Long Distance	Philippines
GLDFY	Goldfields SAF	South Africa
KLOFY	Kloof Gold	South Africa
REP	Repsol	Spain
TEF	Telefonica	Spain
BBV	Bilbao Vizcaya	Spain
ELE	Endesa	Spain
ELUXY	Electrolux	Sweden
ASEAY	ASEA	Sweden
ERICY	Ericsson	Sweden
VOLVY	Volvo	Sweden
BCS	Barclays	United Kingdom
BTI	BAT Industries	United Kingdom
BAB	British Airways	United Kingdom
BRG	British Gas	United Kingdom
BST	British Steel	United Kingdom

Table 5-6. Selection of 60 International Blue-Chip ADRs (*Continued*)

Ticker Symbol	Company	Country
BTY	British Telecom	United Kingdom
CADBY	Cadbury Schweppes	United Kingdom
COU	Courtaulds	United Kingdom
GLX	Glaxo	United Kingdom
NW	National Westminster Bank	United Kingdom
RANKY	Rank Organisation	United Kingdom
SC	Shell Trans. & Trading	United Kingdom
SBH	Smithkline Beecham	United Kingdom
HAN	Hanson Plc.	United Kingdom
ICI	Imperial Chemical Industries	United Kingdom
VOD	Vodafone	United Kingdom
CWP	Cable & Wireless	United Kingdom

Yearly Returns of the Equity Portfolio of the Above		
Year-end	Return	Indexed return
1989		100.00
1990	−16.09%	83.91
1991	22.31%	102.62
1992	−9.02%	93.37
1993	36.28%	127.24
1994	10.29%	140.33
1995	10.40%	154.92

The presence of fast growing economic influences is quite clear in the NASDAQ ADR Index. To its benefit we can attribute the huge interest in emerging markets to excellent results of this investment basket from 1991 to 1995, along with the favorable environment in the stock markets of the world. Offsetting that is 1990, when markets turned strongly bearish, and this index underperformed the others. This switch from underperforming to overperforming results in volatility that is higher than that in the other indices.

In our own index of equally weighted world blue-chip stocks, the emerging markets are not well represented. One reason for this is that we did not want to include extreme situations where overaccelerated growth could give a distorted slant to our analysis. It is always important, nevertheless, to pay attention to what is happening in these markets and not forget their growth potential.

The other reason for not including emerging markets is that we did not have enough historical price data for those stocks to perform a reliable evaluation. Without using these exceptional growth markets, the returns of our basket of 60 foreign stocks fall closer to those of the more conservative AMEX International Index.

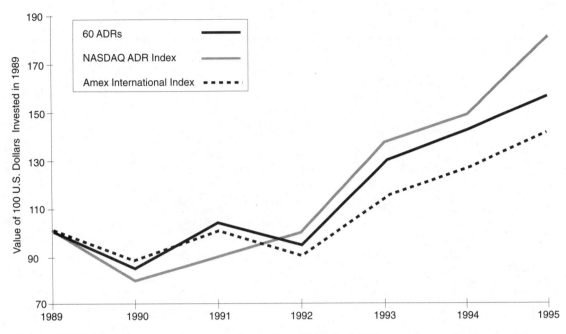

Figure 5-4. Comparison of three ADR indices. Using individual ADRs, we can construct our own representative portfolio.

The Dow Jones Industrial Average and the ADRs

If we compare the results of our ADR basket to that of the U.S. blue-chip companies, as measured by the Dow Jones Industrial Average of 30 industrial stocks, we will see that the American stocks performed better than the foreign basket. We know that by the mid-1990s Wall Street had been strongly outperforming the other world exchanges, but we must not forget the added value that geographic diversification gives to the quality of investment results, as we discussed in the first two chapters of this book.

As shown in Table 5-7, some years were marked by excellent performance in foreign stocks and other years by their underpeformance compared to the U.S. blue-chip companies. In 1990 the Dow Jones resisted the turmoil caused by the Gulf War crisis better than foreign stocks. The Japanese market, highly dependent upon oil prices, suffered more than others. And, while 1992 was a relatively bearish year for the average of foreign blue-chip stocks, 1993 and 1994 would have been a very timely period to diversify into international stocks because our foreign equity basket outperformed the 16% return of the Dow by over 50% during those two years.

Table 5-7. Comparison of Returns among 60 Blue-Chip ADRs and the 30 Stocks Comprising the Dow Jones Industrial Average

Year-end	60 ADRs	Dow Jones	Equal Distribution	Yearly returns 60 ADRs	Yearly returns Dow Jones	Yearly returns Equal Distribution
1989	100.00	100.00	100.00			
1990	83.91	95.50	89.70	−16.1%	−4.5%	−10.3%
1991	102.62	112.65	107.76	22.3%	18.0%	20.1%
1992	93.37	119.90	106.37	−9.0%	6.4%	−1.3%
1993	127.24	136.35	132.96	36.3%	13.7%	25.0%
1994	140.33	139.27	141.23	10.3%	2.1%	6.2%
1995	154.92	185.86	172.19	10.4%	33.4%	21.9%
Six-year return	54.9%	85.9%	72.2%			
Compounded rate of return	7.6%	10.9%	9.5%			
Average yearly return	14.0%	14.7%	14.4%			
Standard deviation of returns	19.4%	13.4%	14.3%			
Risk-adjusted ratio	0.39	0.81	0.66			

A Smaller Foreign Stock Selection for Historical Evaluation

Diversification between the U.S. and foreign stocks would allow us to benefit from less volatile returns, but to evaluate these benefits correctly, six years of price history is simply not enough to be statistically reliable. There are some large, well-known foreign companies, nevertheless, that have been traded as ADRs for many years, and we can analyze a basket of 15 of those stocks from 1981 to 1995. The list of the stocks composing the basket and their returns over 15 years from 1981 through 1995 are shown in Table 5-8.

This selection, which presumes an equal weighting of 6.7% ($^1/_{15}$) for each stock, represents the following distribution of countries: Japan (46.6%), Great Britain (26.7%), and the Netherlands (26.7%). It does well representing the primary foreign companies by including such giants as Toyota, Royal Dutch, Glaxo, Sony, and Philips.

The broader geographic distribution contains 46.6% Asian stocks, represented entirely by Japan, and the remainder in European stocks. It would seem that Europe might be a little overexposed except that companies such as Royal Dutch, Unilever, and Glaxo should be considered as multinational because they are active throughout the world rather than only associated with their country of origin. The most important sectors of the world economy are also represented well and include auto, oil and gas, food and tobacco, electronics, transportation, pharmaceutical, insurance, and telecommunications industries.

The way an investment performed in these important companies during the 15 years from 1981 to 1995 deserves some attention. A basket of stocks comprised of these firms increased the initial investment by 853.7%, equivalent to a com-

Table 5-8. Selection of 15 International Blue-Chip Companies with 15 Years of History as ADRs

Ticker symbol	Company	Country
BTI	Bat Industries	United Kingdom
GLX	Glaxo	United Kingdom
RANKY	Rank Organisation	United Kingdom
SC	Shell Trans. & Trading	United Kingdom
PHG	Philips Electronics	Netherlands
RD	Royal Dutch Petroleum	Netherlands
UN	Unilever	Netherlands
KLM	KLM	Netherlands
KUB	Kubota	Japan
TOYOY	Toyota Motor	Japan
SNE	Sony	Japan
HIT	Hitachi	Japan
HMC	Honda Motor	Japan
TKIOY	Tokio Marine	Japan
MITSY	Mitsui & Co.	Japan

Yearly Returns of the Equity Portfolio of the Above		
Year-end	Return	Indexed returns
1980		100.00
1981	10.6%	110.64
1982	18.7%	131.38
1983	15.6%	151.89
1984	7.5%	163.34
1985	42.4%	232.63
1986	49.7%	348.23
1987	20.5%	419.75
1988	29.7%	544.38
1989	18.1%	643.14
1990	−20.9%	508.98
1991	19.9%	610.37
1992	−11.2%	541.83
1993	28.9%	704.08
1994	15.2%	811.11
1995	17.6%	953.70

pounded yearly rate of return of 16.2%. The 30 American blue-chip companies, given by the Dow Jones Industrial Average, returned only a 429.2% capital increase during the same years, corresponding to a compounded rate of return of 11.7%.

Along with the higher returns of foreign blue-chip companies, there was a predictable increase in investment volatility. The standard deviation of yearly returns was 17.8%, more than 4% higher than the Dow's 13.5%, but the risk-adjusted ratio (the ratio of the compounded yearly rate of return and the standard deviation of yearly returns) was still better (0.91 versus 0.87 for the Dow).

Diversification Is Always Worthwhile

Once again the best results came from diversification. If we had built a portfolio with 40% of the assets in the 30 American blue-chip companies of the Dow and 60% in our 15 ADRs, we would have achieved a geographical distribution of 40% United States, 28% Japan, and 32% Europe. This diversification meant a 679.0% return in 15 years for a compounded yearly rate of return of 14.7% and a standard deviation of yearly returns of 14.5%, therefore giving a very desirable risk-adjusted ratio of 1.01. Table 5-9 and Figure 5-5 give a graphical comparison among investments in the DJIA, in the 15 ADRs, and in a combination of both, with 40% in U.S. stocks and 60% in the 15 ADRs.

The reliability of this selection of 15 ADRs is seen in the comparison of its results, from 1990 to 1995, to those of the AMEX International Index. The correla-

Table 5-9. Comparison of Returns between the DJIA, 15 ADRs, and a Portfolio of 40% U.S. Stocks and 60% ADRs

		Yearly returns					
	Year-end	15 ADRs	Dow Jones	40% DJIA + 60% ADRs	15 ADRs	Dow Jones	40% DJIA + 60% ADRs
	1980	100.00	100.00	100.00			
	1981	110.64	90.54	102.60	10.6%	−9.5%	2.6%
	1982	131.38	108.29	122.19	18.7%	19.6%	19.1%
	1983	151.89	130.24	143.54	15.6%	20.3%	17.5%
	1984	163.34	124.61	147.55	7.5%	−4.3%	2.8%
	1985	232.63	159.67	201.70	42.4%	28.1%	36.7%
	1986	348.23	199.76	282.10	49.7%	25.1%	39.9%
	1987	419.75	200.63	317.36	20.5%	0.4%	12.5%
	1988	544.38	224.40	388.94	29.7%	11.9%	22.6%
	1989	643.14	284.90	473.21	18.1%	27.0%	21.7%
	1990	508.98	272.07	405.46	−20.9%	−4.5%	−14.3%
	1991	610.37	320.94	483.06	19.9%	18.0%	19.1%
	1992	541.83	341.60	462.95	−11.2%	6.4%	−4.2%
	1993	704.08	388.47	571.53	29.9%	13.7%	23.5%
	1994	811.11	396.78	628.55	15.2%	2.1%	10.0%
	1995	953.70	529.50	778.95	17.6%	33.4%	23.9%
15-year return		853.7%	429.5%	679.0%			
Compounded rate of return		16.2%	11.8%	14.7%			
Average yearly return		17.6%	12.5%	15.6%			
Standard deviation of returns		17.8%	13.5%	14.5%			
Risk-adjusted ratio		0.91	0.87	1.01			

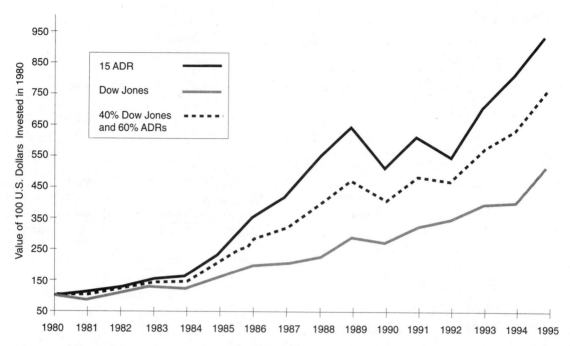

Figure 5-5. Comparison of returns between the DJIA, 15 ADRs, and a portfolio of 40% U.S. stocks and 60% ADRs. Again, results favor diversification, even with a small sample of foreign markets.

tion coefficient between the yearly returns of the two series is extremely high, at 0.985. The total return of the 15 ADRs was 48.3%, while the AMEX Index returned 40.2%. This means that we can comfortably use this smaller selection of stocks as a reliable proxy to evaluate the effects of diversification in international equities.

When we compare the differences between the returns in the U.S. market with those of foreign stocks, we should always remember the effects of the currency swings that occurred over those years. The conclusions from the analysis that was performed in Chapter 4 apply here as well. The appreciation of the yen and the Dutch guilder from 1981 to 1995 made a significant change in the final results.

We also noted that during the 15 years observed, the foreign stocks outperformed the Dow eight times and underperformed it four times. In three of those years their results were almost equal. In four of the eight years when foreign stocks outperformed the U.S. market, 1985, 1986, 1987, and 1994, the dollar's depreciation had a significant impact. In 1992 the 15 ADRs underperformed the Dow because of the 26% fall of the Japanese market in the absence of a substantial U.S. dollar depreciation against the yen. For other years when the returns of the 15 foreign blue-chip companies were disappointing, in comparison with the U.S. stocks, we see that 1990 had a 20.9% loss versus −4.5% for the Dow, while 1989 and 1995 yielded positive but less impressive returns than those of the American blue-chip companies.

A Note on Currency Hedging

It is always possible to apply the currency hedging techniques, described in Chapter 4, to the ADR portion of the portfolio. Because the hedge price is strictly dependent upon the local currency of the foreign stock, currency hedging should be applied to the full investment value of the ADR. The same applies to currency trading strategies.

An investment using ADRs contains the same foreign-market potential as we saw when we analyzed the country index markets in Chapter 3. ADRs have expanded to contain many investment choices among the emerging markets, especially Latin American. The growth potential of these underdeveloped markets is impressive, but the risks of higher price volatility should be taken into consideration when building a stock portfolio. A higher overall volatility is also present in the foreign markets as a whole when you consider currencies. As we discussed in Chapter 4, adding currency swings to normal stock movement adds volatility to any investment in equities.

Foreign-Market Investments through Diversified Products

The purchase of individual stocks, either ADRs or equities traded in their home market, may not always be the best approach to investing abroad. It is not easy to get the investment diversification that you need by owning a few specific stock issues because their price fluctuations do not represent the overall market direction. Also, it is necessary to invest a consistent portion of your capital, otherwise the portfolio created cannot reproduce the world indices that represented the diverse economies in which we want to participate. If the investments target several different countries, this work is even more difficult.

The stock selection process requires significant effort, and it is remarkably time consuming. A broadly diversified portfolio needs to be continuously watched and updated and is not very practical, especially for individuals or for small- or medium-sized managed amounts. The problem is not only in the transaction costs but also in the difficulties of buying numerous stocks and constantly adjusting the portfolio.

The choice to restrict the portfolio selection to a few specific, desirable stocks, in order to catch the market's best performers, is most often a losing game. Traders' experience tells us how difficult it is to beat the market this way. The biggest investment companies develop and use sophisticated asset allocation models focused on just this area. They invest huge amounts of money to maintain large research departments; nevertheless, there is no assurance that, even with careful, calculated stock picking, their investment choices will outperform the markets. Needless to say, for those who have smaller resources at their disposal, the chances of success are even worse.

Trading WEBS

The financial markets are able to provide products that obviate these problems. In the realization of a move toward globalization, the American Stock Exchange introduced the so-called World Equity Benchmark Shares (WEBS) in 1996. They are 17 individual securities especially conceived and designed to provide investors with a targeted exposure to foreign equity markets. Each of the WEBS index series represents an equity portfolio of a specific foreign market that is intended to track the performance of the corresponding Morgan Stanley Capital International (MSCI) country index.

The MSCI indices, used as benchmarks, are market capitalization-weighted indices designed to trace the performance of specific markets. Since they represent nearly two-thirds of the capitalization of a country's equity market, they are quite reliable for this purpose. Morgan Stanley Capital International has been covering the markets of the world for many years, and their indices are well known and widely recognized as benchmarks.

The following WEBS are available at the AMEX (as of July 1996):

Ticker symbol	Country
WBJ	Australia
WPB	Canada
WBQ	Sweden
WBF	France
ING	Germany
INH	Hong Kong
INE	Italy
INJ	Japan
INK	Belgium
INL	Switzerland
INM	Malaysia
INN	Netherlands
INY	Austria
INP	Spain
INR	Singapore
INU	United Kingdom
INW	Mexico

Technical Aspects of WEBS

The World Equities Benchmark Shares series are issued by Foreign Fund, Inc., an investment company registered under the Investment Company Act of 1940. Among the other institutions involved are Morgan Stanley Capital International and the American Stock Exchange. BZW Barclays Global Fund Advisors are responsible for the investment management of each index series, their portfolio construction, basket monitoring, and rebalancing in order to guarantee that the benchmark continues to track the country's market accurately. Morgan Stanley Trust Company is the custodian and lending agent for the portfolio securities that are held in the various foreign countries.

WEBS were launched at the American Stock Exchange on March 1996 at initial prices ranging between $10 and $20, in order to provide easy access to small investors looking to participate to international markets. A round lot of WEBS on an index series is 100 shares. WEBS trade and settle in U.S. dollars three business days after the trade date. Investors can trade during normal market hours in the same way as any other U.S. stock or ADRs. Trading is continuous.

The net asset value of each WEBS is computed daily and determined at the close of the regular trading session on the New York Exchange. The value of each portfolio security is translated into dollars at the prevailing currency rate of each individual country in which they are invested, in just the same manner as an ADR. Just as with an ADR, buying a WEBS exposes the trader to currency risk. In other words, the price movement of a WEBS is the sum of the foreign market price change plus any change in its local currency with respect to the U.S. dollar. If investors wish to participate in the market but want to protect their investment from an eventual weakness of the foreign currency, they must protect themselves by using one of the currency hedging techniques described in Chapter 4.

The performance objective of each WEBS index series is that of the corresponding MSCI index; therefore, the funds are fully invested and not leveraged. Because of technical problems, such as the liquidity of certain securities, the WEBS index series do not generally contain all of the stocks in the corresponding MSCI index. The selection is chosen by the advisor according to analytical models that give a portfolio with the same characteristic of the relevant MSCI index. For this reason a WEBS index series is not expected to track its benchmark index with the same degree of accuracy as it would if it were invested in every stock in the corresponding index. Because of the sophistication of the model that provides a subset of stocks, the tracking error is expected to be less than 5%.

Do WEBS Really Represent the Foreign Markets?

At the time of this writing, the WEBS were only a few months old, and it was not possible to analyze their data over an extended time span. Only the existing four months of price history could be used to verify whether the WEBS index series really tracked the trends of the foreign markets they represent.

As Table 5-10 shows, during the four months from March to July 1996, the correlation between the monthly WEBS returns and those of the local market indices, translated into U.S. dollars, ranged from very high to nearly perfect. We know that some distortion is always possible because the prices used to calculate the WEBS close a few hours after the European markets, and the constant volatility of the currencies, even during the day, makes it likely that some small difference will always exist.

Table 5-10. Correlation between WEBS Returns and Volume of Trading

	Correlation*	Volume in millions		
		Apr. 1996	May 1996	Jun. 1996
Australia	0.997	359	1313	1194
Canada	0.995	383	293	300
Sweden	0.990	376	355	294
France	0.954	209	188	161
Germany	0.999	589	614	1104
Hong Kong	0.982	1500	1170	1471
Italy	0.997	3190	2480	2392
Japan	0.999	4740	2970	3280
Belgium	0.999	0.30	0.27	0.40
Switzerland	0.992	46	33	43
Malaysia	0.996	731	551	442
Netherlands	0.950	400	288	344
Austria	0.991	50	55	7
Spain	0.999	282	219	233
Singapore	0.999	324	445	416
United Kingdom	0.999	6150	5350	5290
Mexico	0.999	1500	1500	1290

*Correlation coefficient between the WEBS monthly returns and the local market indices translated into U.S. dollars from March to July 1996.

Nevertheless, the degree of correlation between the returns of WEBS and the corresponding foreign indices has been, in most cases, very near the value 1.00, which means an almost perfect correlation. In only 3 cases out of 17 was the correlation coefficient below 0.990, but it still fell above 0.950.

Market Liquidity

The volume traded in WEBS, also shown in Table 5-10, indicates good reception by the investors. As we noted for the ADRs, there were many trades in the Japanese market, which is second in the world for size and importance, and among the Anglo-Saxon countries, the United Kingdom came in first but also represented were Australia, Canada, and Hong Kong. It is the famous British tradition that spawned financial interests throughout Southeast Asia; those countries now represent the fusion between the new Far Eastern evolution and the old occidental financial interest in Asia, which attracts a lot of interest from Wall Street.

The American investors were also very interested in Mexico, for natural geographic and economic reasons, but they prefer to use WEBS because they lack the familiarity with the Mexican exchange and are unsure of currency transactions. Therefore they find it easier to trade the Mexican exchange by using a dollar-denominated tool, provided locally.

The Multiple Uses of WEBS

It turns out that because WEBS track the underlying index closely, their use is quite versatile, and they appeal to a variety of market participants. Small, individual investors can easily build a portfolio of foreign stocks, while institutions are more likely to incorporate WEBS within a larger global international portfolio to reduce the volatility of their foreign equity holdings with added diversification or for quick protection.

Imagine the problem of a fund manager who needs to change the exposure in a certain market sector (in this case, geographic) quickly, but cannot possibly act fast because of the complexity of evaluating which and how many specific stocks need to be bought and sold in order to change the allocation correctly. Instead, it is very easy to increase or decrease the allocation in a particular market by trading a basket.

This is the same process that is followed when institutions sell S&P 500 futures or cash in order to hedge part of the risk in their portfolio. It is much cheaper to sell an S&P futures contract with a unit value of about $325,000 for a commission of $15 than to liquidate individual stocks. In addition, the liquidity of the index market is usually far greater for buying and selling than any one stock issue. The convenience and usefulness of trading the whole market at one time attract a much broader participation.

The WEBS are not only useful to Americans. A European wishing to create a small investment portfolio of European stocks can use them as an alternative to the multitude of international equity funds offered by the European institutions. Many equity funds are not traded continuously and can only be subscribed to or redeemed at the time of the next net asset value calculation, which may require notification of up to one week. An investment decision could suffer heavily from this inconvenient delay, especially when markets move fast and your order to buy or sell takes a week to execute.

It is very likely, because of the clear benefits they offer investors, that we will not only see an expansion of these types of market instruments in terms of volume and participation but also a broadening of the products available. It is also likely that, in the near future, new baskets will be issued for other countries and, as interest grows, each of these will have subindices representing specialized business sectors. There is no reason to think that the United States is the only country that has transportation, pharmaceutical, or energy sectors. A benchmark series that crosses borders, allowing investments in Asian technology or European telecommunication stocks, for example, would be very interesting and useful.

The Country Funds

A well-established way to have access to the international markets is the purchase of what is now called *country funds.* Country funds are closed-end mutual funds generally traded at the New York Stock Exchange, although you will find a few traded at other exchanges, including the American Exchange and over the counter.

A closed-end mutual fund has a specific number of shares issued. Unlike ordinary mutual funds that usually sell unlimited shares and that can be redeemed for their net asset value, a closed-end fund is subject to price fluctuations caused by the supply and demand of the fund itself. This volatility is added to that of its net asset value in the same way the currency fluctuation is added to the underlying stock price swings when trading foreign shares.

If an institutional investor decides to buy a massive amount of a closed-end fund, its price will be pushed up just as any other share when it is subjected to a strong demand. In such a case, the value of the assets invested in the fund could be compared to the assets of a company in relation to its share price. It is quite rare, if not impossible, for the per share price of one stock to equal the asset value of the company that it represents.

This same situation can happen with a closed-end fund, where the price is likely to trade at a premium or discount to the net asset value of the fund itself. The consequences of this create disadvantages for those who decide to invest in closed-end funds. For example, shares in a fund may be purchased at a premium, but afterwards, when the assets increase in value, the former premium reverts to a discount because of larger than normal liquidation or other market reasons. The investor does not benefit from the increased value of the underlying assets because the difference between the purchase and selling price, based on the premium and discount, offsets the gain in the assets.

There are times when a large institutional trader will cause these premiums and discounts to occur as the natural result of setting or liquidating a large position. Although the current price of a fund represents a profit for the buyer, a sale at a time of light volume could move prices far enough to take away a large portion of those profits. An institution with very large positions to sell will always depress the price.

The difference between the fund's price and the value of its assets can often vary sharply. These changes in premium or discount are translated into undesired volatility because they extend the range of the price swings. The consequence is that the fund does not track the performance of the market it represents in the way expected by the investor.

The problems arising from asset and price differences as well as liquidity are directly attributed to the fixed number of shares represented by closed-end funds. The fund manager's ability to produce satisfactory investment results is a separate issue because a country fund does not have to track the market it represents exactly, but can be aimed at improving returns over time above that represented by the country's economy. This additional objective can cause both risk and reward to be compounded, but it is not necessarily a disadvantage because there is a good chance that the fund's manager will be successful.

Barron's, the well-known weekly financial newspaper, regularly publishes a list of closed-end funds in its section "Market Week." Among the groups of closed-end funds listed, there is a category called "World Equity Funds," containing nearly 100 names, of which about one-half target single countries and an additional one-third cover groups of foreign countries, such as emerging markets, Latin American, European, or Far Eastern markets. Some funds specialize in small-capitalization stocks or warrants. A list of the World Equity Funds reported by *Barron's* can be found in Table 5-11.

Table 5-11. World Equity Funds Listed Weekly in *Barron's* (1996)

Name	Exchange	Symbol	Premium, June 1996	Investment philosophy
All Seasons Global	NASDAQ	Fund	−23.2%	U.S. and foreign bonds and treasury
Anchor Gold & Currency	Chicago	GCT	−0.5%	Gold and foreign exchange
ASA Limited	NYSE	ASA	−2.1%	South Africa gold mines
Argentina	NYSE	AF	−6.4%	Argentine equities minimum 65%, Argentine bonds up
Asia Pacific Fund	NYSE	APB	−10.8%	Asia Pacific region equities, minimum 80% of assets
Asia Tigers Fund	NYSE	GRR	−10.6%	Asian equities
Austria Fund	NYSE	OST	−21.6%	Austrian equities, Austrian bonds up to 35% of asset
BGR Precious Metals	Toronto	BPT/A	−24.8%	International precious metal shares
Brazil Fund	NYSE	BZF	−10.7%	Brazilian equities, minimum 70% of assets
Brazilian Equity Fund	NYSE	BZL	−13.8%	Brazilian equities, minimum 80% of assets
CDN General Inv.	Toronto	CGI	−26.7%	Canadian equities
CDN World Fund	Toronto	CWF	−21.0%	International equities
Central European Equity	NYSE	CEE	−23.8%	European equities
Chile Fund	NYSE	CH	−8.8%	Chilean equities and bonds, minimum 75% of assets
China Fund	NYSE	CHN	−6.8%	Chinese equities, minimum 50% of assets
Clemente Global Growth Fund	NYSE	CLM	−24.9%	Small- and medium-sized international companies
Czech Republic Fund	NYSE	CRF	−12.6%	Czechian equities
Emerging Mexico Fund	NYSE	MEF	−16.3%	Mexican equities, minimum 65% of assets
Emerging Tigers Fund	NYSE	TGF	NA	Asian and Pacific basin equities
Europe Fund	NYSE	EF	−17.4%	European equities
European Warrant	NYSE	EWF	−23.5%	European equity warrants
Foreign & Colonial Middle East	NYSE	EME	−13.5%	Middle East equities
Fidelity Advisor Korea Fund	NYSE	FAK	−5.3%	Korean equities
Fidelity Advisor Emerging Asia	NYSE	FAE	−13.3%	Asian emerging countries equities
First Australia	AMEX	IAF	−17.9%	Australian equities
First Iberian Fund	AMEX	IBF	−23.0%	Spanish or Portuguese equities
First Israel Fund	NYSE	ISL	−15.7%	Israeli securities, minimum 30% of assets
First Philippine Fund	NYSE	FPF	−20.4%	Philippine equities, minimum 80% of assets
France Growth Fund	NYSE	FRF	−19.3%	French equities, minimum 65% of assets
Germany Emerging	NYSE	FRG	−20.9%	German equities
Germany Fund	NYSE	GER	−22.7%	German equities

Fund	Exchange	Ticker		Description
Germany New	NYSE	GF	−25.9%	German equities
Global Small Cap.	AMEX	GSG	−11.2%	Companies outside U.S.
Greater China	NYSE	GCH	−12.3%	Chinese equities minimum 50% of assets
Growth Fund Spain	NYSE	GSP	−15.8%	Spanish equities minimum 65% of assets
GT Global Developing Mkts.	NYSE	GTD	−19.2%	Emerging markets equities: Europe, Asia, Latin America
Herzfeld Caribbean	NASDAQ	CUBA	12.4%	Caribbean Basin equities
India Fund	NYSE	IFN	−4.0%	Indian equities minimum 65% of assets
India Growth Fund	NYSE	IGF	6.7%	Indian equities minimum 80% of assets
Indonesia Fund	NYSE	IFN	20.2%	Indonesian equities, minimum 65% of assets
Irish Investment Fund	NYSE	IRL	−17.9%	Irish equities, minimum 65% of assets
Italy Fund	NYSE	ITA	−17.3%	Italian equities minimum 65% of assets
Jakarta Growth Fund	NYSE	JGF	−5.1%	Indonesian equities
Japan Equity Fund	NYSE	JEQ	6.3%	Japanese first section equities
Japan OTC Fund	NYSE	JOF	−3.0%	Japanese over the counter equities
Jardine Fleming China Region	NYSE	JFC	−12.2%	China, Hong Kong, Taiwan, and Macau equities
Jardine Fleming India Fund	NYSE	JFI	−5.1%	Indian equities
Korea Fund	NYSE	KF	14.3%	Korean equities
Korea Equity Fund	NYSE	KEF	−1.4%	Korean equities, minimum 65% of assets
Korean Investment Fund	NYSE	KIF	−1.2%	Korean equities
Latin America Discovery Fund	NYSE	LDF	−10.9%	Latin American companies
Latin America Equity Fund	NYSE	LAQ	−10.9%	Argentine, Brazilian, Chilean and Mexican shares
Latin America Growth Fund	NYSE	LLF	−18.1%	Latin American equities, minimum 80%, bonds up to 20%
Latin America Investment Fund	NYSE	LAM	−9.2%	Brazilian, Chilean, and Mexican shares
Malaysia Fund	NYSE	MF	−12.2%	Malaysian equities
Mexico Fund	NYSE	MXF	−15.7%	Mexican equities
Mexico Equity & Income Fund	NYSE	MXE	−17.5%	Mexican equities and bonds
Morgan Stanley Africa Inv. Fund	NYSE	AFF	−22.6%	Equity and debt securities of African issuers
Morgan Stanley Asia Pacific Fund	NYSE	APF	−13.0%	Asian-Pacific equities and bonds
Morgan Stanley Emerging Mark	NYSE	MSF	−7.3%	Emerging countries equity securities
Morgan Stanley India Fund	NYSE	IIF	3.0%	Indian equities, minimum 65% of assets
New South Africa Fund	NYSE	NSA	−22.6%	South African equities
Pakistan Investment Fund	NYSE	PKF	−7.9%	Pakistani equities
Portugal Fund	NYSE	PGF	−18.1%	Portuguese equities, minimum 75% of assets

(*Continued*)

Table 5-11. World Equity Funds Listed Weekly in *Barron's* (1996) (*Continued*)

Name	Exchange	Symbol	Premium, June 1996	Investment philosophy
ROC Taiwan Fund	NYSE	ROC	12.3%	Taiwanese equities
Schroeder Asian Fund	NYSE	SHF	−9.2%	Asian equities and bonds, at least five countries
Scudder New Asia Fund	NYSE	SAF	−8.1%	Asian equities, in particular smaller Japanese cos.
Scudder New Europe Fund	NYSE	NEF	−22.0%	Smaller European companies or emerging European cos.
Singapore Fund, Inc.	NYSE	SGF	6.8%	Singapore equities
Southern Africa Fund	NYSE	SOA	−20.6%	Southern African countries equities and bonds
The Spain Fund, Inc.	NYSE	SNF	−19.4%	Spanish equities, minimum 65% of assets
The Swiss Helvetia Fund	NYSE	SWZ	−15.8%	Swiss equities
Taiwan Fund	NYSE	TWN	9.5%	Taiwan equities
Taiwan Equity Fund	NYSE	TYW	1.1%	Taiwan equities, minimum 65% of assets
TCW/DW Emerging Markets	NYSE	EMO	−19.7%	Emerging markets equities, minimum 65% of assets
Templeton China World Fund	NYSE	TCH	−16.8%	China, Hong Kong, and Taiwan equities
Templeton Dragon Fund	NYSE	TDF	−17.3%	China: minimum 45%, Japan: up to 20%, remainder Asia
Templeton Emerg. Mkts. Apprec.	NYSE	TEA	−7.9%	Emerging markets equities, 65% of assets, bonds 35%
Templeton Emerg. Mkts. Income	NYSE	TEI	10.2%	Securities issued by emerging markets entities
Templeton Russia Fund	NYSE	TRF	11.6%	Russia, minimum 65% of assets
Templeton Vietnam Opportunity	NYSE	TVF	−17.7%	Vietnam equities
Thai Fund	NYSE	TTF	−5.5%	Thailand equities
Thai Capital Fund	NYSE	TCH	−6.7%	Thailand equities
Third Canadian Gnl. Inv. Trust	Toronto	THD	−5.1%	Canadian and foreign equities
Turkish Investment Fund	NYSE	TKF	18.2%	Turkish equities
United Corps, Ltd.	Toronto	UNC	33.3%	Canadian equities and bonds
United Kingdom Fund	NYSE	UKM	−18.9%	British equities, minimum 65% of assets
Worldwide Value Fund	NYSE	VLU	−16.4%	Worldwide equities
Z Seven	NYSE	ZSE	4.0%	Common stocks and securities convertible in stock

The disadvantages of closed-end funds are more than compensated for by their undeniable advantages. In fact, it is often very difficult to access certain markets, especially the very exotic or emerging economies. Countries such as Russia, China, Vietnam, or the Czech Republic are very difficult to trade unless you are a highly organized institution, but closed-end funds provide a way for everyone to invest quickly and easily. Furthermore, these exotic investments are managed by big institutions that know very well the markets in which they are investing, on both the analytic and technical sides, and often have a strong influence on the local financial situation, the result of being substantial investors in the economy. Therefore, it is advantageous to access those countries through specialized funds.

The closed-end World Equity Funds are also traded continuously on the New York Stock Exchange and have all the advantages that we have already discovered about the ADRs and WEBS.

Analysis of Closed-End World Equity Fund Returns

We compared the yearly returns of a sample of closed-end World Equity Funds representing a few important markets, Germany, France, the United Kingdom, Italy, Switzerland, and Japan, to those of local indices converted into U.S. dollars. The yearly returns of these funds were far more volatile than the underlying indices. The standard deviations of yearly results, the accepted measurement of risk, were on average 2.5 times greater than those of the local indices, expressed in dollars. This means that there is much more risk in the closed-end World Equity Funds than the intrinsic risk of the markets in which they are invested.

The funds used in the sample often underperformed the country index. Certain years were marked by strong success, exceeding the country index, as in 1993 in general and in 1989 for the Germany fund. Other years were characterized by noticeable underperformance, most apparent in 1990 and 1994. It seems that these funds overall tend to accentuate the market movements. The result is increased volatility and therefore greater risk.

Table 5-12 shows the yearly returns of the six funds used in the sample noted above and compares them with the local indices, converted to U.S. dollars. The returns shown at the bottom of the table are not very good. The rates of return fall far short of the corresponding local index, and the standard deviations of yearly returns are two to three times higher than that of the market index. It is easy to conclude that this representative sample of closed-end funds invested in the stock markets of industrialized countries is not a good alternative to an indexed basket of the markets themselves.

Figures 5-6 and 5-7 give us a closer look at the comparison between the performance of the closed-end funds and index markets of Germany and the United Kingdom. In the case of Germany, the fund posts corresponding profits and losses in all except 1994 but cannot hold onto its extreme profits of 1990. The U.K. fund has the opposite problem, continually trying to catch up to the U.K. index. The closed-end funds of both markets clearly show greater volatility than the underlying index.

Table 5-12. Comparison of Yearly Returns of Six World Funds with Corresponding Country Indices

Year	Germany fund	German index	France growth fund	French index	United Kingdom fund	British index	Italy fund	Italian index	Japan fund	Japanese index	Swiss Helvetia fund	Swiss index
1987	-40.8%	-23.1%					-34.2%	-22.1%				1.4%
1988	25.0%	14.7%			15.4%	0.3%	25.1%	7.2%			-1.3%	15.0%
1989	156.7%	41.1%			14.6%	20.9%	109.1%	20.3%			59.3%	-4.6%
1990	-42.9%	-7.7%			-16.3%	6.2%	-39.7%	-15.6%			-21.5%	6.8%
1991	9.1%	4.1%	2.9%	14.2%	1.4%	8.5%	-13.4%	-3.5%			11.5%	6.9%
1992	-15.6%	-11.6%	4.2%	-1.0%	1.3%	-5.5%	-15.5%	-31.6%			4.8%	46.3%
1993	23.4%	30.9%	47.4%	14.2%	44.6%	18.3%	36.7%	19.8%	73.8%	15.0%	63.9%	3.6%
1994	-14.0%	3.9%	-33.0%	-8.2%	-18.7%	-4.9%	-20.7%	7.9%	-10.8%	26.8%	-17.0%	38.9%
1995	5.9%	11.9%	8.2%	8.6%	11.5%	18.8%	-6.2%	-4.9%	0.0%	-2.8%	12.6%	
Return	12.30%	60.80%	14.5%	28.7%	49.2%	76.7%	-22.8%	-31.2%	55.0%	41.8%	120.7%	167.5%
Compounded rate of return	1.3%	5.4%	2.7%	5.2%	5.1%	7.4%	-2.8%	-4.1%	15.7%	12.3%	10.4%	13.1%
Standard deviation of returns	59.7%	20.3%	28.5%	9.9%	20.1%	10.7%	46.5%	18.1%	46.1%	14.9%	31.8%	18.4%
Risk-adjusted ratio	0.022	0.267	0.096	0.522	0.255	0.689	-0.061	-0.224	0.342	0.829	0.327	0.710
Correlation fund vs. index	0.853		0.785		0.607		0.742		-0.001		0.702	

	Germany fund		France growth fund		United Kingdom fund		Italy fund		Japan fund		Swiss Helvetia fund	
Year	NAV* returns	Premium or discount	NAV returns	Premium or discount	NAV returns	Premium or discount	NAV returns	Premium or discount	NAV returns	Premium or discount	NAV returns	Premium or discount
1991		9.6%		-16.1%		-12.1%		-17.2%				-3.5%
1992	-10.2%	3.0%	0.4%	-12.9%	-1.3%	-9.7%	-26.3%	-5.1%		-19.9%	6.5%	-5.1%
1993	30.3%	-2.4%	21.6%	5.3%	24.9%	4.6%	21.8%	6.5%	10.6%	25.9%	43.4%	8.5%
1994	2.8%	-18.4%	-10.0%	-21.7%	-1.3%	-13.8%	-3.5%	-12.4%	9.7%	2.4%	-6.7%	-3.5%
1995	2.8%	-16.0%	3.6%	-18.2%	17.0%	-17.9%	-3.6%	-14.8%	-10.2%	19.3%	24.2%	-12.5%
Correlation NAV vs. index	0.965		0.931		0.965		0.944		0.902		0.954	
NAV return deviation	17.1%		13.3%		13.3%		19.6%		11.8%		21.7%	
Index return deviation	17.7%		10.0%		13.7%		22.1%		14.9%		21.8%	

*NAV denotes net asset value.

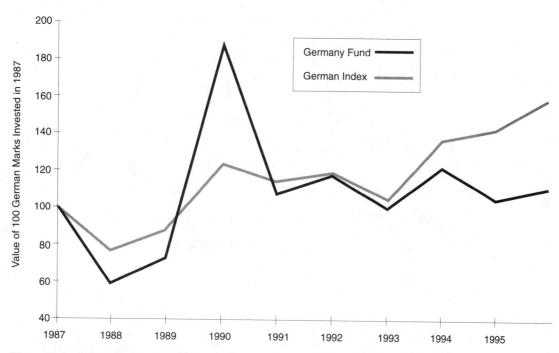

Figure 5-6. Comparison of a German closed-end fund with the German FAZ index. Although similar, the fund cannot keep up with the total market gain.

Is there a reason for this poor performance other than simply blaming it on the skill of the fund managers? It is certainly possible that their investment strategies work in some years and not in others. Surprisingly, the fund managers' ability is not the reason for the erratic performance of these closed-end funds. If we look more carefully at the bottom of Table 5-12 we will see how the net asset values, which are the real values of the invested portfolios, performed from 1991 through 1995. The ratios between the net asset values and the fund prices changed sharply over only a few years. If we analyze the returns of the net asset values, we see that they were closer to those of the indices than the fund prices themselves.

A look at the correlation coefficient clearly quantifies this concept. For all six funds we have examined, the correlation coefficients between the net asset value returns and the market indices were greater than 0.90 and as high as 0.965, showing a very close relationship in the tracking of each pair of asset value and index. The same coefficients calculated with the fund prices were well below that value and significantly less correlated. In the case of Japan it was even negative, showing that the fund often went in the direction opposite to the actual market prices. Furthermore, the deviations of the net asset value returns were not higher than those of the indices.

No, we cannot justify blaming the fund managers but instead should pay more attention to the way the premiums changed into discounts, and discounts into premiums, during the years from 1991 to 1995.

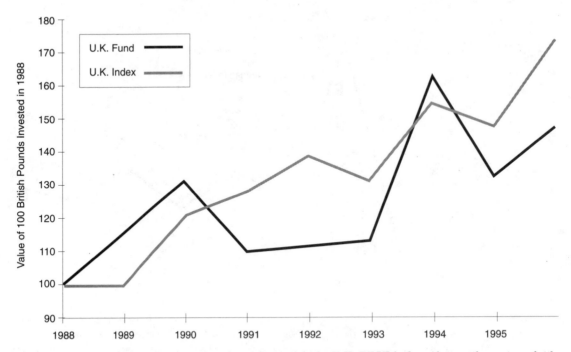

Figure 5-7. Comparison of a U.K. closed-end fund with the U.K. FTSE index. Along with greater volatility, the U.K. fund always seems to be trying to catch up with the market.

Irregular Money Flows to Closed-End Funds

The most obvious example of a change in premium is the Germany fund, where a 10% premium in 1991 turned into an 18% discount in 1994. The other funds we examined traded with double-digit discounts in 1991, turned into a premium in 1993, and then reverted back to a double-digit discount in 1995.

The year 1993 was euphoric for almost all the markets in the world. Because the prices of closed-end funds are influenced by the law of supply and demand, the strong investor interest in the equity markets was an important factor in boosting the value of the funds. The volume of trading in the closed-end fund, which was still modest, did not help to stabilize the volatility. Then, in 1992 and 1994 the overall bad market behavior produced exactly the opposite effect.

Unfortunately, in 1995, a good year for equities, we did not see the same effect. Our best explanation for this is that the closed-end fund became unfashionable and was replaced by other investment alternatives. It is very likely that the enviable performance of the U.S. market was so well known that investors simply moved their resources to the United States, which they considered the best opportunity, combined with safe and easy access.

The reason for the change in the flow of money in and out of the closed-end funds is just conjecture. What is important is that the sharp changes in premiums and discounts characterizing those funds add volatility on top of the volatility that is already part of the natural market movement. It seems wise to avoid buying a closed-end fund when premiums are high, but as with most investment strategies, good advice cannot always be followed. Decisions depend on a combination of the market's trend and the way the money flows to the fund—neither of which are very predictable.

A Good Way to Access Emerging Markets

We have looked at the problems of investing in closed-end funds for developed countries but have intentionally separated the funds for emerging markets. Remembering that there are few ways for outsiders to access the opportunities offered by the far less developed world regions, which have very fast-growing economies, the closed-end funds cannot be brushed aside. Table 5-13 lists 24 emerging market funds together with their performance from 1992 through 1995.

Table 5-13. Four Years of Returns for 24 Closed-End Funds Representing Emerging Markets

	1992	1993	1994	1995	Standard Dev of returns
Europe Fund	−14.1%	31.6%	−17.3%	18.6%	24%
European Warrant Fund	20.4%	106.6%	−54.1%	21.4%	66%
Templeton Emerging	−31.4%	91.4%	−29.7%	−5.1%	58%
Scudder New Asia	−5.8%	92.1%	−25.6%	−28.9%	57%
MS Emerging	25.0%	74.5%	−32.0%	−27.9%	50%
Scudder New Europe	−10.2%	40.9%	−15.1%	23.2%	27%
Worldwide Value	−4.0%	38.6%	−14.3%	18.5%	24%
Argentina Fund	−14.0%	39.8%	−29.2%	−5.2%	30%
Chile Fund	38.7%	34.4%	3.6%	12.7%	17%
Brazil Fund	−7.6%	55.0%	56.2%	−36.0%	46%
Emerging Mexico	−4.2%	49.3%	−50.5%	−51.9%	48%
Mexico Equity and Income Fund	16.5%	64.2%	−37.6%	−43.9%	51%
Mexico Fund	4.5%	67.7%	−42.0%	−43.7%	52%
Latin American Equity Fund	3.7%	83.1%	−31.2%	−26.9%	53%
Latin America Investment Fund	−8.0%	29.2%	−40.5%	−21.3%	29%
Asia Pacific Fund	17.6%	70.0%	−46.1%	0.9%	48%
Korea Fund	10.8%	71.4%	−5.2%	−3.3%	36%
India Growth	14.9%	85.3%	−32.5%	−33.1%	56%
Indonesia Fund	7.4%	130.6%	−42.2%	−15.6%	76%
Jakarta Growth	24.0%	92.8%	−34.5%	−1.3%	54%
Malasia Fund	38.3%	72.3%	−37.9%	−2.2%	48%
Taiwan Fund	−23.9%	108.7%	−26.2%	−29.0%	68%
Thai Fund	18.2%	96.7%	−39.3%	0.0%	57%
Singapore Fund	−4.9%	151.3%	−39.3%	−10.1%	86%
Averages	4.6%	74.1%	−27.6%	−12.1%	48.4%

Once again we note the high volatility, a strong return in 1993, and a plunge in 1994. However, for these funds, that pattern of performance is not surprising. Any emerging market investment is understandably very volatile because of the fast-changing structure and more extreme policies that occur in those countries. Participation should always be weighted as a smaller portion of a portfolio. The closed-end funds invested in emerging markets are a very good way to gain access to those countries if used with a careful valuation of risk.

Conclusion

Closed-end funds contain more risk than a direct investment in foreign markets and are somewhat dependent on the portfolio selection by the fund manager. The reward to risk analysis of the closed-end funds does not show that increased profits offset the higher risk; however, these funds offer one of the few ways to access emerging markets, and the net result of those investments is good.

It is also understandable that we would want to participate in the exceptionally good performance that occurs every few years. Certainly, the closed-end fund seems to have strong upside potential. To use this potential wisely it is necessary to invest only during periods when the negative money flow has caused a discount in the fund value. This should be combined with a smaller investment allocation to in order to manage its higher risk.

6
Adding Sophistication to the Investment

The Use of Stock Index Futures

The financial markets of the world are constantly expanding in the number of participants and the volume of transactions. Every day, they are increasing the supply of tradable products in order to satisfy the increasingly diverse needs of a broad base of investors who, on their part, are becoming more sophisticated daily.

Besides the products that are available for the equity investors around the world, and those that we have reviewed up until now, the major international financial markets offer a broad choice of derivative instruments. These derivative markets add important flexibility to the way we choose to create our equities investment strategy.

The Futures Contracts

One of the most successful, sophisticated, and well-established derivative products available on an exchange is undoubtedly the *futures contract*. It is an obligation to buy or sell a certain commodity (or tangible product) at a specified price on a particular day.

The origin of futures contracts is very old. Beginning with the "fair letter" in the thirteenth century and popularized by the Certificate of Trade issued by the Dutch East India Company, traders have sold their products in advance of their production or delivery. Their reasons are easily understood; they could simply use the money to finance their business, or draw on it to pay their ongoing expenses, and survive the period of no income when they were growing crops or manufacturing products, all the time hoping for a successful delivery against their commitment. The European whale hunters in the sixteenth century sold their anticipated prey even before setting sail. English commodities traders fixed a price for a load of tea that was shipped from India, expecting arrival a few months later on the coast of Great Britain. In America, the farmers as early as 1800 sold their products even before planting the seed.

Exchange-traded futures, as we know them, began with the founding of the Chicago Board of Trade in 1848. The Chicago Mercantile Exchange, originally known as the Chicago Butter and Egg Board, followed in 1874, after Pudd's Exchange in 1868, now known as the MidAmerica Commodity Exchange.

Despite the broad use of these exchanges to price agricultural commodities, we consider "modern" futures markets to have emerged during the early 1970s, when currency futures and interests rates began trading on the two major Chicago exchanges, by far the largest in the world. Beginning with U.S. Treasury bills, 30-year Treasury bonds and GNMA mortgages, the market for interest rate futures has become enormous. In a typical day, about 1 million contracts of Eurodollars trade hands, each representing 1 million U.S. dollars in banks abroad, a total transaction of 1,000,000,000,000 U.S. dollars.

The first stock index futures contract, appearing in 1982 at the Kansas City Board of Trade, was the Value Line Index. It was unique because it did not deliver the product itself, which would be a basket of stocks creating the index, but buyers and sellers satisfied their positions on the final contract date by cash settlement. Instead of delivery of the stocks, you simply paid out any losses or received profits, based on the price at which you bought or sold the index futures. This opened a new, convenient way of using futures when the "product" was not as easy to deliver as a bushel of wheat.

It was soon followed by the most popular stock index futures contract, the Standard & Poor's 500, traded at the Chicago Mercantile Exchange (CME). It gives the right to receive or deliver (corresponding to the purchase or sale of the futures contract) the specific basket of stocks as represented by the S&P 500 index on a fixed date. The value of one contract is calculated as 500 times the value of the index at the New York Stock Exchange. Therefore, if the S&P 500 is at 650, a futures contract has the value of $325,000. In most cases, with proper credit arrangements, a trader only needs to post a 10% good-faith deposit to buy or sell a contract. Clearly, this becomes a very convenient way for an institution to protect its diverse holdings from short-term fluctuations without actually selling and buying back each of its stocks.

European and Pacific Rim futures markets followed the American exchanges, expanding into both interest rates and stock indices during the 1980s and increasing at a faster pace in the 1990s. Now, futures on the most important stock index markets are easily available and actively traded around the world. It is no problem at all to trade a futures contract on the Japanese Nikkei, the German DAX, the French CAC, or many other international indices, including those of smaller markets such as Singapore, Zurich, or Madrid. The exchanges have implemented accounting practices that allow you to buy the U.S. dollar or German mark today on the Chicago International Monetary Market and sell it tomorrow on the Singapore Monetary Exchange, and the profits or losses flow in and out of your account as though it was all done at your local bank.

The Multiple Strategies of Stock Index Futures

Futures trading inevitably is associated with the idea of speculative risk. The good-faith deposit, called *margin* in derivatives trading, allows investors to deposit a relatively small sum in a trading account yet trade contracts valued at 10, 20, and even 40 times that margin. Investors can, in fact, create a profit or loss based on an investment 20 times as great as the deposited funds.

Of course, it is not a requirement that you leverage futures market trades by a factor of 20. You can actually deposit the entire value of the contract to back up the trade, or you can deposit 50% or 25% rather than the typical minimum of 5%. Because of the ability to apply such high leverage, futures markets are used by many speculators whose prime objective is speed rather than safety. Nearly all amateurs fail, along with many experienced traders, when they ignore the risk or forget to evaluate the risk properly, failing to hold enough reserves to provide protection during the greatest losses.

While there are many stories of incredible fortunes, the risk is always proportional to the rewards. If the market does not move in your direction, there is a very strong chance that it will drop by 5%. While a price swing of 5% does not seem especially large for a stock trader, a move from $48.00 a share to $45.60, it means a total 100% loss for a futures trader who is fully leveraged. For many speculators who have been attracted to this apparently easy way to make money, it would be more accurate to say that they were gambling rather than investing.

The futures contracts, if used rationally, are an excellent way to improve the quality of the investment strategies. Instead of increasing the risk with leverage, we should simply evaluate the risk based on the entire value of the investment. If a contract's value is US$100,000 and 10% volatility is anticipated, it means that we can normally expect a $10,000 equity swing. If this is more than the amount that we were required to deposit for margin and it represents all of our resources, we can wave goodbye to our investment.

Hedging

Stock index futures have been very useful for investors. The original purpose for introducing this financial instrument was not for speculative use, but to provide a way to build a hedge position in expectation of a price reversal. Unlike stocks, an index futures contract can be traded in both directions, buying a long position or selling a short one as well; there is no "up-tick" rule for short sales, which restricts all new short sales only to when prices are rising. An investor that owns a portfolio of stocks, concerned that a market correction is likely to come soon yet not wanting to liquidate the portfolio because the correction could be temporary, can easily use one of the index futures contracts for protection.

Such a situation can be managed by entering a short position ("selling short") in stock index futures with a quantity that has a total contract value corresponding to the amount we want to protect. An essential condition for success is that there is a high correlation between the portfolio to be hedged and the futures market index that we choose to sell. If the relationship between these two investments is not close, the group of stocks that make up your investment may go down in value, and at the same time the futures market index, for example, the S&P 500, may go up. In this case we lose in both the stock portfolio and the future's short position because the index that was picked as a hedge did not trace the trend of our portfolio; therefore it proved useless. A hedging strategy implemented using index futures contracts implies a good knowledge of the relationship between the stocks in portfolio and the index itself.

In the past few years there have been more index futures introduced by exchanges, which makes it more likely that one will come closer to tracking one's own stock portfolio. Besides the S&P 500 and Value Line, the NYSE Composite Index is popular on the New York Futures Exchange, and the Chicago Board Options Exchange lists options on the S&P 500 and 100, S&P SmallCap 600, the Russell 2000, and 13 sector indices. The Chicago Mercantile Exchange, Index and Options Market Division, lists futures and options on the S&P 500, S&P MidCap 400, S&P 500/Barra Growth, S&P 500/Barra Value, Russell 2000, and the Major Market Index.

Margining Futures.   To further encourage the use of futures contracts, there is only a small deposit required to participate. As mentioned earlier, the good-faith deposit of about 5% allows speculators to leverage the returns 20 times. For hedgers, it means that the cost of protecting a stock portfolio is very small. This deposit, although called *margin* in the derivatives industry, is not the same margin used for stocks. It is not necessary to borrow the balance and pay interest. The trader is, however, responsible for the full amount of losses should the hedge position go the wrong way. Whenever these funds on deposit fall by 25% of the initial margin amount, the brokerage firm issues a *margin call*, requiring the trader to restore the value of the account to the full 100% level. Of course, when the value of the hedge account declines, the equity in the stock portfolio should increase; therefore the net effect is an offset of profits and losses. When hedging a stock portfolio using futures, the investor has every expectation of having a profitable futures trade to offset interim losses in equities. If this proves true, then a margin call is unlikely.

Alternative Market Investment

Another use of the futures contract is to invest a certain capital in the market without an immediate payment of the corresponding cash. For example, an investor wishes to participate in a bull market that seems to be developing on Wall Street but does not want to buy a basket of stocks, which requires a substantial outlay, because the money is already tied up in other investments. She is aware of the alternative of buying an S&P 500 futures contract that allows her to participate in the movement of the entire market, rather than selecting specific shares. At that moment the price of the S&P 500 cash index is 603, but a contract that "delivers" in about six months costs 613 points. There is always a difference between the cash value and the future value, based mostly on anticipation, but we will describe these reasons a little later.

The Risk Analysis Is Always Paramount. Our investor buys the June S&P futures contract, which has a calculated value of 500 times the current price, now trading at 613.00. The value of the contract purchased is therefore $306,500. This also means that for every one point change in the S&P value, the investor will gain or lose $500 on this contract. Remembering the way that margin works for futures, the investor does not need to produce the full amount of the purchase but only deposit a relatively small amount as a guarantee. At this time, the minimum margin needed to trade one Standard & Poor's contract is $6000, less than 2%, which must be deposited in a special customer "segregated funds" account with a Futures Commission Merchant, who is registered with the Commodity Futures Trading Commission, the U.S. counterpart of the Securities and Exchange Commission.

Over the following week after buying one futures contract, the S&P price falls four full points (a drop of 0.6% in total value). Because each point change in index price represents a change of $500 in the contract value, there is a temporary loss of $2,000 for our investor. But this loss is one-third of the total amount of margin on deposit, and exchange rules require that when the account balance drops below 75% of the initial margin amount (called the *maintenance level*), the investor is required to restore the account balance to the full amount of the initial margin. The broker notifies the client of the *margin call*, and the investor transfers additional funds within 24 hours.

This may seem to be a prime formula for investor anxiety; however, margin calls are a very common and normal procedure when taking advantage of the small margin requirement. Instead of being inconvenienced by regular calls from your broker whenever the price goes up or down, most investors who use the futures market estimate the expected volatility and deposit enough to cover margin variation caused by these price swings. Or, they may decide, in advance, that they will close out the trade if the S&P drops by 3% and deposit $15,500 to cover a 19 point S&P decline ($19 \times 500 = 9500), plus the initial margin of $6000.

When calculating volatility, the investor must consider the time to expiration of the contract. With a market as active as the S&P, it is certainly possible that it will move 8%, or 49 points, during the next six months. If the contract is to represent a buy-and-hold strategy, the margin deposited should be $30,500 ($49 \times $500 + 6000).

If our investor holds the futures contract until it expires in June, she finds that the S&P index now stands at 630. That means a gain of 17 points, or $8500, based on the futures contract value of $500 per point. This gain corresponds to a 2.7% increase in the index, but compared to the $30,500 deposited as margin it means a 27% gain. If our investor had treated the futures market as she would the stock market and committed the whole contract value of $306,500 to the market, then the gain would have been the same as the stock market, 2.7%, with no chance of a margin call. If the $30,500 used as a margin was the only money that the investor had available, then the leveraged profit of 27% is offset by the very possible risk of total loss had the market volatility caused prices to drop during the short period to expiration. The use of futures as an alternative to direct investment must be considered in evaluating the whole picture of risk.

Fast Investing Decisions

Suppose we want to increase our stock market exposure from 50% to 60% of our assets and we must act quickly. If the stock index is our benchmark, then we should buy a selection of equities, each one weighted properly, in order to replicate the index itself. This requires both effort and considerable time. It may be that the amount of money to be invested does not allow this to be done easily. Futures contracts provide an alternative that takes only a few minutes to execute. The purchase of a futures contract is simple, fast, and very inexpensive. You can pay as little as $15 for a round-turn commission (paid when you liquidate the trade) on each contract, valued at more than $300,000. That comes to a very small percentage. Two other factors make this very attractive:

1. The liquidity of the U.S. S&P 500, the French CAC-40, the German DAX, and the British FTSE-100 are all far greater than any individual shares traded; therefore, the ability to get in and out quickly at the market price is very easy.

2. You receive interest on the money deposited in your margin account. Because this is not the same margin as the equities markets but a deposit on the full value of the contract, the brokers normally pay interest on the amount in excess of the funds needed for daily settlement. This reserved amount may be only 25% of the required margin, but it can be transferred out of your account daily if the price of the S&P moves down when you are holding a long position. On the other hand, if you are profiting, daily settlement means that those profits are transferred into your account at the end of the day, and you can earn interest on those profits according to the arrangement with your broker.

The Fair Value

Since the futures contracts are forward commitments, their values are different from the cash prices of the same goods they represent. The main components of this difference are the cost of money and the anticipated value of dividends. If the buyers do not have to pay for the goods immediately, then they can earn interest on that money until the time of delivery. This advantage is recognized by the futures market and discounted in the futures contract price, normally to the extent of the current three-month government rate. If an investor buys an S&P contract when the cash price is $600 and the delivery is in three months, there will be a premium of about 7.50 points [(600 × 5% annual interest)/4]. Therefore, the buyer should expect to pay $607.50 for the futures contract. In reality, stock index futures are slightly different, and the premium is based on expected dividends paid over the next three months. In general, this is similar to the three-month fixed rate because the stock market and the government compete for the same investors.

There is an exact way to measure the future value of the stock index, at least based on what we know today. Many professional traders use this calculation to decide whether the index is under- or overvalued, and this effects their decisions and strategy. The theoretical value of a future contract, called *fair value*, is calculated as

$$\text{Fair value} = Ie^{rt} - D$$

where I = underlying value of the cash index

r = current annual interest rate

t = time to expiration (in decimal years, where 0.25 is 3 months)

e = the "exponential" constant 2.71828...

D = total dividends expected to be paid by the stocks comprising the index, expressed as index points, for the period today through the expiration of the futures contract

For example, on the day we plan to invest, the cash value for the S&P index is 640 points. At that time the three-month Treasury bill has an annual yield of 4.8%, and the expected dividend on the index is 4 points (an annualized return of 2.5%). According to the formula, the theoretical value for a three-month futures contract is

$$640^*2.71828\wedge(0.048^*0.25) - 4 = 643.73$$

The real price for a three-month contract was $646.50, 0.43% higher than the fair value. The difference between the fair value and the traded price of the futures contract is always anticipation, or *market sentiment*. At that moment the majority of investors expected prices to continue higher, and they were willing to pay a premium to participate. When investors as a whole see the end of a bull market or experience a sharp drop in share prices, we find that the market trades significantly below the fair value, and in the most severe cases can even trade below the cash value.

Futures Premium and Discount: Market Sentiment

Figure 6-1 shows the percentage difference between the nearest expiring futures contract for the S&P 500 and the cash index value from June 1993 to April 1996. The S&P 500 futures always expire in March, June, September, and December, in line with most other financial markets. When the contract approaches the expiration date, the difference between cash and futures effectively disappears, although

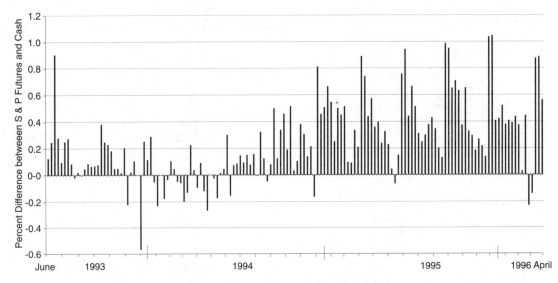

Figure 6-1. Percentage differences between futures and cash S&P prices. Premiums always decline as the quarterly expiration date approaches, and during stock market declines the premiums often disappear.

there is usually a small difference at the time of expiration. In our chart, in which the futures contract value is represented by a joined series of three-month contracts, this causes the ratio to increase suddenly every three months and then decrease slowly toward zero on the expiration dates.

Even with this distortion, it is clear from the chart that in a period when the stock market declined, in the trends of early 1994, the premium of the futures over the cash index was almost flat or negative; it often traded at a discount between December 1993 and June 1994. In 1995, when the bull market resumed, the premium increased again to a level of about 1%.

The sentiment of the market is the key to the futures and cash price relationship. It is so strong that it can overwhelm the effects of interest and dividends. But it is equally hard to quantify; it depends on the emotional factors that influence the market—and these change every day.

The S&P 500 contract that expired in March 1996 traded on March 17, 1995, a full year before, at $514.5, while the cash price was $495.42, almost 4% lower. By the time of expiration on March 15, 1996, both prices were equal at $641 because the premium declines to zero on the expiration date. The premium paid for the futures contract reduces the 29% profit that would have been gained in an outright stock investment to 24.4%, based on the beginning and ending price of the futures contract. To offset this loss, the investor can add the interest that could be earned on the cash that was not put into the stock market. This might be as much as 90% of the total amount, translating into 90% of the current one-year fixed income returns. By adding the interest on cash back to the return in the futures market, we get nearly the same return as being fully invested in the stock market.

In terms of return, the purchase of futures is technically nearly equal to the physical investment; nevertheless, it is much easier and more practical to execute for relatively short-lived strategies used to optimize the global investment results. For those countries with special long-term capital gains tax rules, the use of futures as a hedging vehicle avoids liquidation of the underlying stocks, which can change their status from long-term to short-term gains. Investors wishing to participate in the stock market's long-term growth will not need to use futures, which is ideal for getting in and out on short notice and may have different tax consequences. They would do well to buy an equity fund or a basket of stocks and keep that portfolio; however, if they want to protect this portfolio from market turmoil, then index futures will be a priceless tool.

There is a lot to consider before choosing to use futures contracts instead of direct investment in stocks. Above all, it is the investor's need that will drive the choice. It is only necessary to remember that futures contracts offer flexibility and the ability to speed up the decision process when market conditions are changing.

Index Futures around the World

Futures became extremely popular in the mid-1970s when the U.S. agricultural markets reflected tremendous price increases based on the U.S.–Russian wheat trade agreement, which was immediately followed by a bad crop year that drove the price to twice the level seen before. Following that publicity, the Chicago Mercantile Exchange created the International Monetary Market (IMM), which traded futures contracts in six major currencies, the Swiss franc, German mark, British pound, Canadian dollar, Japanese yen, and Mexican peso. From there the exchanges began trading interest rate futures and then stock index futures. Now, there are an incredible variety of markets to choose from (see Table 6-1).

During the 1980s the popularity of these markets boomed. Major corporations, banks, and other financial institutions began to actively hedge their risk using futures. In a financial world that is becoming more global every day, thanks to the impressive progress of computerized telecommunications, all the major financial centers of the world have developed a futures exchange: London, Osaka, Frankfurt, Paris, Singapore, Hong Kong, Sidney, Amsterdam, Zurich, Milano, Madrid, Brussels, as well as many others. It is possible to trade the principal equity indices and also contracts in interest rates, from the long-term maturity of domestic Treasury bonds and Germany's bund, to the short-term yield of France's three-month PIBOR, the U.K.'s short sterling, or the continent's Eurodollars, Euroyen, or Euromarks. Some markets also list international instruments that are not of their country; the Italian Treasury bonds were traded in London before being listed in Milano. The futures contract on the Japanese Nikkei index is traded in Osaka, in Singapore, and in Chicago. When a European trader awakens, the trading day in Tokyo is about to end, but there is still some time to place an order in Singapore. If he oversleeps and misses that trade, he can wait for the market opening in Chicago, which for the Europeans corresponds to the early afternoon.

To consolidate all of this trading, the Chicago Mercantile Exchange introduced *Globex*, a computerized trading facility that is open whenever normal exchange

Table 6-1. The Most Actively Traded International Index Futures as of 1996

| Index | Futures market | Currency | Value of one contract; July 1996 | | Multiplier (one index point) | Trading hours (local) | Trading hours (New York) | Months traded |
			U.S. dollars	Original currency				
United States								
Value Line	Kansas City Board	U.S. dollar	295,000	295,000	500	8:30–15:15	9:30–16:15	Mar., Jun., Sep., Dec.
Major Market XMI	Chicago Merc. Exch.	U.S. dollar	275,000	275,000	500	8:15–15:15, 15:45–8:15	9:15–15:15, 16:45–9:15	All
S&P 500	Chicago Merc. Exch.	U.S. dollar	315,000	315,000	500	8:30–15:15, 15:45–8:15	9:30–16:15, 16:45–9:15	Mar., Jun., Sep., Dec.
Nasdaq 100	Chicago Merc. Exch.	U.S. dollar	310,000	310,000	500	8:30–15:15, 15:45–8:15	9:30–16:15, 16:45–9:15	Mar., Jun., Sep., Dec.
NYSE Index	New York Futures Exch.	U.S. dollar	165,000	165,000	500	9:30–16:15	9:30–16:15	Mar., Jun., Sep., Dec.
Mini Value Line	Kansas City Board	U.S. dollar	58,000	58,000	100	8:30–15:15	9:30–16:15	Mar., Jun., Sep., Dec.
MidCap 400	Chicago Merc. Exch.	U.S. dollar	109,000	109,000	500	8:30–15:15, 15:45–8:15	9:30–16:15, 16:45–9:15	Mar., Jun., Sep., Dec.
Pacific S.E. Technology	New York Futures Exch.	U.S. dollar	94,000	94,000	500	9:30–16:15	9:30–16:15	Mar., Jun., Sep., Dec.
Russell 2000	Chicago Merc. Exch.	U.S. dollar	156,000	156,000	500	8:30–15:15, 15:45–8:15	9:30–16:15, 16:45–9:15	Mar., Jun., Sep., Dec.
Canada								
TSE 100	Toronto Futures Exch.	Canadian dollar	110,000	150,000	500	9:15–16:15	9:15–16:15	Mar., Jun., Sep., Dec.
Toronto 35 Index	Toronto Futures. Exch.	Canadian dollar	95,000	130,000	500	9:15–16:15	9:15–16:15	Mar., Jun., Sep., Dec.
Mexico								
Mexican IPC	Chicago Merc. Exch.	U.S. dollar	75,000	75,000	25	8:30–15:15, 15:45–8:15	9:30–16:15, 16:45–9:15	Mar., Jun., Sep., Dec.
Brazil								
Bovespa Index	Bolsa de Mercadorias	Brazilian real	11,500	12,000	0.20	9:00–14:45	8:00–13:45	Feb., Apr., Jun., Aug., Oct., Dec.
Japan								
Nikkei 225	Singapore Intl. Monetary Exch.	Japanese yen	97,000	10,400,000	500	8:00–10:15, 11:15–14:15	20:00–22:15, 23:15–2:15	Mar., Jun., Sep., Dec.
Nikkei 225	Osaka Securities Exch.	Japanese yen	195,000	20,800,000	1,000	9:00–11:00, 12:30–15:00	20:00–22:00, 23:30–2:00	Mar., Jun., Sep., Dec.
Nikkei 225	Chicago Merc. Exch.	U.S. dollar	104,500	104,500	5	8:00–15:15	9:00–16:15	Mar., Jun., Sep., Dec.
Nikkei 300	Singapore Intl. Monetary Exch.	Japanese yen	28,000	2,950,000	1,000	8:00–10:00, 11:15–14:15	20:00–22:00, 23:15–2:15	Mar., Jun., Sep., Dec.
Nikkei 300	Osaka Securities Exch.	Japanese yen	28,000	2,950,000	1,000	9:00–11:00, 12:30–15:15	20:00–22:00, 23:30–2:15	Mar., Jun., Sep., Dec.
Topix	Tokyo Stock Exch.	Japanese yen	152,000	16,250,000	10,000	9:00–11:00, 12:30–15:10	20:00–22:00, 23:30–2:10	Mar., Jun., Sep., Dec.

Index	Exchange	Currency				Trading Hours		Contract Months
					Malaysia			
KL Composite	Kuala Lumpur Futures Exch.	Malaysian ringit	42,000	105,000	100	9:30–12:45, 14:30–17:15	21:30–0:45, 2:30–5:15	All
					Hong Kong			
Hang Seng Index	Hong Kong Futures Exch.	Hong Kong dollars	68,000	525,000	50	10:00–12:30, 14:30–15:45	22:00–0:30, 2:30–3:45	All
					Australia			
Aus. All Ordinaries	Sydney Futures Exch.	Australian dollar	40,000	52,000	25	9:50–12:30, 14–16:10	0:50–3:30, 5–7:10	Mar., Jun., Sep., Dec.
					New Zealand			
NZSE Top 10	New Zealand Futures Exch.	New Zealand dollar	21,000	27,000	25	8–12, 13–16:30, 2–8	16–20, 21–)0:30, 10–16	Mar., Jun., Sep., Dec.
					South Africa			
JSE Industrial	South African Futures Exch.	South African rand	16,500	75,000	10	24 h	24 h	Mar., Jun., Sep., Dec.
All Gold	South African Futures Exch.	South African rand	2,800	12,600	10	24 h	24 h	Mar., Jun., Sep., Dec.
All Share	South African Futures Exch.	South African rand	13,500	61,000	10	24 h	24 h	Mar., Jun., Sep., Dec.
					Austria			
ATX	Austrian Futures Exch.	Austrian shilling	10,000	101,000	100	9:00–14:00	3:00–8:00	All
					Belgium			
BEL 20	Belgian Futures Exch.	Belgian franc	55,000	1,650,000	1,000	9:00–16:00	3:00–10:00	All
					Denmark			
KFX Index	Copenhagen Exch. Exch.	Danish krona	20,000	115,000	1,000	9:00–15:30	3:00–9:30	All
					France			
CAC 40	MATIF France	French franc	80,000	400,000	200	24 h	24 h	All
					Germany			
DAX	DTB Germany	German mark	167,000	245,000	100	9:00–17:00	3:00–11:00	Mar., Jun., Sep., Dec.

(*Continued*)

Table 6-1. The Most Actively Traded International Index Futures as of 1996 (*Continued*)

Index	Futures market	Currency	Value of one contract; July 1996		Multiplier (one index point)	Trading hours (local)	Trading hours (New York)	Months traded
			U.S. dollars	Original currency				
Germany								
DAX	DTB Germany	German mark	167,000	245,000	100	9:00–17:00	3:00–11:00	Mar., Jun., Sep., Dec.
Great Britain								
FT 100	LIFFE London	British pound	140,000	91,000	25	8:35–16:10, 16:30–17:30	3:35–11:10, 11:30–12:30	Mar., Jun., Sep., Dec.
FT250	LIFFE London	British pound	65,000	42,000	10	8:30–16:05	3:30–11:05	Mar., Jun., Sep., Dec.
Italy								
MIB 30	Milano Futures Exch.	Italian lira	92,000	140,000,000	10,000	9:30–17:30	3:30–11:30	Mar., Jun., Sep., Dec.
Netherlands								
EOE	Financieie Termijnmarkt	Dutch guilder	64,000	105,000	200	9:30–16:30	3:30–10:30	All
Top 5	Financieie Termijnmarkt	Dutch guilder	98,000	162,000	200	7:20–14:00	1:20–8:00	All
Norway								
OBX	Oslo Stock Exchange	Norwegian krona	7,000	45,000	100	10:00–15:00	4:00–9:00	All
Spain								
IBEX 35	Mercado Español Futuros	Spanish peseta	3,200	395,000	100	10:45–17:15	4:45–11:15	All
Sweden								
OMX	OMLX London	Swedish krona	22,000	145,000	100	10:00–11:30, 19:30–21:00	5:00–6:30, 14:30–16:00	All
Switzerland								
Swiss Market Index	Swiss Futures Exch.	Swiss franc	154,000	185,000	50	9:30–13:00, 13:55–16:15	3:30–7:00, 7:55–10:15	All

trading is not in session. By including other world futures markets into this program, a trader in nearly any place in the world can place an order and execute it any time of day or night. Financial arrangements between the clearinghouses of these exchanges allows you to enter a trade in the United States during the day and liquidate it in Singapore at night, without worrying about the accounting or margin. Everything shows up in your normal brokerage statement the next day. For the financial world, the borders are disappearing rapidly.

The Use of Trading Techniques

A passive investment in equities, which means buying stocks and holding them for many years, gave reasonably good rewards in the past, if we consider them as long-term revenue. The way those returns have been reached, nevertheless, has not been as smooth as we would have wanted, and we have tried to show this in the previous chapters. The periods of poor performance, which can be short or extend for many months, are unavoidable. However long they actually last, these capital drawdowns always seem to go on forever and are often hard to live with.

Trying to Improve the Market's Returns

It is a common belief that the smart investors, whether we call them specialists, professionals, or gurus, are able to catch the maximum move from bull markets and, at the same time, manage their way through market tumbles as if they were experienced sailors facing the storms, yet in view of a safe haven at all times.

This is only partly true. A good specialist has many tools available to decide when to invest and when to get out of the market, but even the most experienced professionals have to fight with uncertainties. Nobody can know the next market movement. Those who claim to see the market's future do not deserve your confidence. The expertise of the specialists resides in their ability to take sensible risks and, what is more important, to correctly evaluate and manage them.

We know that prices move according to rules of supply and demand and are driven by specific events. What is most difficult is giving the right weight to the news. The impact of a certain fact on stocks prices can be very different according to each situation. It is not uncommon to see the stock market plunge on the news that the economy is doing well! In a reversal of logic, good news can be inflationary, resulting in a tighter monetary supply by the central bank that discourages further investments. This happened in 1984, 1986, 1995, and again in 1996 after very strong bull markets. If positive economic news comes after a period of recession, the stock prices would undoubtedly rise. At the same time in Germany, where the economic health was not as good as in the United States yet interest rates continued to rise at an unreasonable if not suicidal rate, the financial markets reacted in almost the same way.

In Italy, also during 1996, the central bank lowered the discount rate by almost one full point. It is this type of news that normally causes stock prices to ignite; instead, the Italian exchange plunged on that day, even following a long-lasting weakness.

The moral of the story is that the forces of supply and demand that drive the markets are only magnified by such news. If the global sentiment is negative, then good news will only serve as a temporary relief; sooner or later the prevailing economic forces will overcome to drive prices lower. The same will happen when the buyers dominate the market. The reasons may be many, including liquidity, political factors, confidence, and interest rates; whatever factors surface, the market knows more than we do, and it acts faster, often reacting with logic that is only apparent with hindsight.

Improving the Quality of Revenues

Having now portrayed the market as irrational and complex, it is not beyond our grasp. We must only be realistic about overanalyzing it, and expecting too much. Timing the market is very difficult; to find the best price levels to buy and sell, many traders apply timing methods, sometimes with success, other times not so.

Trading activity in investments is clearly aimed at maximizing the profits that the market can provide and reducing possible losses to a minimum. We believe that the long-term returns of the equity markets are good enough to satisfy the average investor. Yet, if the negative returns of the worst periods could be somehow avoided, then a greater number of investors would feel more confident about committing their savings to the equity market.

We do not mean to give you the impression that we, or anyone else, will satisfy the universal dream of buying at the lowest prices and selling at the highest prices; that is only a naive and unrealistic expectation, unfairly imposed on so-called market wizards. We see an undeniable advantage if the same returns of the market can be achieved in a smoother way, avoiding the need to be fully exposed during those periods that produce double-digit losses and which, when they happen, last several months and cause long and painful capital drawdowns. By having less exposure during drawdowns, there would be an improvement in the quality of returns; if we could obtain the same long-term revenues from stocks while not suffering, or at least minimizing, those temporary sharp losses that cyclically depress the market, then the investment technique would be successful.

Identifying the Trend

The secular upside trend of the equity markets is often interrupted by sustained sideways movement or, even worse, by sharp downtrends that can be devastating in certain particularly bad periods. The long-term growth of the market is generally achieved by a limited number of strong up moves followed by corrections and consolidation phases. It is in remembering the negative periods that has discouraged many people from investing in stocks.

It is almost impossible to identify the price trends before they develop and equally difficult to forecast their exhaustion. There is no way to identify the start of a new trend, or its end, until after each has occurred; this makes it impossible to benefit from the entire trend because, when it finally becomes clear to us and we decide to invest, we have already missed the start of the movement. The same problem applies at the exhaustion of the trend. We understand that the period of profit is over only after prices have deteriorated more than expected. This pattern of missing by lagging both the beginning and end of a move is the price we pay for using a trend-following approach.

The Use of Trend-Following Techniques

An investing method aimed at benefiting from the largest possible portion of a trend is called *trend following*. It assumes that the factors driving the prices in a certain direction persist and that, once a trend has begun, it will continue somewhat smoothly until it reverses. The investment decision is made after the new trend is identified; the opposite decision is driven by the evidence that the trend is over. The technical analysts' rules on this subject are very popular and prophetic:

- Follow the trend.
- Let profits run.
- Cut losses short.

The trend-following approach is intended to ride the existing trend until it shows signs of exhaustion. Because trends are caused by new and developing fundamental factors, normally accompanied by a shift in government policy, and are often started by the anticipation of a change in policy, there are few market "mavens" who will fight with the trend once it is recognized.

Before adopting a trend-following strategy it is essential to define an operating horizon for the investment. The short-term trader, wishing to time the market and to act quickly on short-lived movements, will adopt a short time horizon and identify the moves that occur as part of an historical trend. If the goal is to catch the big trends and only concentrate on avoiding the sharp corrections, then it is wiser to look at the whole market picture from a longer-term perspective. In this case the natural small corrections that occur along the way should be ignored because they are a necessary part of the pattern. Their negative influence on the invested capital will be almost insignificant in proportion to the profit objectives.

Introduction to Technical Methods

The most reliable information at our disposal for measuring the market direction is the price, and the best-known methods to evaluate the price patterns belong to technical analysis. There is a long-standing conflict between advocates of technical and fundamental analysis. Most analysts will classify themselves as *fundamentalists* or *technicians*, but the modern evolution of the evaluation methods, thanks to the enormous progress in computer technology, gives everyone access to sophisticated, yet cheap, tools, causing the line between the two philosophies to fade. In practice, both camps will use any computerized method to reach their goal of determining the next possible market direction.

There are still some differences in their underlying approaches. The fundamentalists analyze the causes that are likely to drive the market; they evaluate the market fair value (based on earnings, price level, supply and demand, and policy) and, if the current price levels are too low they can declare it "undervalued" and buy; if the price level is too high, they would be wise to sell. The technicians study only the price movement itself, assuming that whatever fundamental reasons are important have already been included, or discounted, in the price move. For the technicians, the market always leads the fundamentals.

Our own opinion is that trends are driven by *anticipation* of policy decisions. If the Producer Price Index has been exceeding 6% annually, we expect the chairman of the Federal Reserve to announce a tightening of money and an increase in rates. The stock market will usually move lower on expectation of any government report or statistic that will eventually result in raising interest rates, and when the final policy action is announced, prices are corrected to the "right" level, either higher or lower.

It is important to consider that technical analysis is no longer simply charting. The subjective and empirical chart analysis that has been associated with the classic technician is being displaced by the quantitative evaluation methods in the modern decision-making process. In fact, technical analysis now includes many factors that we all consider important to trading but do not always think of as technical. It can be used to measure volatility and therefore risk. It can relate volume to liquidity in order to estimate transaction costs and compare sector relationships or intermarket spreads for strength and weakness. Many of these items are commonly used by fundamentalists, yet they are purely mathematical. Technical analysis is now encompassing many areas once classified as econometric, statistical, and even fundamental. Instead, we might do better talking about this as *computerized* or *systematic* analysis and not worrying about what facts or data go into the solution.

Today's technology has made technical analysis essential for large-scale investing. With hundreds of opportunities each day in markets all over the world, it is impossible to qualify the best without some rules and a computer. The need to sort, select, quantify, and then qualify markets from such a broad database makes some form of technical analysis a necessity. It is essentially a massive data-reduction problem, rapidly approaching the same magnitude as interpreting the photographs and scientific data transmitted back to Earth from space missions.

The Need for a Systematic Approach

The investment strategy can be approached in a systematic way. A "mechanical," programmable, or well-defined system consists of specific rules for buying and selling and their successful validation by testing historical data. While there are some complaints about the value of systems that have been poorly tested, it would be unwise to use a set of trading rules without knowing if they have some chance of producing good returns. Even a very rational and apparently smart trading idea can be an open door to catastrophic losses.

Many institutional investors are introducing the mechanical approach in the trading decision process, principally for the following three reasons:

1. The method adopted is backtested and, if done properly, its chances of success are statistically good.

2. The discretionary decision is replaced by systematic signals; therefore, there is less room for subjective trading, better anticipation, and improved operational control.

3. The risk is well defined by mathematic rules and acceptable procedures. In addition, the actual results can be compared with expectations, allowing good and bad features to be identified and the bad ones improved.

The Long-Term Trend-Following Approach for Stocks

It is very difficult to find a simple technique, applied to the equity market, that beats the buy-and-hold returns over the long run. The reason is found in the volatility that occurs inside the historical uptrends. If we use a method that buys after an upmove has begun and sells after a predetermined retracement of that upward move, we are going to miss a certain portion of that move. But this is the price that is paid in order to avoid extended losses when the market is in a bearish phase.

The problem is that the market often moves sideways and prices stay inside a trading range. This appears as a pattern, where prices consolidate and rise after having reached the bottom, reversing their trend again as the top of the range approaches. Trend-following techniques do not work during these periods because they require a more sustained move in one direction to capture a profit. This is because of the lag, which causes both buy and sell signals to occur after the trend has changed. If the lag is larger than the price move, the trade is going to be a loss. This very rigorous strategy will suggest that you sell just as the end of the down move is near or buy around the top of the range; therefore the losses caused by the trend technique compromise the benefits produced by the same method when the trends are clear. It would be easy, but entirely unrealistic, to create perfect trends and consistent profits, if we could expect stock prices to increase by 100% and then immediately decline by 50% without any erratic movement. Unfortunately we have to live with markets that often change their pattern; therefore, a technique that works fine during certain periods reveals itself as completely inadequate in others. Using any systematic method requires learning about that program's patterns of profits and losses, and accepting them as a means to an end.

To help understand what we should expect in the way of advantages and disadvantages, we can look at the most popular trend-following technique, the moving average. Figure 6-2 is a simplified chart showing the way a moving average gives signals for different market conditions. The typical rules for using a moving average as a trading system is to *buy* when the price crosses from below to above the moving average and to *sell* when the price does the opposite. You may also use a more conservative rule and *buy* when the moving average itself moves up, then

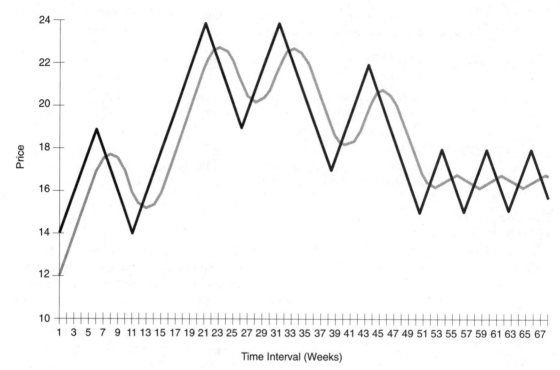

Figure 6-2. A moving average example. The average (gray line) lags the market movement (bold line) and performs worse when price swings are small.

sell when the moving average declines. For either method, until the trends are clear and well established, there are frequent incorrect trading signals given by the prices crossing over the average value (called the *trendline*). When the market becomes erratic, which we can see toward the right edge of the chart, this happens quite often. Frequent buying and selling without any sustained price move translates into a series of losses.

An investment method must be conceived for the correct time span. An indicator that responds quickly to change is not right for the investor with a long-term view because it gives frequent signals that cause you to jump in and out of your position. A classic shareholder, using the market for its long-term value, does not have the means or the desire to follow these signals, which requires that the prices be constantly watched. Their orders will get to the market too late, and brokerage commissions will only contribute to the penalty.

Long-Term Trading Techniques

The use of a long-term technique is more appropriate for most investors. It should be a method that requires no more than a few interventions over the years, just to prevent catastrophic risk, and in the meantime takes the maximum advantage of sustained trends.

We have chosen a few simple long-term trading techniques, and backtested them on 25 years of history for three popular stock indices, to see how using these tactics would have affected an investment. The choices represent the three main equity markets in the world, the United States, Japan, and Germany.

We have adopted the following criteria for backtesting.

Use of Historical Weekly Data from 1971 to 1995.   The use of weekly data allows the status of signals to be checked only once per week, and is therefore more convenient for people not continuously involved in trading activity. The negative effects of daily volatility are also avoided. This is often the result of simple market noise and causes false and contradictory signals. Equally important is that viewing prices weekly actually makes the direction of prices appear smoother and accentuates the underlying trend.

Only Long Trades.   The methods are not intended for traders wishing to take advantage of the downward price moves by selling short, but for those investors needing to know when to stay invested in the market and when to reduce that investment by holding more cash. The goal is not speculation but rather the quality of investment.

No Entry or Exit Commission.   The methods we have tested are usually out of the markets about 30% to 40% of the time. We assume that during these periods the capital can be invested as cash at the current, short-term riskless fixed interest rate. Because the number of trades required by these systems are on average less than two per year, we can be safe in assuming that the revenues from cash will cover the transaction costs, that is, 30% of a 5% fixed-income return will cover two transactions each at about 1%.

Indices Used for Backtesting

United States.   The S&P 500 represents a broad range of stocks and can be traded as derivative instruments, such as a future contract or option.

Japan.   The evergreen Nikkei 225, which closely represents the total market, is also available for trading in a broad range of futures and option contracts and can be traded in the United States.

Germany.   The new DAX, which replaced the FAZ index, does a better job representing the German market, but the DAX has a short history and could not be backtested sufficiently; therefore, we stayed with the FAZ index. The techniques shown, however, can be adopted to the DAX because the correlation between the two indices is very high.

Simple Methods Are Robust

Before describing in detail the techniques we have tested, let us briefly mention the reasons that led us to use simple criteria. A trading system may be much more complex than those we are going to describe. Its degree of complexity depends on the needs of the final user; it may take in account some sophisticated money management techniques or mathematical self-adapting variables designed to automatically alter the way the system responds to the natural relationship of price change and volatility.

The simple techniques that we used as examples have the most important overriding quality—robustness. The robustness of a trading method is measurable by its success under many different market conditions, or even better, by its success in different markets as well. We chose this broad-brush approach over the use of many highly specific trading strategies because it is more practical. To experience a broad sampling of conditions, there is no substitution for long-term testing. Therefore, we selected 25 years of market history, from the erratic 1970s through the bullish 1980s, including crashes and minicrashes, and finally the highly changeable 1990s. We tested three markets that were, and still are, often very different from one another in both trend behavior and volatility.

Overfitting: The Collateral Effect of Optimization

We know that we could optimize the techniques, that is, we could use the computer to search for the best number of weeks to calculate the trend in the past, but we did not want to follow that procedure intentionally. We could have found that a certain parameter worked better for the German market and another for the Japanese. Our simulated results would have appeared more attractive, but the robustness of the technique would have suffered. In other words, to be able to show the reader the best example of past performance, we would have risked *overfitting* the data. A system is called *overfit* if it has been tailored to work on a specific series of historic data over a specific time.

Overfitting is the undesired effect of optimization. It is the result of the search for a set of parameters for the trading strategy that are as statistically "reliable" as possible. This search easily leads to an excessive adaptation of the rules for what happened in the past. The result is a system that worked perfectly in the past, but has no predictive ability for the future. Because the rules were decided after the fact, it is so precisely tuned to past patterns that it will only succeed as expected if the future market movements are identical to the past—a situation that has not yet happened.

Overfitting is most often caused by testing short periods of data or using too many rules. A trading method that proves to be satisfactory when backtested over many different conditions, for many years, and for an assortment of markets, has a much greater chance of working in the future the way it did in the past. You will find that a system that works under such broad conditions, one that is robust, will not be perfect. You will need to compromise your expectations to find a realistic set of rules that work to improve overall market returns.

System Rules

Even though we have devised simple trend-following trading strategies, there are a number of logical rules that we should test. We used the computer to validate these methods, rather than letting the computer tell us the best alternative rules. We also chose to use a "breakout" strategy, in addition to a moving average, for identifying the trend direction. This technique defines an uptrend when a price occurs that is higher than all those in some past interval, for example, the last 20 weeks. The advantage of this popular trend definition is that there is no lag in the identification of the trend direction. At the moment that prices move to a new high, the system tells you to buy. We tested four popular trend periods, 10 and 18 weeks for the breakout strategy and 20 and 40 weeks for the moving average.

Every system needs risk control. Using a trend method, the built-in risk control is when the trend changes direction; however, that may be too slow and may generate losses that are too large for many investors. We also tested a trailing equity stop of 7% to control losses. As an alternative, we used a weekly high–low criteria to create a variable risk control.

We allowed a moving average system to have a filter of 1%, a popular technique which improves the percentage of correct trend signals but adds a little more risk. Because there is so much market noise, it is very likely that the price will pass through the trendline more than once before prices settle on a new direction. A filter of 1% is a commitment to hold each new trade a little longer.

Finally, we tested a classic pattern based on a strong market move in January. It is important to repeat that we simply *validated* these popular concepts, we did not look to change the number of weeks in the breakout rule, the percent of risk, or the month in which the market posted its best gains. That would be taking a step in the direction of overfitting.

System A

Buy when the weekly closing price moves above the high of the previous 18 weeks.

Sell when the weekly closing price moves below the low of the previous 18 weeks.

This is the simplest trend-following technique called a *weekly breakout system.* It assumes that, because a significant event must have caused prices to move to a new high level, compared to the past period of N weekly prices, the trend is now up and should be followed. The same logic is true when prices decline to new lows and a downward trend has begun. We used an 18-week time span because it is slow enough to select and (often) signals the strongest trends.

System B

Buy when the weekly closing price moves above the high of the previous 10 weeks.

Sell when weekly close falls more than 7% from the highest price recorded during the trade.

The same entry method as system A is used, although with a much faster, 10-week trend interval. The exit applies the money management criteria of a 7% drawdown in total equity and requires that the position be liquidated and funds held in cash until the next buy signal.

System C

Buy when the weekly close is 1% above the average of the last 40 weekly closing prices.

Sell when the weekly close is 1% below the average of the last 40 weekly closing prices.

This system is based on the moving average technique. It assumes that when prices are above the average, then an uptrend exists and is likely to continue. Conversely, if prices are below average, then the price trend is down. The 40-week moving average is considered one of the most reliable long-term trend indicators. Nevertheless, when the market is chaotic and moves in an erratic, sideways pattern, even this slow indicator gives repeated false signals; the flip-flopping of prices causes frequent changes in the direction of the moving average trendline. For this reason we used a 1% filter to reduce the false signals. This rule requires the price to close 1% above or below the moving average trendline to confirm a buy or sell signal.

System D

This is exactly the same as system C but uses a 20-week moving average instead of 40. The filter has been left at 1%.

System E

If the weekly close is above the average of the past 40 weekly closes, place a buy stop order for next week just above the high of the past five weeks.

If the weekly close is below the average of the past 40 weekly closes, place a sell stop order for next week just below the low of the past five weeks.

This method is similar to system C, but instead of a 1% filter the trend confirmation is given by the short-term breakout of the high or low price over the past five weeks. This is another alternative to satisfy the need to eliminate the frequent false signals generated by a pure moving average system.

System F

Buy at the end of January only if the monthly close is higher than the year-end close.

Sell (close out) at the end of December and wait for the next confirmation at the end of January.

The technique used in this system differs greatly from the mathematical approach of the others. Rather, its foundation is the pattern of psychological behavior of investors. Called the *January rule,* it is based on the observation that years beginning with January gains are likely to be winners for the stock market. There is a good statistical evidence that this is true, at least on Wall Street; therefore, we also tested the rule on the Japanese and German markets to check its effects.

Evaluating the Results

Tables 6-2, 6-3, and 6-4 show the returns that could have been obtained using systems A through F, trading each on the U.S., Japanese, and German markets from 1971 to 1995. Revenues were reinvested and the currency, in the case of foreign markets, was assumed to be fully hedged because the test returns are calculated in the domestic currencies. The trades generated by each technique for the three markets are illustrated in Tables 6-5 through 6-10.

The evaluation of the results leads to the following conclusions:

1. The final returns obtainable by the use of these systems are not normally better than the long-term buy-and-hold results; on the contrary, they are often noticeably worse. For the S&P 500 in Table 6-2, the buy-and-hold result of 568% was well above the average of 311% for the other six systems.

2. In contrast to the disappointing rates of return, the risk-adjusted ratios show that the quality of the returns improves. In fact, despite lower returns, the volatility of results are clearly lower that of the indices. For the Japanese market, every one of the six systems had a better risk-adjusted ratio than the buy-and-hold approach.

The technique that proved to be best over the three markets tested is the one used in system B, which buys after a 10-week breakout of the high price, and exits the position after a 7% retracement of the maximum price recorded during the trade. It illustrates the importance of using a money management rule to close out the investment, instead of using the *reverse signal* given by a classic technical indicator. It is interesting to observe that a price drawback is not just a pure money management rule but a slightly more complex trend indicator because it shows when the trend has started to reverse in terms of net equity.

It should also be noted that a 7% drawdown is very large. This teaches us that market movement contains a great deal of noise—erratic price movement that is meaningless for determining the trend direction. When a stop loss, or risk control, is too close to the current price level, we are likely to be triggered more often simply due to noise.

Although system B was the best overall among those we tested, in terms of risk-adjusted ratio, the January rule, applied only to the U.S. market, posted the highest single risk-adjusted ratio of 0.73 for the S&P 500. This last technique deserves a special mention, even though its exceptional success was limited to the U.S. market. When applied to the German market it gave buy signals for more years that had losses, and in other years that started with poor January returns, we see that

Table 6-2. Results of Six Systems Applied to the United States Market (S&P 500 Index)

Year	Buy & hold	System A	System B	System C	System D	System E	System F
1971	10.8%	5.3%	11.9%	1.3%	12.0%	1.4%	6.5%
1972	15.6%	14.3%	15.6%	15.6%	10.0%	11.5%	13.6%
1973	−17.4%	−18.3%	−12.1%	−10.8%	−15.4%	−13.1%	0.0%
1974	−29.7%	0.0%	−11.1%	0.0%	−4.9%	0.0%	0.0%
1975	31.5%	11.5%	21.2%	11.1%	23.3%	3.4%	17.2%
1976	19.1%	10.9%	8.1%	15.6%	9.2%	11.9%	6.5%
1977	−11.5%	0.0%	−12.9%	−5.1%	−7.7%	−5.9%	0.0%
1978	1.1%	−1.6%	−0.6%	−2.7%	4.0%	−1.7%	0.0%
1979	12.3%	12.2%	3.3%	−5.6%	−4.4%	−5.0%	8.0%
1980	25.8%	5.5%	17.1%	16.3%	21.1%	24.1%	18.9%
1981	−9.7%	−10.1%	−8.6%	−6.7%	−12.5%	−6.7%	0.0%
1982	14.8%	15.9%	5.8%	19.5%	8.1%	16.0%	0.0%
1983	17.3%	17.3%	17.3%	17.3%	11.1%	17.3%	13.5%
1984	1.4%	−3.9%	−3.0%	−2.0%	−3.4%	0.9%	0.0%
1985	26.3%	26.1%	20.4%	22.8%	17.5%	20.9%	17.6%
1986	14.6%	10.7%	11.4%	17.8%	6.2%	12.2%	14.4%
1987	2.0%	−13.6%	14.5%	−8.9%	25.3%	−8.9%	−9.9%
1988	12.4%	3.7%	1.6%	2.3%	−9.6%	3.9%	8.0%
1989	27.3%	27.3%	21.1%	27.2%	15.1%	27.2%	18.8%
1990	−6.6%	−16.4%	−5.1%	−12.7%	−12.1%	−15.5%	0.0%
1991	26.3%	20.9%	23.7%	17.0%	10.1%	16.4%	21.3%
1992	4.5%	8.2%	−1.4%	4.1%	1.0%	5.4%	0.0%
1993	7.1%	6.1%	6.1%	6.1%	6.1%	6.1%	6.3%
1994	−1.5%	−5.4%	−4.6%	−11.5%	−2.6%	−5.8%	−4.6%
1995	34.1%	34.1%	34.1%	32.2%	30.9%	33.1%	30.9%
Total return	568%	289%	352%	294%	224%	258%	451%
Compounded rate of return	7.9%	5.6%	6.2%	5.6%	4.8%	5.2%	7.1%
Standard deviation of returns	16.0%	13.5%	12.7%	13.1%	12.6%	12.8%	9.7%
Risk-adjusted ratio	0.49	0.41	0.49	0.43	0.38	0.41	0.73

Table 6-3. Results of Six Systems Applied to the Japanese Market
(Nikkei 225 Index)

Year	Buy & hold	System A	System B	System C	System D	System E	System F
1971	37.4%	15.4%	20.6%	14.3%	18.7%	13.8%	29.3%
1972	91.9%	91.9%	91.9%	91.9%	91.9%	91.9%	82.7%
1973	−17.3%	−10.9%	−16.6%	−13.9%	−16.6%	−13.1%	−18.7%
1974	−11.4%	−4.6%	−0.7%	−3.8%	−0.7%	−3.8%	−14.5%
1975	14.2%	5.1%	12.6%	−1.8%	11.4%	−0.1%	10.8%
1976	14.4%	6.6%	5.9%	10.5%	10.5%	10.5%	6.5%
1977	−2.4%	−7.4%	−8.7%	−0.3%	−2.3%	1.1%	−2.8%
1978	23.4%	16.2%	19.1%	17.0%	17.0%	18.5%	19.0%
1979	9.5%	9.5%	6.4%	9.5%	6.4%	9.5%	6.6%
1980	7.5%	7.5%	2.2%	7.5%	4.6%	7.5%	4.4%
1981	8.5%	3.8%	3.3%	−2.5%	2.6%	−0.4%	5.9%
1982	4.6%	0.5%	−1.0%	7.2%	3.1%	2.4%	1.2%
1983	23.4%	23.4%	23.4%	23.4%	23.4%	23.4%	22.1%
1984	16.7%	16.7%	10.5%	8.5%	12.2%	8.5%	13.2%
1985	13.3%	13.3%	13.3%	13.3%	7.7%	13.3%	9.1%
1986	43.9%	26.3%	37.1%	43.9%	37.0%	43.9%	0.0%
1987	17.5%	15.3%	23.3%	18.0%	18.0%	16.4%	7.6%
1988	35.8%	30.2%	23.4%	20.9%	19.0%	20.9%	27.2%
1989	29.5%	29.5%	29.5%	29.5%	29.5%	29.5%	23.2%
1990	−38.7%	−13.0%	−10.3%	−14.4%	−19.9%	−14.4%	0.0%
1991	−5.9%	−19.2%	−2.5%	−13.7%	−8.0%	−16.8%	0.0%
1992	−21.3%	−6.4%	−8.2%	0.0%	−10.7%	−0.3%	0.0%
1993	−1.3%	3.0%	11.6%	−1.8%	−0.1%	−2.4%	2.3%
1994	13.2%	−7.1%	3.1%	−4.8%	8.5%	−11.5%	−2.5%
1995	0.7%	10.4%	12.5%	10.4%	19.9%	8.6%	0.0%
Total return	906%	675%	1101%	769%	895%	668%	577%
Compounded rate of return	9.7%	8.5%	10.5%	9.0%	9.6%	8.5%	7.9%
Standard deviation of returns	25.2%	21.6%	21.3%	21.8%	21.6%	22.2%	19.2%
Risk-adjusted ratio	0.38	0.40	0.49	0.41	0.45	0.38	0.41

Table 6-4. Results of Six Systems Applied to the German Market (FAZ Index)

Year	Buy & hold	System A	System B	System C	System D	System E	System F
1971	5.6%	−8.6%	−5.7%	−3.7%	0.3%	−4.1%	−7.5%
1972	13.6%	9.4%	9.9%	6.0%	12.0%	5.7%	7.9%
1973	−21.1%	−3.1%	−5.3%	−14.0%	−14.6%	−0.1%	−25.2%
1974	−0.1%	−1.9%	−4.2%	−1.9%	−4.1%	0.5%	−7.9%
1975	35.7%	35.8%	24.7%	35.8%	24.4%	35.7%	24.4%
1976	−7.7%	−3.0%	−2.3%	−3.1%	−3.0%	−3.0%	−8.5%
1977	8.4%	2.8%	3.1%	6.7%	1.8%	2.7%	7.5%
1978	6.9%	0.9%	4.5%	1.3%	1.3%	3.5%	5.4%
1979	−11.6%	−2.5%	−6.7%	−2.4%	−4.8%	−2.5%	−12.7%
1980	−2.1%	−3.0%	−8.5%	−7.4%	−5.9%	−5.9%	−2.2%
1981	−0.7%	−6.2%	3.9%	−4.7%	3.6%	−0.2%	0.0%
1982	14.4%	3.7%	9.9%	2.3%	7.8%	6.5%	12.0%
1983	39.1%	39.1%	31.6%	39.1%	31.8%	39.1%	0.0%
1984	8.3%	5.1%	5.3%	3.2%	0.7%	3.2%	4.4%
1985	64.3%	70.3%	70.3%	70.3%	70.3%	70.3%	58.4%
1986	8.0%	−7.5%	−0.2%	−11.1%	−3.8%	−11.4%	3.7%
1987	−37.1%	−18.3%	−6.5%	−26.1%	−9.5%	−20.6%	0.0%
1988	29.3%	16.4%	11.7%	15.7%	19.2%	15.6%	0.0%
1989	34.7%	34.8%	32.7%	34.8%	20.2%	34.7%	33.2%
1990	−18.6%	−1.3%	−3.5%	−1.3%	−4.3%	−1.3%	−20.8%
1991	6.2%	−6.1%	8.5%	−7.8%	1.2%	−2.4%	5.2%
1992	−5.8%	4.6%	2.5%	−5.7%	2.9%	−1.8%	−11.7%
1993	40.6%	31.9%	35.5%	31.9%	35.7%	31.8%	37.6%
1994	−7.4%	−10.6%	−11.9%	−15.3%	−12.0%	−10.2%	0.0%
1995	4.0%	−3.7%	−3.1%	−0.6%	−2.4%	0.7%	0.0%
Total return	335%	288%	388%	157%	276%	319%	96%
Compounded rate of return	6.1%	5.6%	6.5%	3.8%	5.4%	5.9%	2.7%
Standard deviation of returns	22.5%	20.2%	18.5%	21.4%	18.5%	20.1%	18.3%
Risk-adjusted ratio	0.27	0.28	0.35	0.18	0.29	0.29	0.15

Table 6-5. Simulated Trades for System A from 1971 through 1995

Rules: Buy when the weekly close moves up to a new 18-week high;
sell when the weekly close moves down to a new 18-week low.

	Standard & Poor's 500 (U.S.)	FAZ (Germany)	Nikkei 225 (Japan)
Number of trades	13	16	16
% of winning trades	77	50	56
Largest % gain in one trade	42.64	64.48	124.19
Largest % loss in one trade	-13.62	-18.3	-15.81
Average trade results	12.50	11.18	17.17
Number of trades per year	0.52	0.64	0.64

Standard & Poor's 500 (U.S.)

Entry date	Price	Exit date	Price	% Result of trade
01/01/71	91.09	08/06/71	95.96	5.35
01/14/72	103.32	03/30/73	109.84	6.31
10/19/73	110.05	11/30/73	96.58	-12.24
02/21/75	80.93	10/29/76	100.07	23.65
05/05/78	97.67	04/04/80	102.09	4.53
07/25/80	122.51	09/04/81	122.79	0.23
09/10/82	121.37	02/17/84	154.95	27.67
08/10/84	162.60	09/19/86	231.94	42.64
01/16/87	260.30	10/23/87	224.84	-13.62
03/04/88	267.82	02/02/90	327.22	22.18
05/25/90	354.40	08/31/90	320.17	-9.66
02/01/91	336.06	04/08/94	445.66	32.61
08/26/90	463.61	12/29/95	615.93	32.86

FAZ (Germany)

Entry date	Price	Exit date	Price	% Result of trade
12/25/70	187.49	01/01/71	187.42	-0.04
02/05/71	213.33	09/17/71	194.91	-8.63
01/28/72	205.39	05/18/73	217.87	6.08
12/13/74	180.51	05/07/76	233.21	29.20
04/22/77	233.91	05/05/78	236.29	1.02
07/28/78	250.43	02/16/79	250.60	0.07
08/01/80	234.51	10/31/80	227.41	-3.03
04/17/81	232.99	10/02/81	218.57	-6.19
03/05/82	230.54	06/25/82	222.23	-3.60
09/24/82	235.11	06/08/84	354.13	50.62
09/28/84	365.18	07/11/86	600.63	64.48
07/03/87	624.68	10/30/87	510.36	-18.30
03/25/88	472.57	08/17/90	731.24	54.74
03/01/90	678.31	07/24/92	666.46	-1.75
02/12/93	642.41	07/01/94	757.51	17.92
07/21/95	807.7	11/03/95	777.82	-3.70

Nikkei 225 (Japan)

Entry date	Price	Exit date	Price	% Result of trade
12/25/70	1973.59	08/27/71	2278.44	15.45
01/07/72	2713.74	04/20/73	4640.93	71.02
04/26/74	4613.59	08/09/74	4403.31	-4.56
02/14/75	4046.66	08/15/75	4252.41	5.08
01/02/76	4358.6	10/29/76	4604.03	5.63
12/31/76	4942.27	06/17/77	4927.55	-0.30
08/19/77	5176.5	11/25/77	4853.42	-6.24
03/03/78	5166.46	03/20/81	7124.33	37.90
04/10/81	7447.74	03/19/82	7078.68	-4.96
10/22/82	7370.2	10/24/86	16523.40	124.19
01/23/87	19188.7	09/09/88	27341.60	42.49
11/18/88	28520.9	03/09/94	33845.20	18.67
03/01/91	26462.8	06/28/91	23765.50	-10.19
11/08/91	24950.9	01/31/92	21007.10	-15.81
03/19/93	18086.1	11/12/93	18625.20	2.98
06/10/94	20726.7	11/18/94	19261.40	-7.07

Table 6-6. Simulated Trades for System B from 1971 through 1995

Rules: Buy when the weekly closing price moves up to a new 10-week high; sell when the weekly close is 7% below the highest price recorded during the trade.

Standard & Poor's 500 (U.S.)

Number of trades	27
% of winning trades	56
Largest % gain in one trade	33.86
Largest % loss in one trade	-11.15
Average trade results	6.53
Number of trades per year	1.08

Entry date	Price	Exit date	Price	% Result of trade
01/01/71	92.15	06/25/71	97.99	6.34
12/03/71	97.06	02/02/73	114.35	17.81
07/27/73	109.59	11/23/73	99.44	-9.26
03/15/74	99.28	05/17/74	88.21	-11.15
01/10/75	72.61	08/01/75	87.99	21.18
01/09/76	94.95	10/22/76	99.96	5.28
12/10/76	104.70	02/11/77	100.22	-4.28
06/24/77	101.19	08/26/77	96.06	-5.07
11/25/77	96.69	01/13/78	89.69	-7.24
04/14/78	92.92	10/20/78	97.95	5.41
01/12/79	99.93	10/19/79	101.60	1.67
11/30/79	106.16	03/21/80	102.31	-3.63
05/23/80	110.62	07/03/81	128.64	16.29
12/04/81	126.26	01/15/82	116.33	-7.86
04/23/82	118.64	06/04/82	110.09	-7.21
08/27/82	117.11	02/10/84	156.30	33.46
08/03/84	162.35	09/13/85	182.91	12.66
11/01/85	191.53	09/12/86	230.67	20.44
10/31/86	243.98	10/16/87	282.70	15.87
02/19/88	261.61	08/19/88	260.24	-0.52
09/30/88	271.91	10/13/89	333.65	22.71
12/01/89	350.63	01/26/90	325.80	-7.08
03/16/90	341.91	08/03/90	344.86	0.86
11/30/90	322.22	04/03/92	401.55	24.62
04/17/92	416.05	10/09/92	402.66	-3.22
11/20/92	426.65	04/01/94	445.76	4.48
06/03/94	460.13	12/29/95	615.93	33.86

FAZ (Germany)

Number of trades	36
% of winning trades	50
Largest % gain in one trade	86.88
Largest % loss in one trade	-8.33
Average trade results	5.66
Number of trades per year	1.44

Entry date	Price	Exit date	Price	% Result of trade
01/15/71	203.4	04/23/71	206.86	1.70
07/30/71	214.58	09/10/71	196.70	-8.33
12/24/71	195.66	10/13/72	226.86	15.95
11/17/72	234.46	05/04/73	226.05	-3.59
10/19/73	198.69	11/16/73	186.99	-5.89
01/18/74	192.11	05/31/74	177.83	-7.43
11/15/74	171.00	05/30/75	206.59	20.81
07/11/75	218.90	09/19/75	213.54	-2.45
10/10/75	219.47	04/30/76	234.82	6.99
01/07/77	227.22	03/11/77	217.07	-4.47
03/25/77	222.74	04/21/78	238.39	7.03
06/09/78	243.77	02/09/79	253.18	3.86
08/10/79	237.86	11/09/79	225.33	-5.27
02/08/80	233.62	03/21/80	217.11	-7.07
05/16/80	224.26	09/12/80	229.32	2.26
10/10/80	236.19	10/24/80	227.54	-3.66
03/13/81	221.59	09/11/81	230.23	3.90
01/29/82	255.91	05/21/82	228.42	1.11
09/17/82	232.62	09/16/83	308.38	32.57
10/07/83	326.03	03/09/84	344.81	5.76
04/27/84	353.20	06/01/84	340.71	-3.54
09/07/84	342.09	05/30/86	639.31	86.88
08/15/86	667.07	01/09/87	634.32	-4.91
06/19/87	615.73	10/16/87	613.67	-0.33
02/26/88	455.51	05/13/88	428.06	-6.03
06/03/88	462.61	10/20/89	645.30	39.49
11/24/89	655.28	06/15/90	759.24	15.86
06/22/90	791.73	08/10/90	745.56	-5.83
02/08/91	620.23	07/26/91	672.77	8.47
01/17/92	678.64	06/26/92	695.83	2.53
01/15/93	610.00	05/07/93	639.25	4.80
06/11/93	655.63	06/03/94	808.75	23.35
08/05/94	827.84	09/30/94	764.22	-7.69
02/10/95	791.97	03/10/95	741.39	-6.39
05/12/95	773.44	10/06/95	793.97	2.65
12/01/95	809.24	12/29/95	815.66	0.79

Nikkei 225 (Japan)

Number of trades	29
% of winning trades	62
Largest % gain in one trade	91.24
Largest % loss in one trade	-9.13
Average trade results	10.69
Number of trades per year	1.16

Entry date	Price	Exit date	Price	% Result of trade
01/15/71	2112.13	08/20/71	2278.44	7.87
11/26/71	2426.75	04/13/73	4640.93	91.24
07/13/73	4960.43	09/14/73	4644.12	-6.38
01/25/74	4466.43	07/12/74	4436.83	-0.66
01/31/75	3935.22	07/18/75	4327.37	9.97
10/17/75	4257.86	04/16/76	4475.10	5.10
04/30/76	4668.73	10/22/76	4604.03	-1.39
12/10/76	4769.62	04/08/77	4928.03	3.32
04/22/77	5135.02	06/10/77	4927.55	-4.04
07/08/77	5057.66	07/29/77	4923.71	-2.65
08/05/77	5095.65	10/28/77	5041.00	-1.07
01/13/78	5040.08	10/26/79	6292.37	24.85
11/30/79	6474.06	03/28/80	6475.93	0.03
04/18/80	6811.39	03/13/81	6956.52	2.13
03/27/81	7303.04	09/04/81	7662.50	4.92
01/22/82	7823.36	02/26/82	7548.51	-3.51
05/07/82	7518.78	07/02/82	7084.87	-5.77
10/08/82	7361.57	06/01/84	9913.20	34.66
07/06/84	10461.90	10/03/86	17240.20	64.79
11/28/86	18083.00	10/23/87	23201.20	28.30
01/29/88	23622.30	09/02/88	27116.50	14.79
11/04/88	27953.30	02/23/90	34891.00	24.82
02/08/91	24296.10	06/07/91	25035.10	3.04
09/27/91	23969.50	11/29/91	22687.30	-5.35
08/28/92	17970.70	11/13/92	16330.70	-9.13
11/27/92	17470.60	10/29/93	19703.00	12.78
01/21/94	19307.40	09/09/94	19897.90	3.06
12/30/94	19723.10	01/27/95	18104.30	-8.21
07/07/95	16213.10	12/29/95	19868.20	22.54

Table 6-7. Simulated Trades for System C from 1971 through 1995

Rules: Buy when the weekly close is 1% above the average of the last 40 weekly closing prices; sell when the weekly close is 1% below the average of the last 40 weekly closing prices.

	Standard & Poor's 500 (U.S.)					FAZ (Germany)					Nikkei 225 (Japan)				
Number of trades	23					26					21				
% of winning trades	52					35					48				
Largest % gain in one trade	34.35					69.08					112.85				
Largest % loss in one trade	-5.73					-21.49					ms]10.89				
Average trade results	6.90					5.36					12.33				
Number of trades per year	0.92					1.04					0.84				
Entry date	Price	Exit date	Price	% Result of trade		Entry date	Price	Exit date	Price	% Result of trade	Entry date	Price	Exit date	Price	% Result of trade
01/01/71	91.09	08/13/71	93.53	2.68		02/05/71	213.33	09/03/71	205.53	-3.66	02/12/71	2127.06	08/27/71	2278.44	7.12
08/27/71	99.25	10/22/71	97.35	-1.91		01/28/72	205.39	10/27/72	222.99	8.57	10/08/71	2432.50	10/15/71	2359.54	-3.00
12/24/71	101.55	03/30/73	109.84	8.16		11/24/72	232.21	12/08/72	226.80	-2.33	12/10/71	2466.97	05/04/73	4598.47	86.40
10/19/73	110.05	11/09/73	105.52	-4.12		01/26/73	242.42	02/16/73	230.08	-5.09	07/20/73	4960.43	08/24/73	4834.45	-2.54
02/14/75	78.36	12/12/75	87.07	11.12		03/23/73	244.28	05/11/73	221.38	-9.37	04/26/74	4613.59	07/19/74	4436.83	-3.83
01/02/76	90.13	10/22/76	101.47	12.58		12/13/74	180.51	05/21/76	232.97	29.06	02/28/75	4136.34	08/29/75	4143.60	0.18
12/17/76	104.63	02/04/77	102.03	-2.49		04/15/77	225.38	04/28/78	234.49	4.04	11/07/75	4346.86	11/28/75	4261.38	-1.97
05/05/78	97.67	11/03/78	95.06	-2.67		06/23/78	247.40	02/23/79	250.73	1.35	01/02/76	4358.60	10/29/76	4604.03	5.63
01/19/79	100.69	02/16/79	98.20	-2.47		02/22/80	236.03	03/14/80	224.19	-5.02	12/17/76	4769.62	11/18/77	4971.54	4.23
03/23/79	101.06	05/18/79	98.06	-2.97		06/27/80	232.50	11/07/80	226.55	-2.56	03/27/81	7293.57	10/02/81	7037.12	-3.52
06/15/79	101.91	10/26/79	100.71	-1.18		04/10/81	229.41	10/02/81	218.57	-4.73	11/27/81	7647.00	03/05/82	7548.51	-1.29
11/30/79	106.80	03/21/80	102.26	-4.25		03/12/82	233.80	06/25/82	222.23	-4.95	10/22/82	7370.20	07/27/84	9703.35	31.66
05/30/80	111.40	07/10/81	127.37	14.34		09/24/82	235.11	06/22/84	338.24	43.86	08/10/84	10431.10	10/30/87	22202.60	112.85
09/03/82	117.66	02/10/84	158.08	34.35		09/21/84	355.24	07/11/86	600.63	69.08	02/26/88	24846.70	03/02/90	33321.90	34.11
08/10/84	162.60	10/04/85	182.08	11.98		08/22/86	676.97	09/26/86	661.03	-2.35	03/15/91	26669.40	06/28/91	23765.50	-10.89
10/25/85	186.96	10/23/87	224.84	20.26		12/05/86	687.17	01/16/87	636.42	-7.39	10/25/91	25016.80	11/15/91	24233.00	-3.13
06/17/88	271.43	02/02/90	327.22	20.55		07/24/87	650.02	10/30/87	510.36	-21.49	12/25/92	17645.40	01/08/93	16994.00	-3.69
05/18/90	353.36	08/17/90	333.13	-5.73		07/01/88	475.39	08/17/90	731.24	53.82	02/12/93	17281.70	02/19/93	17117.90	-0.95
02/01/91	336.06	11/29/91	374.57	11.46		03/15/91	671.77	03/29/91	643.65	-4.19	03/19/93	18086.10	11/12/93	18625.20	2.98
12/27/91	387.05	10/16/92	402.66	4.03		04/12/91	672.44	10/18/91	647.13	-3.76	03/04/94	19997.20	10/07/94	19650.00	-1.74
11/06/92	418.66	04/08/94	445.66	6.45		01/24/92	677.06	07/31/92	638.30	-5.72	08/25/95	17999.90	12/29/95	19868.20	10.38
10/21/94	469.11	12/02/94	452.26	-3.59		02/12/93	642.41	06/24/94	761.11	18.48					
01/20/95	465.97	12/29/95	615.93	32.18		08/12/94	826.13	08/19/94	807.04	-2.31					
						09/09/94	824.29	09/23/94	796.15	-3.41					
						06/09/95	789.20	11/03/95	777.82	-1.44					
						12/08/95	809.08	12/29/95	815.66	0.81					

Table 6-8. Simulated Trades for System D from 1971 through 1995

Rules: Buy when the weekly close is 1% above the average of the last 20 weekly closing prices; sell when the weekly close is 1% below the average of the last 20 weekly closing prices.

	Standard & Poor's 500 (U.S.)	FAZ (Germany)	Nikkei 225 (Japan)
Number of trades	43	39	27
% of winning trades	26	44	52
Largest % gain in one trade	39.74	37.12	88.12
Largest % loss in one trade	-7.57	-10.09	-10.51
Average trade results	2.89	2.38	9.77
Number of trades per year	1.72	1.56	1.08

Entry date	Price	Exit date	Price	% Result of trade	Entry date	Price	Exit date	Price	% Result of trade	Entry date	Price	Exit date	Price	% Result of trade
01/01/71	91.09	06/25/71	97.87	7.44	01/22/71	202.22	04/30/71	206.77	2.25	01/22/71	2112.13	08/27/71	2278.44	7.87
12/17/71	97.97	07/21/72	105.88	8.07	08/06/71	214.72	08/27/71	209.26	-2.54	12/10/71	2466.97	04/20/73	4640.93	88.12
08/11/72	110.61	10/13/72	109.90	-0.64	12/31/71	196.65	07/14/72	228.39	16.14	07/20/73	4960.43	09/21/73	4644.12	-6.38
11/03/72	110.59	03/02/73	112.19	1.45	07/28/72	236.66	09/22/72	229.70	-2.94	02/01/74	4466.43	07/19/74	4436.83	-0.66
08/03/73	109.25	08/17/73	103.71	-5.07	01/12/73	233.07	05/11/73	221.38	-5.02	02/07/75	3935.22	07/25/75	4327.37	9.97
09/28/73	107.36	11/23/73	100.71	-6.19	11/02/73	207.89	11/23/73	186.91	-10.09	10/31/75	4301.02	10/29/76	4604.03	7.05
03/22/74	98.05	04/05/74	93.25	-4.90	01/25/74	188.29	03/01/74	181.02	-3.86	12/17/76	4769.62	06/17/77	4927.55	3.31
01/10/75	71.07	08/08/75	87.15	22.62	04/12/74	187.87	05/31/74	181.55	-3.36	08/12/77	5095.65	11/04/77	5041.00	-1.07
10/31/75	89.73	06/11/76	98.63	9.92	11/22/74	171.51	06/06/75	208.52	21.58	02/10/78	5130.96	11/02/79	6292.37	22.64
06/25/76	104.28	10/22/76	101.47	-2.69	07/18/75	221.10	09/26/75	213.77	-3.32	03/27/81	7293.57	09/18/81	7542.82	3.42
12/17/76	104.63	02/04/77	102.03	-2.49	10/17/75	219.97	05/07/76	233.21	6.02	12/11/81	7789.16	03/05/82	7548.51	-3.09
07/01/77	100.98	08/19/77	98.18	-2.77	01/14/77	228.18	03/18/77	217.07	-4.87	05/21/82	7619.39	06/04/82	7325.65	-3.86
04/21/78	94.45	10/27/78	98.18	3.95	04/08/77	224.73	04/28/78	234.49	4.34	10/15/82	7361.57	05/25/84	10165.00	38.08
02/02/79	101.55	05/18/79	98.06	-3.44	06/23/78	247.40	12/29/78	256.88	3.83	08/31/84	10568.70	08/16/85	12372.90	17.07
06/15/79	101.91	10/26/79	100.71	-1.18	09/07/79	240.48	11/02/79	228.97	-4.79	10/18/85	13017.30	10/10/86	17435.30	33.94
12/14/79	107.67	03/14/80	106.51	-1.08	02/15/80	234.62	03/14/80	224.19	-4.45	12/05/86	18308.00	10/30/87	22202.60	21.27
05/30/80	111.40	01/30/81	129.84	16.55	06/20/80	230.89	10/31/80	227.41	-1.51	02/19/88	24207.40	09/09/88	27341.60	12.95
04/03/81	134.28	07/10/81	127.37	-5.15	03/27/81	223.29	09/11/81	231.33	3.60	11/18/88	28520.90	03/02/90	33321.90	16.83
12/04/81	126.35	01/15/82	116.78	-7.57	02/12/82	227.93	05/28/82	228.42	0.21	07/13/90	32538.30	08/03/90	30442.90	-6.44
04/30/82	119.26	06/04/82	111.68	-6.36	09/24/82	235.11	09/02/83	309.94	31.83	02/15/91	24934.00	06/14/91	24598.40	-1.35
08/27/82	116.11	09/02/83	162.25	39.74	10/14/83	327.17	03/16/84	341.10	4.26	10/04/91	23916.40	11/29/91	22868.70	-4.38
09/16/83	165.48	11/04/83	163.55	-1.17	05/11/84	355.66	05/18/84	344.24	-3.21	09/04/92	18061.10	11/20/92	16162.90	-10.51
12/02/83	166.54	12/23/83	162.32	-2.53	03/14/86	658.73	05/23/86	647.10	-1.77	12/04/92	17683.60	01/08/93	16994.00	-3.90

01/13/84	168.90	02/03/84	162.87	−3.57	08/22/86	676.97	01/09/87	671.71	−0.78	02/12/93	17281.70	02/19/93	17117.90	−0.95
08/10/84	162.60	12/14/84	162.83	0.14	06/26/87	625.44	10/23/87	569.85	−8.89	08/06/93	20343.50	11/05/93	19438.20	−4.45
01/18/85	170.51	09/20/85	182.88	7.26	03/04/88	456.82	05/20/88	444.09	−2.79	01/28/94	18353.20	09/16/94	19917.30	8.52
11/08/85	191.25	07/25/86	236.24	23.52	06/03/88	448.57	11/03/89	615.09	37.12	07/21/95	16573.80	12/29/95	19868.20	19.88
08/22/86	247.38	09/19/86	231.94	−6.24	12/08/89	689.55	06/01/90	772.66	12.05					
11/07/86	245.80	10/16/87	309.39	25.87	07/13/90	816.23	08/10/90	749.06	−8.23					
02/26/88	265.64	05/27/88	250.83	−5.57	02/22/91	658.84	08/02/91	667.02	1.24					
06/10/88	267.05	08/26/88	256.98	−3.77	01/24/92	677.06	07/03/92	696.85	2.92					
09/23/88	268.82	11/25/88	266.22	−0.97	01/08/93	602.31	05/28/93	635.25	5.47					
10/27/89	347.79	11/03/89	336.45	−3.26	07/09/93	658.83	03/04/94	801.28	21.62					
12/08/89	350.84	01/19/90	338.22	−3.60	03/25/94	815.87	06/10/94	816.66	0.10					
04/20/90	347.24	04/27/90	333.45	−3.97	08/12/94	826.13	08/19/94	807.04	−2.31					
05/18/90	353.36	08/10/90	336.82	−4.68	09/09/94	824.29	09/30/94	784.86	−4.78					
12/14/90	327.75	07/05/91	371.18	13.25	02/17/95	790.40	03/17/95	749.76	−5.14					
07/26/91	384.21	11/29/91	374.57	−2.51	05/19/95	773.16	10/13/95	792.30	2.48					
01/03/92	407.47	06/26/92	403.64	−0.94	12/22/95	812.19	12/29/95	815.66	0.43					
07/17/92	414.68	10/16/92	402.66	−2.90										
11/06/92	418.66	04/01/94	460.58	10.01										
08/05/94	458.28	12/02/94	452.26	−1.31										
02/03/95	470.39	12/29/95	615.93	30.94										

Table 6-9. Simulated Trades for System E from 1971 through 1995

Rules: If weekly close is above the average of 40 weekly closes, put a buy order with a stop at the highest of 5 weeks; if weekly close is below the average of 40 weekly closes, put a sell order with a stop at the lowest of 5 weeks.

Standard & Poor's 500 (U.S.)

Number of trades	27
% of winning trades	48
Largest % gain in one trade	34.31
Largest % loss in one trade	-6.39
Average trade results	5.30
Number of trades per year	1.08

Entry date	Price	Exit date	Price	% Result of trade
01/08/71	92.99	08/06/71	95.08	2.25
08/27/71	101.00	10/01/71	97.61	-3.36
12/24/71	101.55	10/13/72	107.35	5.71
10/27/72	111.35	04/27/73	107.41	-3.54
10/12/73	110.46	11/09/73	105.52	-4.47
02/07/75	78.69	09/19/75	82.21	4.47
10/10/75	87.42	12/12/75	86.54	-1.01
01/09/76	92.58	10/22/76	100.02	8.04
12/10/76	103.78	02/04/77	101.08	-2.60
04/28/78	95.89	11/03/78	94.30	-1.66
01/12/79	99.79	03/02/79	96.51	-3.29
03/16/79	100.58	05/18/79	97.92	-2.65
06/15/79	102.54	10/26/79	100.71	-1.78
11/23/79	104.94	03/14/80	105.99	1.00
05/23/80	108.12	07/10/81	127.37	17.80
09/03/82	121.23	02/03/84	162.82	34.31
08/10/84	162.60	09/27/85	180.78	11.18
10/25/85	188.52	09/19/86	228.74	21.33
10/31/86	240.18	10/23/87	224.84	-6.39
06/10/88	267.43	02/02/90	321.44	20.20
03/23/90	341.91	04/27/90	333.41	-2.49
05/18/90	353.36	08/10/90	336.82	-4.68
02/01/91	336.92	11/29/91	374.52	11.60
12/27/91	388.24	10/09/92	410.43	5.72
11/06/92	421.16	04/01/94	457.67	8.67
08/19/94	462.77	12/09/94	444.18	-4.02
01/13/95	462.73	12/29/95	615.93	33.11

FAZ (Germany)

Number of trades	24
% of winning trades	42
Largest % gain in one trade	69.08
Largest % loss in one trade	-19.41
Average trade results	7.81
Number of trades per year	0.96

Entry date	Price	Exit date	Price	% Result of trade
01/22/71	204.13	05/14/71	204.67	0.26
07/16/71	211.58	09/10/71	/202.43	-4.32
01/28/72	205.39	10/20/72	225.13	9.61
11/17/72	233.10	12/08/72	224.81	-3.56
01/12/73	233.07	05/04/73	232.72	-0.15
12/06/74	176.19	05/14/76	233.02	32.25
01/14/77	228.18	02/25/77	219.05	-4.00
04/08/77	224.73	04/28/78	234.49	4.34
06/09/78	242.15	02/16/79	250.60	3.49
02/15/80	234.62	03/14/80	224.19	-4.45
06/20/80	230.89	10/31/80	227.41	-1.51
04/10/81	229.41	09/25/81	228.90	-0.22
03/05/82	230.73	05/28/82	228.42	-1.00
09/24/82	235.11	06/22/84	338.24	43.86
09/21/84	355.24	07/11/86	600.63	69.08
08/22/86	676.97	10/03/86	651.29	-3.79
11/28/86	679.31	01/09/87	666.10	-1.94
07/17/87	633.29	10/30/87	510.36	-19.41
06/24/88	475.65	08/17/90	731.24	53.73
04/19/91	680.28	10/04/91	664.07	-2.38
01/24/92	678.64	07/24/92	666.46	-1.79
02/12/93	643.00	06/24/94	761.11	18.37
02/17/95	791.97	03/10/95	756.53	-4.47
05/19/95	773.44	12/29/95	815.66	5.46

Nikkei 225 (Japan)

Number of trades	22
% of winning trades	50
Largest % gain in one trade	110.05
Largest % loss in one trade	-11.02
Average trade results	12.83
Number of trades per year	0.88

Entry date	Price	Exit date	Price	% Result of trade
01/22/71	2112.13	08/27/71	2278.44	7.87
10/08/71	2432.50	10/15/71	2333.07	-4.09
12/10/71	2466.97	04/27/73	4640.93	88.12
07/20/73	4960.43	08/24/73	4834.45	-2.54
04/26/74	4613.59	07/19/74	4436.83	-3.83
02/21/75	4107.63	08/29/75	4143.60	0.88
10/31/75	4301.02	12/12/75	4261.38	-0.92
01/02/76	4358.60	11/05/76	4604.03	5.63
12/17/76	4769.62	11/04/77	5041.00	5.69
02/03/78	5064.10	11/02/81	7037.12	38.96
01/22/82	7719.34	03/05/82	7548.51	-2.21
05/21/82	7619.39	06/04/82	7325.65	-3.86
10/15/82	7361.57	07/27/84	9703.35	31.81
08/17/84	10431.10	11/13/87	21910.10	110.05
02/26/88	24846.70	03/02/90	33321.90	34.11
03/15/91	26709.80	06/28/91	23765.50	-11.02
10/25/91	25016.80	11/22/91	23400.10	-6.46
12/18/92	17704.70	01/08/93	16891.90	-4.59
03/19/93	18104.60	11/12/93	18470.30	2.02
02/11/94	20509.90	04/08/94	19082.80	-6.96
05/27/94	20568.70	09/23/94	19554.10	-4.93
09/08/95	18299.70	12/29/95	19868.20	8.57

Table 6-10. Simulated Trades for System F from 1971 through 1995

Rules: Buy at the end of January only if the monthly close is higher than the year's end close; sell at the end of the year.

Standard & Poor's 500 (U.S.)

Number of trades	16
% of winning trades	88
Largest % gain in one trade	30.93
Largest % loss in one trade	−9.85
Average trade results	11.69
Number of trades per year	0.64

Entry date	Price	Exit date	Price	% Result of trade
01/29/71	95.88	12/31/71	102.09	6.48
01/31/72	103.94	12/29/72	118.05	13.58
01/31/75	76.98	12/31/75	90.19	17.16
01/30/76	100.86	12/31/76	107.46	6.54
01/31/79	99.93	12/31/79	107.94	8.02
01/31/80	114.16	12/31/80	135.76	18.92
01/31/83	145.30	12/30/83	164.93	13.51
01/31/85	179.63	12/31/85	211.28	17.62
01/31/86	211.78	12/31/86	242.17	14.35
01/30/87	274.08	12/31/87	247.08	−9.85
01/29/88	257.07	12/30/88	277.72	8.03
01/31/89	297.47	12/29/89	353.40	18.80
01/31/91	343.93	12/31/91	417.09	21.27
01/29/93	438.78	12/31/93	466.45	6.31
01/31/94	481.61	12/30/94	459.27	−4.64
01/31/95	470.42	12/29/95	615.93	30.93

FAZ (Germany)

Number of trades	19
% of winning trades	53
Largest % gain in one trade	58.41
Largest % loss in one trade	−25.19
Average trade results	5.43
Number of trades per year	0.76

Entry date	Price	Exit date	Price	% Result of trade
01/29/71	213.83	12/31/71	197.89	−7.45
01/31/72	208.33	12/29/72	224.74	7.88
01/31/73	237.08	12/31/73	177.36	−25.19
01/31/74	192.30	12/31/74	177.20	−7.85
10/31/75	193.28	12/31/75	240.41	24.38
01/30/76	242.49	12/31/76	221.89	−8.50
01/31/77	223.70	12/30/77	240.45	7.49
01/31/78	243.90	12/29/78	257.00	5.37
01/31/79	260.24	12/31/79	227.27	−12.67
01/31/80	227.63	12/31/80	222.56	−2.23
01/29/82	225.91	12/31/82	252.95	11.97
01/31/84	365.14	12/31/84	381.18	4.39
01/31/85	395.31	12/31/85	626.21	58.41
01/31/86	652.08	12/31/86	676.37	3.72
01/31/89	556.15	12/29/89	740.93	33.22
01/31/90	761.48	12/31/90	603.06	−20.80
01/31/91	608.59	12/31/91	640.31	5.21
01/31/92	683.17	12/31/92	602.97	−11.74
01/29/93	615.83	12/31/93	847.57	37.63

Nikkei 225 (Japan)

Number of trades	20
% of winning trades	53
Largest % gain in one trade	82.66
Largest % loss in one trade	−18.65
Average trade results	11.62
Number of trades per year	0.80

Entry date	Price	Exit date	Price	% Result of trade
01/29/71	2099.37	12/31/71	2713.74	29.26
01/31/72	2851.22	12/29/72	5207.94	82.66
01/31/73	5294.26	12/31/73	4306.80	−18.65
01/31/74	4466.43	12/31/74	3817.22	−14.54
01/31/75	3935.22	12/31/75	4358.60	10.76
01/30/76	4684.25	12/31/76	4987.47	6.47
01/31/77	5007.66	12/30/77	4865.60	−2.84
01/31/78	5044.58	12/29/78	6001.85	18.98
01/31/79	6165.32	12/31/79	6569.73	6.56
01/31/80	6768.16	12/31/80	7063.13	4.36
01/30/81	7254.01	12/31/81	7681.84	5.90
01/29/82	7918.82	12/31/82	8016.67	1.24
01/31/83	8103.47	12/30/83	9893.82	22.09
01/31/84	10196.10	12/31/84	11542.60	13.21
01/31/85	11992.30	12/31/85	13083.20	9.10
01/30/87	20048.30	12/31/87	21564.00	7.56
01/29/88	23622.30	12/30/88	30050.90	27.21
01/31/89	31581.30	12/29/89	38915.90	23.22
01/29/93	17023.70	12/31/93	17417.20	2.31
01/31/94	20229.10	12/30/94	19723.10	−2.50

profitable market moves were missed. It is easy to conclude that the statistical value of this indicator is very poor for Germany. It was also disappointing for trading of the Japanese Nikkei.

It was interesting to include the "January effect" in the tests; however, the results confirm that the indicator is not robust. Because it does not work in all conditions, and in this case all markets, we must question the rationale, or lack of substance, behind it. We should not overlook the possibility that specific rules work in isolated markets because of unique tax regulations, or other special situations, but this technique clearly cannot be applied to our world market approach without varying the parameters.

A Closer Look at System B's Performance

A look at the charts in Figures 6-3 through 6-5 will give you an understanding of the smoothness of the equity curves derived from the use of system B. This set of rules seems to have avoided the sharp losses of the worst years. The declines of 1973 and 1974 on Wall Street (−17.4% and −29.7%, respectively) were reduced to −12% and −11%. The same improvement can be seen for Japan in Figure 6-4 during the bear market of the early 1990s, where 55% of the investment capital, which deteriorated from 1989 to 1993, could have been held to a 20% loss by using this system.

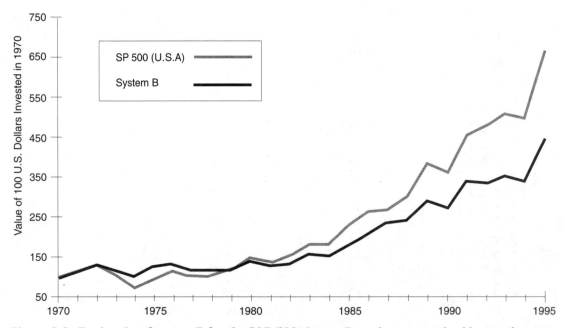

Figure 6-3. Equity plot of system B for the S&P 500. System B results are considerably smoother.

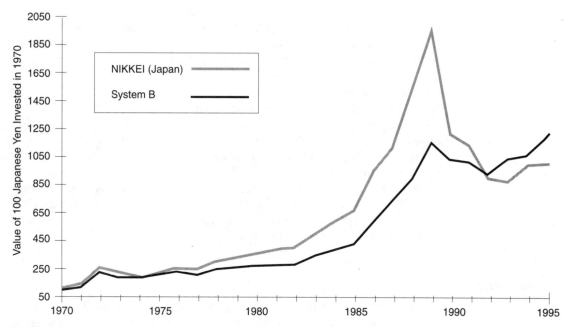

Figure 6-4. Equity plot of system B for the Nikkei 225. System B sharply reduced the losses of the early 1990s.

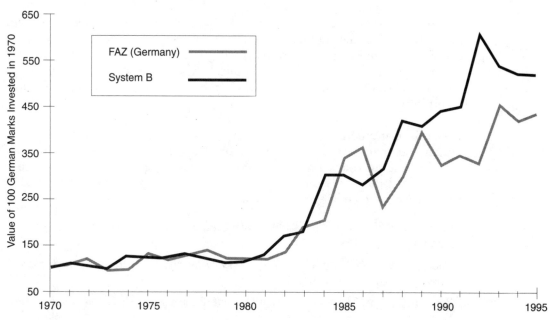

Figure 6-5. Equity plot of system B for the FAZ. While holding the 1987 loss to only 7%, the moving average system missed a large part of the bull-market profits during the last three years.

The heavy loss on the German market in 1987, a drop of 37% caused by the crash, is reduced to only a 7% loss (see Figure 6-5). But the price to pay for lower risk is always lower reward. As we should expect, not all the profits of the bullish years could be captured, but we can say that all the large moves produced profits.

This characteristic of the systems to behave the way we expect (avoiding the sharp losses and staying in the market when the trend is strong), throughout many unique market periods, shows that simple techniques are robust. It is interesting to observe that all the trend-following techniques using indicators of similar speed tend to behave more or less in the same manner. This means that there is no indicator better than any other. Everything depends on the way we manage it. An indicator that gives a signal ahead of another may give too many bad signals afterward. All the trend-following tools lag the market and confirm a situation that has already started. Their qualities and disadvantages are more or less the same. What really makes the difference is not the indicator used but the way it is used.

Conclusion

Our goal was not to provide the "solution" but just to set the basis for a better investment decision. We think the concepts that we just described are a good starting point for those who want to enhance their trading techniques. The systems we have illustrated are unpolished and are intended to demonstrate the usefulness of trend-following methods; they are not intended or expected to be adopted by traders exactly as they are presented.

The true benefit of the systematic approach is that the trade-off of lower risk for lower profits gives a smoother equity curve. And, being out of the market up to 30% of the time means that you have a much lower chance of a capital drawdown due to an unexpected political or economic price shock. These shocks are always unpredictable and the largest ones always drive stock prices down, and offer little opportunity to react.

There is good literature available on the subject of analysis, and this material can be readily computerized; we encourage readers to look more closely at this intriguing domain of technical information. These books will provide tools and ideas for creating your own trading programs. We suggest the following, which cover a broad range of systems and concepts, as a good place to start for those readers wishing to go deeper into this area.

Bruce Babcock, *The Business One Irwin Guide to Trading Systems* (Business One Irwin, Chicago, 1989).

Robert Colby and Thomas Meyers, *The Encyclopedia of Technical Market Indicators* (Dow-Jones-Irwin, Chicago, 1988).

Perry Kaufman, *The New Commodity Trading Systems and Methods* (Wiley, New York, 1987).

Perry Kaufman, *Smarter Trading* (McGraw-Hill, New York, 1995).

John Murphy, *Technical Analysis of the Futures Markets* (New York Institute of Finance, New York, 1986).

Robert Pardo, *Design, Testing and Optimization of Trading Systems* (Wiley, New York, 1992).

Jack Schwager, *Schwager on Technical Analysis* (Wiley, New York, 1996).

Diversification Applied to Trading Methods

One Robust Trading Strategy Helps to Reduce Risk Further

When the investor has a buy-and-hold attitude toward the equity market, then a strategy of diversification proves to be a successful way to gain risk reduction. But would we adopt a single trading strategy and always apply it to a portfolio of diversified international markets? In the previous section we evaluated the results of six systems applied to three major world equity markets. One system in particular was better than the others.

We know that if we had equally allocated an investment to the U.S., Japanese, and German markets we would have improved the quality because of the decrease in the volatility of the equity. If we kept each country allocation at one-third, and we traded each market using system B, which proved the best, the result that we would have achieved is given in Table 6-11.

The compounded yearly rate of return given by the passive, diversified portfolio was 8.7% with a standard deviation of yearly returns of about 16%. The global return obtainable by using system B is a little lower than that of the buy-and-hold strategy (8.2% versus 8.7%), but the single yearly returns, which showed a standard deviation of about 13%, were also less volatile. The result is a better risk-adjusted ratio, 0.63 instead of the 0.54 for the buy-and-hold approach. That means you can get the same returns for a lower risk using a simple trading strategy.

It is particularly interesting to note the way the number and size of negative yearly returns are sharply reduced by the use of a robust trend-following system applied to an international portfolio that is already diversified. In fact, only one year, 1973, shows a double-digit loss of about 11.3% while the average return of the three markets was a loss of 19% in that year.

In 1987, a very bad year for most markets, the use of the trend-following method turned losses into double-digit profits because the system was able to partially freeze the market gains that occurred before the October crash by signaling an exit from the market at a timely moment. In 1990, which was a bad year where even diversification could not prevent a loss of 21%, the use of the trend-following method in our example held losses to only 6%. On the other side, the gains from most of the bull-market trends were somewhat lower, but still good.

Table 6-11. Comparison between an Equally Weighted Investment in the U.S., Japanese, and German Equities and the Use of System B Applied to the Same Investment (returns in local currencies)

Year	Buy & hold	System B
1971	17.9%	8.9%
1972	40.4%	39.1%
1973	−18.6%	−11.3%
1974	−13.7%	−5.3%
1975	27.1%	19.5%
1976	8.6%	3.9%
1977	−1.9%	−6.2%
1978	10.4%	7.7%
1979	3.4%	1.0%
1980	10.4%	3.6%
1981	−0.6%	−0.4%
1982	11.3%	4.9%
1983	26.6%	24.1%
1984	8.8%	4.3%
1985	34.7%	34.7%
1986	22.2%	16.1%
1987	−5.9%	10.4%
1988	25.9%	12.2%
1989	30.5%	27.8%
1990	−21.3%	−6.3%
1991	8.9%	9.9%
1992	−7.6%	−2.4%
1993	15.4%	17.7%
1994	1.4%	−4.5%
1995	12.9%	14.5%
Total return	706%	623%
Compounded rate of return	8.7%	8.2%
Standard deviation of yearly returns	16%	13%
Risk-adjusted ratio	0.54	0.63

We know that even within a trending global portfolio, the movements of each market are different. This means that one specific trading technique can be successful at a certain moment in one market and not in another. A technical trend-following method cannot be perfect because the markets never behave the same way. When we adopt a trading technique we must always be prepared to live with unsuccessful periods; it is an unavoidable price that must be paid. In many cases, however, when a system does not work on one market, it can be giving compensating results in another. The conclusion is that the simultaneous use of trading techniques on several markets improves the global result, in the same way that passive diversification increases the quality of the buy-and-hold returns.

Using Multiple Methods to Reduce Risk

Almost all the trading systems that we presented earlier in this chapter are based on following the trend. Although one in particular proved to be better, it still has a lot in common with the others. All of them try to catch the maximum possible part of the price trend but are unable to profit from the entire move. During downtrends these methods all have rules that are intended to cut losses, and while they do this fairly well, they all act in more or less the same way. This observation can be supported by the degree of statistical correlation that exists when comparing the simulated yearly returns that each of the systems applied to the indices. The average value for the correlation coefficient is near 0.9. This tells us that, if we had to use all those systems simultaneously we could hardly obtain a better result than using only the best method, system B.

If we were to use a totally different system strategy, one not related to trend following, which was also able to provide positive returns and would be less correlated with the returns of the trend-following systems, we could take advantage of additional diversification in the trading methods. In order to clarify this concept we performed a unique experiment. We built a system that has very little in common with a classic trend-following technique, but still includes a very strong element of risk control. The rules for this new system are the following:

Buy the market at the beginning of the year.

Sell only if one of the following two cases occurs: a 3% loss or a 15% profit.

If the long position is closed out because of either profits or losses, the system will not reenter the market again before the next January.

The simulated results of this method, which we called the UC system (UC stands for uncorrelated) are shown in Table 6-12. It has less outright profits than system B, the trend-following technique of our former examples, but its simulated returns are less correlated with the normal trend-following type of system. In backtested results on the single indices, the correlation coefficient between the system's yearly returns and those of the respective markets ranged between 0.65 and 0.70.

As we pointed out, the returns of this new system UC were lower compared with both a buy-and-hold strategy and system B. The very conservative nature of the system's rules toward risk and profit taking resulted in an even lower level of equity volatility (the standard deviation of yearly returns). This profile of return and risk pushed the risk-adjusted ratio to one of the highest levels, at 0.69, despite a compounded yearly rate of return of only 4.9%.

When we combine systems B and UC, which are different in nature, both with very favorable return-to-risk patterns, we get an even better result due to system

Table 6-12. Simulated Returns Comparing System UC with System B

	System UC			Average System UC	System B	50% B and 50% UC
Year	United States	Japan	Germany			
1971	10.8%	16.0%	18.3%	15.0%	8.9%	12.0%
1972	4.0%	17.5%	15.7%	12.4%	39.1%	25.8%
1973	−4.6%	−10.2%	−4.9%	−6.6%	−11.3%	−9.0%
1974	−3.6%	−4.9%	−4.0%	−4.2%	−5.3%	−4.7%
1975	15.3%	17.0%	16.4%	16.2%	19.5%	17.8%
1976	15.5%	10.4%	−3.8%	7.4%	3.9%	5.6%
1977	−4.6%	4.7%	−3.2%	−1.0%	−6.2%	−3.6%
1978	−4.0%	15.9%	−3.1%	2.9%	7.7%	5.3%
1979	8.8%	9.5%	−3.5%	4.9%	1.0%	3.0%
1980	6.8%	5.1%	−4.3%	2.5%	3.6%	3.1%
1981	−4.2%	8.5%	0.2%	1.5%	−0.4%	0.5%
1982	−4.3%	−10.6%	14.0%	−0.3%	4.9%	2.3%
1983	16.5%	15.1%	2.6%	11.4%	24.1%	17.7%
1984	−4.9%	15.1%	−4.1%	2.0%	4.3%	3.2%
1985	15.0%	13.2%	16.7%	15.0%	34.7%	24.8%
1986	17.3%	2.0%	−3.2%	5.3%	16.1%	10.7%
1987	15.8%	15.1%	−13.5%	5.8%	10.4%	8.1%
1988	12.4%	16.7%	16.6%	15.2%	12.2%	13.7%
1989	6.9%	15.9%	−3.6%	6.4%	27.8%	17.1%
1990	−6.0%	−8.8%	−5.5%	−6.8%	−6.3%	−6.6%
1991	15.4%	−3.8%	16.3%	9.3%	9.9%	9.6%
1992	−3.6%	−3.8%	−6.2%	−4.5%	−2.4%	−3.4%
1993	7.1%	17.5%	15.1%	13.2%	17.7%	15.5%
1994	−1.5%	15.6%	−4.7%	3.1%	−4.5%	−0.7%
1995	10.3%	5.0%	−3.4%	0.6%	14.5%	7.5%
Total return	248%	427%	163%	227%	623%	396%
Compounded rate of return	5.1%	6.9%	3.9%	4.9%	8.2%	6.6%
Standard deviation of yearly returns	9%	10%	10%	7%	13%	9%
Risk-adjusted ratio	0.59	0.69	0.40	0.69	0.63	0.70
Correlation between system UC and index returns	0.70	0.65	0.67			

diversification. The risk reduction due to volatility control eliminated all years with double-digit losses. But, as should be expected, the cost for this was that only about 60% of the positive market trends were converted to profits. In this case, the improvement in the risk-adjusted ratio was not as great as the loss in total profitability, an 11% gain in the risk-adjusted ratio versus a 20% reduction in returns.

This is only one of the thousands of possible market strategies that could be customized for investors with a specific degree of risk aversion. In this case the sec-

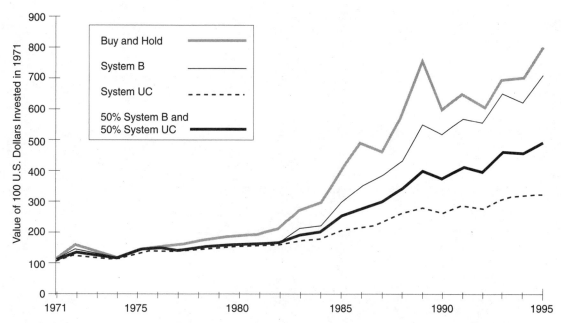

Figure 6-6. Comparison of portfolio strategies. Systems allow a wide range of risk and reward combinations, but generally with lower risk.

ond system used for diversification was good, but not good enough. We really wanted to show the potential for combining uncorrelated trading methods in a way that will improve the quality of the investment's results—its level of risk compared to its return.

Figure 6-6 gives you a final look at the combinations that we have discussed, and compares the equity curves of

- passive diversified investment
- simulated diversified investment using system B
- simulated diversified investment using system UC
- simulated diversified investment combining 50% system B and 50% system UC.

The most volatile strategy, the buy-and-hold, is at the top of the chart, and the most conservative system, UC, is at the bottom.

7

Building an International Portfolio

Balancing World Risk

We know that there are always investment opportunities throughout the world, and we have shown the advantages of the international diversification in the previous chapters. If we could find the best combination of markets for an international portfolio, in order to create an optimal mix between expected return and risk, then diversification would be even more successful. Of course, we will not spend time trying to find the combination that would work better in the *future* because we try to be realistic and believe that we cannot predict the next market developments, such as its effect on price, its future volatility, the intramarket relationships, or patterns such as relative strength or correlation. Instead, we will use historical data to show how past patterns would have worked under conditions that we understand. We can then apply these same principles to our current portfolio, provided we watch for sudden structural changes that occur in the economies of each country and adjust the portfolio from time to time because of gradual changes.

The stocks that are traded in the recently developed countries offer incredible profit potential that we would not want to miss, but when a market tumble occurs in a South American country, for example, it leaves a scar that is not forgotten. It is not unusual for an emerging market to produce a three-digit percent rise in a few months and then to quickly lose half of the previous gain. It seems best to limit the influence of the emerging markets to a relatively small percentage of the portfolio if we want to keep volatility under control.

The European markets also offer good opportunities, although some of them behave as if they were emerging. Spain and Italy, considered developed economies, frequently exhibit the volatility and patterns of less stable countries. To balance this, Germany, Switzerland, and The Netherlands appeal to U.S. investors because their currencies are historically strong.

Will the dollar's downtrend continue on endlessly? Are we safe always betting against the dollar? We have seen that the fluctuations of the currencies in which the foreign markets are denominated also produce an important element of added volatility that should not be ignored. And how do we handle the "King of Extremes," the Japanese market, second in the world in size, with persistent periods of volatility that are even larger than some emerging markets?

There is no single answer to all of these questions. The ideal mix for investors depends on many factors, the first of which is their preference for expected returns related to risk, especially their specific degree of risk aversion. When we build a portfolio of varied stocks, or, even more specifically, a portfolio of multiple markets, we combine different characteristics of volatility. Because the risks and expected returns are often very different, we must measure them carefully to find the weight of the component markets in the investment, remembering that the characteristics of each market change over time. The size of the allocations to each and even the allocation rules are part of a process that needs continuous updating.

Before we can assign part of an investment portfolio to either a single stock or a market we need to establish rules for the way we will allocate. The results of international diversification of equities will depend mostly on the markets we choose, but the weights that we attribute to one market in the portfolio can dramatically change those returns. If we had combined the U.S. market equally with the German and Japanese markets for the past 20 years, from 1976 to 1995, there would have been a 849% profit in U.S. dollars. This result is clearly better than the 495% performance of the Dow's 30 blue-chip Industrial Average during the same period. By now we have also learned to look at the risk, and the equally weighted international portfolio had higher volatility, posting an 18.4% standard deviation of yearly returns compared to the Dow's 13.9%.

Figure 7-1 relates the key figures, the compounded rates of return, and standard deviations of yearly revenues for the three markets, from 1976 to 1995, all in U.S. dollars. Each point represents one market, and the open circle near the center is the result of the equally weighted diversification. The combined portfolio shows a better expectation of return but also an increased risk when compared to the U.S. market alone, which has the lowest levels of both risk and return. The Japanese and German markets are located at the extreme right of the chart because their underlying volatility is higher, and when the results are converted to U.S. dollars the currency swings produce even more volatility for the investment, as we concluded in Chapter 2.

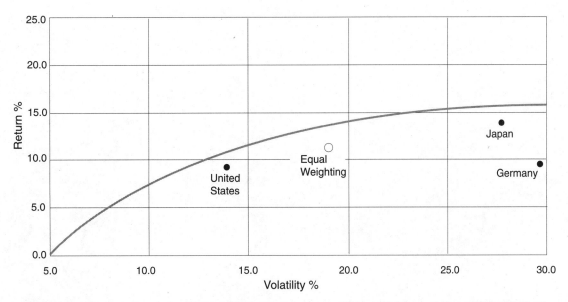

Figure 7-1. Returns and risk of three markets and an equally weighted portfolio, 1976–1995. The diversified portfolio, shown in the center, has nearly the best returns and has much lower than average volatility, or risk.

Table 7-1. Returns of a Portfolio of Three Markets with Selected Weightings

	Weightings, %									
United States	33	66	50	50	30	30	75	15	50	50
Japan	33	17	35	15	50	20	15	75	0	50
Germany	33	17	15	35	20	50	10	10	50	0
Total return	850.17%	687.83%	846.52%	692.45%	978.29%	738.38%	655.36%	1142.81%	568.68%	945.29%
Compounded return	11.2%	10.9%	11.9%	10.9%	12.6%	11.2%	10.6%	13.4%	10.0%	12.5%
Standard deviation	18.4%	14.6%	15.9%	17.0%	18.9%	20.1%	13.8%	22.7%	19.2%	16.6%
Risk-adjusted return ratio	0.61	0.75	0.75	0.64	0.67	0.56	0.77	0.59	0.52	0.75

We tested several different weights for each market and found very different investment performances, as shown in Table 7-1. It is clear that if we had given more weight to the markets with the highest returns, Japan and Germany, we would have increased the portfolio volatility along with its return. If we had added weight to the less volatile market, the United States in this case, then the quality of returns would have improved based on better risk control, but the returns would have declined.

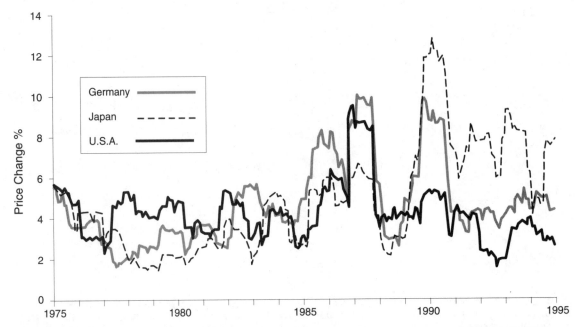

Figure 7-2. Twelve-month rolling standard deviation of price changes for Germany, Japan, and U.S. markets. There are frequent shifts in the most volatile market.

The statistical principles we followed by using more than 20 years of data for our examples are more meaningful than a short period, but realistically it does not ensure that future decisions will be dependable. The markets often change over time, and part of this change is their characteristic volatility and strength. A look at Figure 7-2 gives a better idea of this transformative process. Each line on the chart represents the average standard deviation over the past 12 months for each market; it is quite clear that volatility can be cyclical. The Japanese index was the least volatile of the three in the very early 1980s and then turned into the most volatile in the early 1990s. In order to build a portfolio that would use volatility to control a predefined level of risk, we would have no choice but to adapt the weighting of each market to the changing periods of volatility.

Having illustrated the problems, we are now going to see how useful it could be to consider three major market characteristics—volatility, risk-adjusted ratio, and correlation—and their changes over time when making an investment decision using the three major markets of the world.

Use of Volatility for Investment Weightings

Concept. In the scale of priorities the first goal of any investor is capital preservation and the second is profit. The use of volatility to decide the weighting factor for the allocation of investments puts risk control above the maximization of profits.

Each investor has a certain degree of risk aversion, so he or she should balance the investments to target the acceptable level of risk. More risk-averse investors will assign more weight to those markets in their portfolio that tend to be less volatile, reducing the exposure of the most risky, even if they offer potentially greater returns.

Method. In the following example the market exposure is varied among the three major countries, the United States, Japan, and Germany. Our simulated weightings are based on the following rule:

Volatility Allocation Rule. Allocate two-thirds of the investment to the one market (out of three) that had the lowest standard deviation of yearly returns, in U.S. dollars, based on the average of the last three years. Allocate the remaining one-third equally to the other two markets, giving each one-sixth of the total investment.

Results. In Table 7-2 the results of this simulation are seen to be very successful. Using the volatility allocation rule gave better returns than either the equally weighted allocation or an investment in the U.S. stocks alone. In most cases throughout the test the U.S. stocks were given more weight, which should be expected because Wall Street was often the least volatile of the three markets included. This had already been shown in Figure 7-2. Because the method is unable to *anticipate* the shifts in volatility but instead lags the changes, we cannot expect to get the lowest possible deviation in the total portfolio. The improvement in the quality of results does show that the market characteristic of volatility tends to persist over time. Therefore when we allocate more to a market that has shown the lowest volatility over the past three years, despite its variability from time to time, we can expect that level of volatility to continue long enough to improve the quality of the portfolio.

Use of Risk-Adjusted Ratio for Investment Weightings

Concept. The risk-adjusted ratio uses both the compounded rate of return and the deviation of results, making it a more complex measurement than just volatility. If the volatility of one market is higher than average but we expect a significantly better relative return from it, then we will increase its weight in our international portfolio. In this case, a higher volatility is considered a reasonable price to pay if the returns are better.

Method. Using a portfolio of U.S., Japanese, and German stocks, weight the components according to the risk-adjusted ratio rule.

Risk-Adjusted Ratio Rule. Allocate two-thirds of the portfolio investment to the market with the best risk-adjusted ratio, calculated over the past three yearly

Table 7-2. Results in U.S. Dollars, of a Diversified Portfolio of Three Markets, with Weightings Based on Changing Volatility

Year	Allocations, % United States	Japan	Germany	Return in U.S.$	Most weighted country
1976	0.1666	0.1666	0.6666	8%	Germany
1977	0.1666	0.1666	0.6666	15%	Germany
1978	0.1666	0.6666	0.1666	39%	Japan
1979	0.1666	0.1666	0.6666	−6%	Germany
1980	0.6666	0.1666	0.1666	12%	United States
1981	0.6666	0.1666	0.1666	−8%	United States
1982	0.1666	0.1666	0.6666	8%	Germany
1983	0.1666	0.6666	0.1666	3%	Japan
1984	0.1666	0.6666	0.1666	3%	Japan
1985	0.1666	0.6666	0.1666	52%	Japan
1986	0.6666	0.1666	0.1666	37%	United States
1987	0.6666	0.1666	0.1666	5%	United States
1988	0.6666	0.1666	0.1666	16%	United States
1989	0.6666	0.1666	0.1666	27%	United States
1990	0.6666	0.1666	0.1666	−10%	United States
1991	0.6666	0.1666	0.1666	13%	United States
1992	0.6666	0.1666	0.1666	−2%	United States
1993	0.1666	0.1666	0.6666	25%	Germany
1994	0.6666	0.1666	0.1666	7%	United States
1995	0.6666	0.1666	0.1666	24%	United States

	Performance Comparisons Volatility adjusted	Only U.S.	Equal allocation
Total return	1092%	495%	849%
Compounded yearly rate of return	13.2%	9.3%	11.9%
Standard deviation of returns	16.3%	13.9%	18.4%
Risk-adjusted return ratio	0.81	0.67	0.65

results. Allocate the remaining one-third equally to the other two markets, giving each one-sixth of the total investment.

Results. The risk-adjusted ratio posted for the highest returns so far is shown in Table 7-3. Because this technique looked at relative rather than absolute volatility, the final tests show that volatility was higher than when we chose the low-risk alternative; therefore it should not be surprising that the risk-adjusted ratio of the portfolio is lower. If we remember that the allocation rule is based on an informa-

Table 7-3. Results in U.S. Dollars, of a Diversified Portfolio of Three Markets, with Weightings Based on the Risk-Adjusted Ratio

Year	Allocations, % United States	Japan	Germany	Return in U.S.$	Most weighted country
1976	0.1666	0.1666	0.6666	8%	Germany
1977	0.1666	0.1666	0.6666	15%	Germany
1978	0.1666	0.6666	0.1666	39%	Japan
1979	0.1666	0.6666	0.1666	−8%	Japan
1980	0.1666	0.1666	0.6666	−3%	Germany
1981	0.1666	0.6666	0.1666	−3%	Japan
1982	0.6666	0.1666	0.1666	14%	United States
1983	0.6666	0.1666	0.1666	21%	United States
1984	0.6666	0.1666	0.1666	−3%	United States
1985	0.0666	0.1666	0.1666	45%	United States
1986	0.1666	0.6666	0.1666	65%	Japan
1987	0.1666	0.6666	0.1666	29%	Japan
1988	0.1666	0.6666	0.1666	28%	Japan
1989	0.1666	0.6666	0.1666	20%	Japan
1990	0.1666	0.6666	0.1666	−25%	Japan
1991	0.6666	0.1666	0.1666	13%	United States
1992	0.6666	0.1666	0.1666	−2%	United States
1993	0.6666	0.1666	0.1666	17%	United States
1994	0.6666	0.1666	0.1666	7%	United States
1995	0.6666	0.1666	0.1666	24%	United States

	Performance Comparisons		
	RAR adjusted	Only U.S.	Equal allocation
Total return	1103%	495%	849%
Compounded yearly rate of return	13.7%	9.3%	11.9%
Standard deviation of returns	20.5%	13.9%	18.4%
Risk-adjusted ratio (RAR)	0.67	0.67	0.65

tion lag and that volatility has demonstrated the characteristic of persistence under this situation (shown by its success in the first method), then we can conclude that the other element in the risk-adjusted ratio, the past returns, are not as predictable. This seems to be what happened in this allocation model in 1990 when Japan was given two-thirds of the portfolio weight on the basis of its previous high returns; this was then followed by a show of worst performance. Choosing markets based on the promised return for the anticipated risk was much better than the standard alternatives but exposed the portfolio to much higher volatility. This decision helps to increase returns but also tends to increase volatility. In the first allocation method, based only on lower volatility, the Japanese market was carefully avoided after 1985 despite its good returns because the risk was too great. The use of the risk-adjusted ratio is therefore a more aggressive allocation approach.

Use of Correlation for Investment Weightings

Concept. The correlation among markets plays a key role in traditional portfolio allocation for ensuring diversification. Consider the situation where Germany and Japan show very similar volatility, a standard deviation of yearly returns between 28% and 30% in U.S. dollars, much higher than the corresponding 13.9% shown by the Dow. If we had invested 50% in the United States and 50% in Japan, rather than 50% in the United States and 50% in Germany, we would have had a better return, lower volatility, and therefore a sharply higher reward-to-risk ratio.

This conclusion is not obvious unless you see the correlation coefficients. The correlation coefficient was 0.48 for the German market (compared to the U.S. market after converting foreign returns into U.S. dollars) and 0.19 for the Japanese market. A lower correlation decreases portfolio volatility because the returns of one market, whether positive or negative, tend to be partially offset by a different result produced by a market with low correlation.

Method. As U.S.-based investors, we will diversify our American stock selection by investing in one of the two other major markets, Germany or Japan, whichever has been less correlated with Wall Street.

We calculate the correlation coefficient for the United States and Japan and for the United States and Germany, over the past three years. We always allocate 70% of our investment to the U.S. market and the remaining 30% to the one other market, either the Japanese or German, that has shown the least correlation to the Dow over the past three years—in other words, the one that has the lowest correlation coefficient.

Results. It is interesting to observe in the results given in Table 7-4 that, despite the fact that 30% of the capital was allocated to one of two markets that were quite volatile and whose returns were often less than the Dow, the resulting volatility of 12.8% was far lower than the other two examples of diversification discussed previously and even lower than the 13.9% given by the Dow alone. The return of 593% was better than a 100% investment in the U.S. stocks.

This confirms the basic principles of diversification. When you combine more than one market with different patterns, confirmed by a reasonably low correlation coefficient, the result should be improved investment returns and reduced volatility. The specific amounts that we chose to use for allocating assets to each market, which were arbitrary here, were not as important to us as the principle.

Table 7-4. Results, in U.S. Dollars, of Market Diversification, 70% in the United States and 30% in the Less Correlated Market of the Last Three Years

Year	Allocations 70% to United States and 30% to:	Return in U.S.$	Year	Allocations 70% to United States and 30% to:	Return in U.S.$
1976	Germany	13%	1986	Germany	29%
1977	Germany	−6%	1987	Japan	15%
1978	Japan	14%	1988	Japan	19%
1979	Germany	1%	1989	Japan	23%
1980	Germany	6%	1990	Japan	−14%
1981	Germany	−10%	1991	Japan	14%
1982	Germany	16%	1992	Germany	1%
1983	Japan	22%	1993	Germany	19%
1984	Japan	−1%	1994	Germany	3%
1985	Japan	32%	1995	Japan	23%

	Performance Comparisons		
	Based on correlations	Only U.S.	Equal allocation
Total return	593%	495%	849%
Compounded yearly rate of return	10.1%	9.3%	11.9%
Standard deviation of returns	12.8%	13.9%	18.4%
Risk-adjusted ratio	0.79	0.67	0.65

Combining Methods

If diversification is a winning concept for a passive investment, it should also improve the allocation methods that have just been described. We have tried to establish a foundation for the benefits of diversification of markets in the earlier part of this book, and later, in Chapter 6, we discussed the applications of technical market strategies to improve the passive portfolio. We now combined the three allocation methods, volatility, risk-adjusted ratio, and correlation, by simply averaging the allocations that we would get for each market according to the three methods, taken individually. For example, in 1976, the first year of the table, we had the following allocations:

Method	United States	Japan	Germany
1. Volatility	0.1666	0.1666	0.6666
2. Risk-adjusted ratio	0.1666	0.1666	0.6666
3. Correlation	0.7000	0.0000	0.3000
Average	0.3444	0.1110	0.5444

Table 7-5. Results, in U.S. Dollars, of a
Portfolio of Three World Markets, Each Weighted
by Averaging the Three Allocation Methods

Year	Allocations United States	Japan	Germany	Return in U.S.$
1976	34%	11%	54%	9%
1977	34%	11%	54%	8%
1978	34%	54%	11%	30%
1979	34%	28%	38%	−4%
1980	51%	11%	38%	5%
1981	51%	28%	21%	−7%
1982	51%	11%	38%	13%
1983	51%	21%	28%	22%
1984	51%	38%	11%	−0%
1985	51%	38%	11%	43%
1986	51%	28%	21%	43%
1987	51%	38%	11%	16%
1988	51%	38%	11%	21%
1989	51%	38%	11%	23%
1990	51%	38%	11%	−16%
1991	68%	21%	11%	14%
1992	68%	11%	21%	−1%
1993	51%	11%	38%	20%
1994	68%	11%	21%	5%
1995	68%	21%	11%	23%

	Performance Comparisons Combined methods	Only U.S.	Equal allocation
Total return	926%	495%	849%
Compounded yearly rate of return	12.4%	9.3%	11.9%
Standard deviation of returns	15.6%	13.9%	18.4%
Risk-adjusted ratio	0.79	0.67	0.65

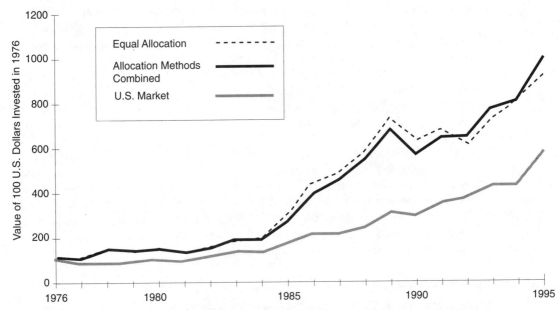

Figure 7-3. Comparison of a U.S. market investment, an equal weighting of three world markets, and an average of three allocation techniques. A diversified strategy of even a small group of world markets will reduce risk and improve returns.

The average of the three techniques becomes the new allocation for 1976, seen in Table 7-5. The results are exceptionally good. To see this more easily, Figure 7-3 compares how US$100 performed in the past 20 years, from 1976 to 1995, if invested in the following:

1. The Dow Jones Industrial Average only

2. A portfolio where the investment is equally distributed among the U.S., Japanese, and German equity markets

3. A portfolio that combines the three allocation weighting methods

It confirms that a diversified strategy among only a limited number of major markets of the world are enough to improve returns and reduce the risk normally associated with stock investing. Without a sound method of allocation, even one as simple as that shown here, investors are exposed to much greater risk.

Investing in the Emerging Economies

The vital energy for wealth and progress in the world is a continuous process of transformation. The investors that diversify their holdings throughout the world improve their profit potential because the simultaneous investment in different markets increases the chances of participating in all of the important changes. The risk of failure derived from having chosen only underperforming markets will be offset by a share of profits from the best performing ones.

An equal geographic distribution of stocks in a portfolio is likely to give the best chance of a good return and, at the same time, have lower volatility. The diversification that we have frequently evaluated throughout this book, which assumes only the most basic information, will create better returns by improving the quality of results.

The greatest contribution to better performance is caused by the large differences among the major economies of the world. Such differences promote enormous capital movements; business tends to flow to those countries where there is the most opportunity to develop and where the reception is friendly. In this way, the roles that each country plays in the world scenario gradually shifts, based on sound, sustained economic forces, and causes corresponding long-lasting price trends in equities, currencies, and interest rates.

A Vital Transformation

We have repeatedly illustrated the way such shifts generated very different market performance in the past from country to country. Our examples have been mostly focused on the major geographical blocs which represent the most efficient and well-developed economies and financial markets, the United States, Japan, and Europe.

A strong world social and political transformation has again occurred toward the end of the twentieth century, favoring an impressive acceleration of an old phenomena, the development and growth of the emerging countries. We say this is an old phenomena because there really has been nothing new in the way trade evolves. In the ancient world, before it became the biggest power, Rome appeared as an emerging country to the Greeks; while we tend to forget, even England and Germany were barbarian lands only 1000 years ago. For the Europeans of the eighteenth century, the United States of America held a small people of adventurers, but hindsight confirms how successful the investments could be in this country. How will China, Malaysia, and even Pakistan look when our grandchildren are trading the markets?

New Horizons in the World

In the economic sense, the word *emerging* should be applied to those countries that are raising themselves up from a subordinate condition compared to the current economic powers, in a gradual evolution toward progress and efficiency. The financial industry is somewhat more casual about the way it uses the label *emerging*. It describes the countries in which the economy, industry, and finance have not yet reached contemporary development. This may simply be the inability to provide proper financial guarantees for international trade. These countries are therefore excluded from the international financial circle. Until a new period of fast growth makes them desirable to the world's investors, they remain *underde-veloped*. We could just as easily call these countries *recently developed, newly indus-trialized,* or *new horizon economies*.

The recent evolution of these countries is essentially a political phenomenon. The most relevant events that stimulated this new course were first decolonization and more recently the fall of the Communist bloc. In the case of Latin America, which is different from most other regions, its true change is the shift from obscure dictatorships to democracy and modernization. The fall of communism was also a factor, because the United States, needing to control the whole continent for strategic reasons, often conditioned the democratic development of this geo-graphic area.

The changing political and economic structures have left many very poor com-munities behind, with people wishing to work and improve their condition. The unlimited reach of modern mass media has accelerated the desire of the men and women to improve their living standards. They believe that, in this modern era, there are opportunities open to industrious people, even though the visible results may take a long time to achieve.

Something similar happened at the end of the World War II. Those countries that were defeated, such as Japan, Germany, and Italy, but also some of those that won, such as France, were extremely poor and needed to rebuild their entire coun-try. This created an above average growth that made those countries the booming economies of the 1950s. Nevertheless that growth was driven by domestic invest-ments. In the boom of today's emerging countries there is a massive influx of funds from all over the world.

New Developments Are Fast

In a rapid change of economic winds, exceptional growth is sweeping many underdeveloped countries. From the view of the major economies, these emerging nations offer needed opportunities for new businesses because of low labor costs, cheap real estate, government incentives, and an impressive potential of increas-ing local demand. But the process of evolution in the economy is a hard and cir-cuitous route. In most cases the early phase of the growth is quite sudden and generates inflation. The authorities find this hard to control because it compro-mises a fragile growth during its most delicate phase.

The macroeconomic data of the emerging countries are often a crucial issue, and one that discourages all but institutions. The investments in emerging mar-kets are risky and volatile until world pressure stabilizes the inflation, public deficit, and exchange rates. The trend of newly developed countries is toward a progressive improvement in economic data. The inflation in Argentina was 2314% in 1990 and only 3.4% in 1995. Peru and Brazil witnessed a similar downtrend in consumer prices, as did the eastern European countries that were pressured by a very high inflation after their democratization. In Russia, for example, the infla-tion was 1542% in 1992. Later, in 1995, it still showed a three-digit rise (205%), but the trend pointed unequivocally to the downside. The rest of the world measures this process by the exchange rate. There were 450 rubles to the dollar in 1992, about 5000 in 1995.

These examples are not intended to be blind to the very different social and economic realities; they simply are intended to show that every country can move down the path to normalization and progress, and take advantage of its opportunities. It is true that the turbulence that characterizes the transformation phases in these countries often discourages the investors, even when the opportunities are large. The emerging markets represent an exciting potential for large returns with equally large risk. This volatility in equities prices will decline slowly as the process of evolution transforms them into primary markets.

Risks and Weightings

A clear example of risk and reward is illustrated in Table 7-6. It compares the yearly returns of the Southeast Asia equity markets, using a Morgan Stanley Index (that excludes Japan), with the Dow. It shows that the investment in Asian countries from 1987 to 1995 gave a 237% return, sharply higher than the respectable 163% of the 30 blue-chip companies of the Dow. A closer look at volatility, as measured by the standard deviation of yearly returns, shows that the average risk for these Southeast Asian countries was almost three times higher for the United States.

It is not unusual to see three-digit returns in those countries, often followed by breathtaking corrections. It is also interesting to note the low correlation between the Southeast Asian markets and the United States over the long run, even if there is a high positive correlation with Wall Street during some periods. After the stock market crash in 1987 the exchange in Hong Kong remained closed for about one

Table 7-6. Diversifying with Southeast Asian (ex-Japan) and U.S. Markets

	Yearly returns	Asia (ex-Japan)	United States DJIA	Allocations		
				50% U.S. + 50% Asia	85% U.S. + 15% Asia	15% U.S. + 85% Asia
	1988	62.69%	11.86%	37.28%	19.49%	55.07%
	1989	35.72%	26.92%	31.32%	28.24%	34.40%
	1990	−28.72%	−4.32%	−16.52%	−7.98%	−25.06%
	1991	14.90%	20.31%	17.61%	19.50%	15.72%
	1992	8.53%	4.17%	6.35%	4.82%	7.87%
	1993	93.66%	13.72%	53.69%	25.71%	81.67%
	1994	−9.80%	2.13%	−3.84%	0.34%	−8.01%
	1995	−1.50%	33.46%	15.98%	28.22%	3.75%
Total return		237.71%	163.90%	222.65%	185.66%	238.01%
Compounded return		16.43%	12.90%	15.77%	14.02%	16.44%
Standard deviation		40.26%	12.88%	22.78%	13.90%	34.81%
Risk-adjusted return ratio		0.41	1.00	0.69	1.01	0.47

week and reopened on October 26, recording a 33% loss in one day. When a catastrophic loss occurs in the primary market, the emerging ones often amplify it; they do not represent any protection, but an added risk. In 1990, when the world was shocked by the crisis in the Persian Gulf, Wall Street declined about 7%, and the Southeast Asian countries almost 30%. Those economies were far more vulnerable because of geographic proximity to the critical area, energy dependence, and weak political structure. When an equity market has a relatively small number of market participants compared to the primary markets, it is much easier to drive prices quickly toward a well-defined direction.

The 1990 Persian Gulf War example is just one case, but such vulnerability to macroevents explains the price volatility in emerging markets. In another situation, in Hong Kong, in June 1989, the overall market fell because of the sudden violence in Beijing; however, the stocks that did best in resisting the decline were those of the airlines. Why? Because their major assets, the aircraft, could be sheltered abroad in case of repercussions in Hong Kong, and in particular, a hostile attitude by the Chinese government following the takeover of Hong Kong in 1997.

Such events are unthinkable in the United States or in Sweden; therefore, the higher volatility frequently produced by the emerging markets must be offset by a modest investment allocation weighting of those countries.

We have normally concluded that the diversification between the two indices shown in Table 7-6 could be the best of the choices. But a more careful look at weighting distribution is needed in this case. The sharply higher volatility of the emerging markets is a more serious concern and must be treated with greater care if we want to improve the quality of the investment results.

The comparison between a 50-50 and an 85-15 distribution is clear evidence that, when diversifying in markets with higher risk and greater volatility, the benefits occur when we allocate just a fraction of the assets to the riskier side. The "optimal" weighting cannot be defined as an absolute factor; it all depends on how much risk the investor is disposed to take in the stock portfolio. The 85-15 percentage distribution is quite reasonable for an average investor, while the 50-50 option is advisable for people who have a preference for more risk. The 50-50 portfolio has nearly the same return as the emerging markets alone, and only half the risk—but that risk is a healthy 22%.

The concepts we have described throughout this chapter should be applied here in the same way. If the emerging markets are to be part of the plan, then they must be considered properly in terms of the relationship of risk to potential profit. The effects that the two sample weighting factors, 50-50 and 85-15, produce on the investment can be understood better if we compare the single yearly returns of the Dow to those of the Asian (except Japan) Index. In a bad year, such as 1990, the loss in the Southeast Asian market was nearly 30%, while in 1995, a very good year for Wall Street, the Asian Index still posted a loss. Conversely, in 1988 and 1993 the Southeast Asian markets performed spectacularly, posting gains of 63% and 94%, a feat that could never be achieved in the United States, which showed its own steady increases of 12% to 14%.

Table 7-7. Standard Deviations of 12 Monthly Returns for Six Southeast Asian Stock Markets Compared to Wall Street

	United States	Hong Kong	Singapore	Taiwan	Thailand	Malaysia	Indonesia	Average (ex-United States)
1993	1.7	9.7	5.6	14.0	11.0	8.2	5.5	9.0
1994	3.6	6.8	5.1	7.1	7.5	7.7	7.1	6.9
1995	2.4	6.3	3.6	5.6	6.6	5.7	5.7	5.6

With uncorrelated and significantly more volatile results there is an excellent chance of improving the investment performance in the long term, but the allocation to each market exposure must be decided after careful risk analysis. Table 7-7 compares the standard deviation of monthly returns for some Southeast Asian markets with that of the Dow for the three years from 1993 through 1995. It shows that volatility is clearly higher for the emerging markets but not unmanageable. We also note a certain trend to lower volatility in the average of these markets, but we all know that specific events of a particular market could well make volatility quickly rise and that three years of data do not include enough possible outcomes to feel that the measurement of risk will include all future volatility. Even in the United States, the standard deviation of the 12 monthly returns of the Dow in 1987 was 8.8, certainly higher than any of these sample emerging markets in 1994 and 1995. Our common sense, however, makes us reason that 1987 was close to the high end for volatility in the United States, while that same value could be the low end for an emerging market.

New Outlooks in Emerging Economies

The regions of the world to which most private capital flows, and the main focus of this new economic development process, can be grouped as

- Southeast Asia and the Pacific Rim
- Latin America
- Eastern Europe (ex-Communist countries)
- Mediterranean and Middle East
- Africa

The prospects of these regions for the twenty-first century are exceptional, but the major political transitions they are facing are likely to surface as having high volatility. An overview is not easy because of the deep structural differences that characterize every interpretation of economic situations, but some global considerations are possible, based on the realities of the mid-1990s.

Growth has tended to accelerate, while at the same time the countries that have already witnessed strong economic improvements, such as the most progressive in Southeast Asia, have also shown a trend toward stabilization. This is a signal of health because it means that the excesses are being controlled. Extreme inflation, which is actually a tribute that every emerging economy must pay for its growth, has slowed. Inflation presents one of the greatest risks for those emerging economies, besides the obvious one of politics, and it can be very different from region to region and from country to country.

In Latin America, where extreme inflation has been well publicized, 1995 showed a 76% increase in Brazil and 61% rise in Venezuela; in contrast, Argentina posted only 3.4% inflation and Chile, 8.2%. Some ex-Communist countries were more affected than others by inflation, with 205% in Russia, 360% in the Ukraine, and 62% in Bulgaria. As of 1995, Russia and Ukraine were still in the middle of recession.

These Eastern European countries have very complex problems that have been difficult to resolve. As we watch, their evolutionary process is very slow, and in all likelihood they will develop later than other geographic areas. The liberalization of the Eastern European countries has not been easy: they had to struggle with a recession in the early 1990s while in the most delicate phase of their new development, and it took until 1994 for most of them to witness some form of growth. Other European countries, such as the Czech Republic, Slovakia, and Croatia, were able to control inflation throughout the transition despite decades of communism, giving them an excellent perspective of growth. Their historical Austro-Hungarian tradition, with all its political severity, can be credited for the rigorous rebuilding of these economies by their people.

The inflation in Southeast Asia was generally below two digits in 1995 with the exception of China (14.8%), Pakistan (12.9%), and Vietnam (12.7%). At the same time, those countries with higher inflation also showed the sharpest growth in the region. These figures indicate that the countries of Southeast Asia are further along the road of free enterprise than those of Eastern Europe.

Tables 7-8 and 7-9 show significant key data, inflation, and GDP growth from 1988 through 1995, for a broad selection of emerging economies. Figures 7-4 and 7-5 plot the average consumer price inflation in the emerging countries of the world. The numbers shown in these tables and figures indicate that the trend for the emerging countries is toward improvement and stabilization. This is reflected in the lowering volatility in the stock markets.

We can conclude that the transformation we have been discussing is moved by a strong economic energy that will reflect significantly in the financial markets of tomorrow. The capital flows into those markets are constantly growing, and the gaps these countries must fill to bring them closer to the primary markets are so wide that very large price moves will be generated by this process.

Table 7-8. Consumer Price Inflation (%) for Emerging Markets, 1988–1995

	1988	1989	1990	1991	1992	1993	1994	1995
Asia								
Hong Kong	7.5	10.1	9.8	11.6	9.3	8.5	8.1	8.7
Singapore	1.5	2.3	3.5	3.4	2.3	2.3	3.1	1.7
South Korea	7.1	5.7	8.6	9.3	6.2	4.8	6.3	4.5
Taiwan	1.3	4.4	4.1	3.6	4.5	2.9	4.1	3.7
China	18.5	17.8	1.7	2.8	5.3	13.1	21.8	14.8
India	10.7	5.7	6.3	8.9	13.9	11.8	7.5	8.1
Indonesia	8.0	6.4	7.8	9.5	6.9	9.7	8.5	9.4
Malaysia	2.5	2.8	3.1	4.4	4.7	3.6	3.7	3.4
Pakistan	6.3	10.4	9.6	12.7	9.6	9.3	11.2	12.9
Philippines	8.9	12.2	14.2	18.7	8.9	7.6	9.1	8.1
Thailand	3.8	5.4	6.0	5.7	4.1	3.3	5.1	5.8
Vietnam	308.2	95.8	36.4	83.1	37.8	8.4	10.2	12.7
Latin America								
Argentina	342.7	3079.2	2314.0	171.7	24.9	10.6	4.4	3.4
Brazil	682.8	1386.0	2901.0	411.0	965.0	1920.0	2149.0	76.0
Chile	14.7	21.3	26.0	21.9	15.4	12.7	11.5	8.2
Colombia	28.1	25.8	29.1	30.4	27.0	22.4	22.9	20.9
Ecuador	58.2	75.6	48.5	48.7	54.6	45.0	27.3	23.0
Mexico	114.2	20.0	26.7	22.7	15.5	9.8	7.0	34.8
Panama	0.0	0.0	0.8	1.3	1.8	0.5	1.3	1.0
Peru	666.3	3399.0	7483.0	409.2	73.5	48.5	21.0	11.2
Venezuela	29.5	84.3	40.7	34.2	31.4	38.1	60.8	61.2
Eastern Europe								
Bulgaria	2.4	6.4	26.3	333.5	82.0	73.0	96.3	62.1
Croatia	200.0	1200.0	609.5	123.0	665.5	1517.0	97.5	2.0
Czech Republic	0.3	1.5	9.4	56.3	11.1	20.8	10.0	9.1
Estonia	NA	5.5	17.2	210.6	1069.3	89.4	47.7	28.9
Hungary	11.9	16.9	28.5	35.0	23.0	22.5	18.8	28.2
Latvia	3.6	4.7	10.5	124.5	951.2	109.1	36.6	25.0
Lithuania	2.4	2.1	8.4	224.7	1020.5	409.2	70.0	39.7
Poland	60.2	251.1	558.3	70.3	45.3	36.7	32.2	27.8
Romania	2.8	0.8	4.2	166.6	210.0	256.1	136.8	32.0
Slovakia	0.1	1.4	8.4	62.0	10.1	23.2	13.4	9.9
Slovenia	NA	1306.0	549.7	117.7	201.3	32.8	19.8	12.6
Russia	NA	2.0	5.6	92.5	1542.1	878.1	433.4	205.2
Mediterranean								
Greece	13.5	13.7	20.4	19.5	15.9	14.4	10.9	9.3
Israel	16.3	20.2	17.2	19.0	10.9	11.0	12.3	10.0
Morocco	2.4	3.3	6.8	8.0	5.7	5.2	5.2	6.2
Turkey	73.7	63.3	60.3	66.0	70.1	66.1	106.3	89.0

Table 7-9. Real GDP Growth for Emerging Countries (%), 1988–1995

	1988	1989	1990	1991	1992	1993	1994	1995
Asia								
Hong Kong	8.0	2.6	3.4	5.1	6.3	6.1	5.5	4.6
Singapore	11.6	9.6	9.0	7.3	6.2	10.4	10.1	8.8
South Korea	11.3	6.4	9.5	9.1	5.1	5.8	8.6	9.0
Taiwan	7.8	8.2	5.4	7.6	6.8	6.3	6.5	6.1
China	11.2	4.3	4.0	8.2	13.0	13.4	11.8	10.2
India	4.8	9.9	6.9	5.7	0.5	4.6	5.0	6.3
Indonesia	5.8	7.5	7.2	7.0	6.5	6.5	7.5	8.1
Malaysia	8.9	9.2	9.7	8.6	7.8	8.3	9.2	9.5
Pakistan	6.4	4.8	4.6	5.6	7.7	2.3	3.8	4.7
Philippines	6.8	6.2	3.0	−0.6	0.3	2.2	4.3	4.8
Thailand	13.3	12.2	11.2	8.5	8.1	8.3	8.8	8.7
Vietnam	5.2	8.0	5.1	6.0	8.3	8.1	8.8	9.5
Latin America								
Argentina	−2.5	−4.5	0.4	7.9	8.7	6.0	7.1	−4.4
Brazil	−0.1	3.3	−4.4	0.2	−0.8	4.1	5.8	4.2
Chile	7.4	9.9	3.3	7.3	11.0	6.3	4.2	8.5
Colombia	4.1	3.4	4.3	2.1	3.8	5.3	5.7	5.3
Ecuador	10.5	0.3	3.0	5.0	3.6	2.0	4.3	2.3
Mexico	1.2	3.3	4.4	3.5	2.7	0.4	3.5	−6.9
Panama	−15.6	−0.4	4.6	9.3	8.6	5.6	3.7	1.9
Peru	−8.8	−11.9	−4.4	2.7	−2.8	5.6	13.0	6.9
Venezuela	6.2	−7.8	6.9	9.7	6.1	−0.4	−2.8	2.2
Eastern Europe								
Bulgaria	11.1	−1.6	−6.5	−11.7	−7.3	−2.4	1.4	2.5
Croatia	NA	−1.9	−8.5	−20.9	−9.7	−3.7	0.8	−1.4
Czech Republic	0.2	6.5	−1.2	−14.2	−6.4	−0.9	−2.6	−4.8
Estonia	NA	NA	10.3	−11.8	−19.3	−2.1	−3.2	3.0
Hungary	−0.1	0.7	−3.5	−11.9	−3.0	−0.8	2.9	1.7
Latvia	5.1	5.7	−3.5	−8.3	−33.8	−11.7	−0.6	−1.6
Lithuania	9.5	1.1	−6.3	−13.4	−35.0	−16.5	1.0	2.0
Poland	4.1	0.2	−11.6	−7.6	2.6	3.8	5.2	7.0
Romania	−0.5	−5.8	−5.6	−12.9	−8.8	1.5	3.9	6.9
Slovakia	1.9	1.1	−2.5	−14.5	−7.0	−4.1	4.8	7.4
Slovenia	NA	−2.7	−4.8	−9.4	−5.4	1.3	4.9	3.5
Russia	4.5	3.0	−3.6	−11.0	−20.0	−12.0	−15.0	−4.0
Mediterranean								
Greece	4.5	4.0	−1.0	3.2	0.8	−0.5	1.5	2.0
Israel	3.2	1.1	6.0	6.2	7.2	3.4	6.5	7.1
Morocco	10.4	2.5	3.5	4.8	−3.0	−1.1	11.0	−6.5
Turkey	2.1	0.3	9.3	0.9	6.0	8.0	−5.5	7.3

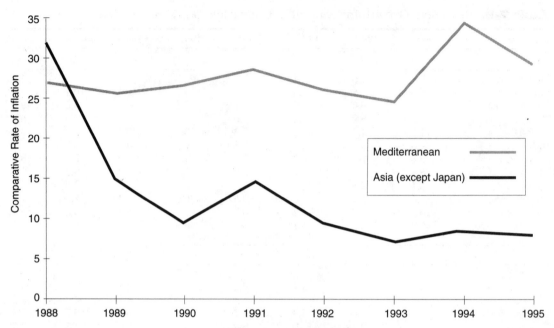

Figure 7-4. Average Consumer Price Inflation for the Mediterranean and Southeast Asia (except Japan), 1988–1995. Emerging countries are becoming more stable.

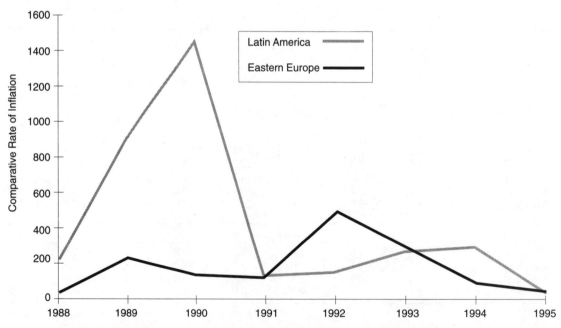

Figure 7-5. Average Consumer Price Inflation for Latin America and Eastern Europe, 1988–1995. Trends toward lower volatility.

Summary and Conclusion

The stock market, along with bonds and real estate, shares the privilege of having to provide sound returns for the long-term investor. Its yield exceeds the risk-free income of bonds; therefore, it has added risk. But this extra uncertainty is an acceptable form of risk because the stock market represents an investment in a country. Taken as a whole, a rising stock market reflects economic growth.

The governments of every nation encourage growth and use a measure of GDP, or a combination of industrial production and international trade to judge its outcome. But the stock market itself is a bellwether for its success. In the United States and in other developed countries, the stock market reaction to new monetary policy is always a concern. It is not good policy to scare the public away from the market because they provide the financing for many of the nations' businesses, and, in turn, the stock market represents a share of the accumulated wealth of the people.

Seeing the Market through the Eyes of Others

It is the knowledge that the government will try its best to maintain a stable economic policy that allows the small investor to sit through years of poor returns in equities. Of course, many investors receive steady dividend checks that provide income, and a modest drop in the share price, or a prolonged sideways period, may not even be noticed, or affect their dividends.

The government, over the past 50 years, has accepted the responsibility of being the caretaker of these investments. It has encouraged, through lower long-term capital gains taxation and pension programs that defer taxes, the investment of savings and retirement money by a broad sample of hard-working people, rather than the wealthier few. It has put comprehensive rules and regulations into place to allow individuals to place substantial portions of their retirement plans in the market through professionally managed funds. Having done this, the government must now make sure that these savings do not disappear, a situation that would have drastic economic effects, not to mention losses of the incumbent political party in the next election.

This awareness to their political, financial, and ethical responsibilities could be seen in the quick response by the government to the 1987 stock plunge. Policy makers immediately stepped in to assure the public there was nothing wrong and that it was "not their fault," that this unfortunate event was caused by "program trading" and that they would correct it and make the market safer. The market responded with confidence and fully recovered in only a few months. It would not be surprising if more investors now feel that government intervention will make the next sudden market drop into a buying opportunity.

Naturally, for readers in the United States, these comments sound as though we are talking exclusively about the U.S. government and its monetary arm, the Federal Reserve. But a German reader would have assumed this was their government and the Bundesbank, which have been struggling to find a fine balance between inflation and growth since 1945, and more recently with the union of East Germany. A British citizen would clearly recognize these same policies and concerns, controlled by the Bank of England, that gave rise to a very similar economic structure in America. Even a Chinese businessperson, living in a communist, rather than a democratic state, will think that these policies could be those of Beijing and its central bank, the Bank of China. Nearly all investors are most comfortable investing in their own country. A European investor thinks of Mercedes Benz before General Motors, and neither a U.S. nor a European investor would readily consider the opportunities in Thailand on their own.

If each of the primary economies sees its stock markets in the same way, orchestrating its growth and protecting the investments of its citizens, there should be some comfort for the international investor, who places funds strategically throughout the world, that each country is trying to maintain a safe, stable growth of their marketplace—within their own limitations, of course. Perhaps this was not as safe 20 years ago, but communications have changed everything.

Economic Variations and Diversification

We have spent considerable time showing that each country has both a domestic and a global aspect to its economy, and the domestic factors cause unique short-term price movements in its stock market. Even though the macroeconomic forces driven by the largest powers may define the direction of interest rates for the longer period, the local policies and problems cause noticeable variations in one market from another. Especially when two countries are physically distant, such as Great Britain and Japan, or economically different, such as India and France, they have market patterns that bear no resemblance to each other.

These differences can provide an investor with diversification and safety. We have shown that diversification improves the quality of an investment portfolio by lowering the risks more than it lowers the returns. Essentially, you can get the same return with less risk, or a greater return with the same risk. The more diverse, the better the results.

With a diversified portfolio, profits are always lower than if you had been fully invested in the best market. Of course, choosing the best market in advance has always been a problem. By diversifying, you are sure of participating in the best, and the worst, to some degree all of the time. When most nations are experiencing growth, your portfolio increases in value rapidly; and when there are global doldrums, your investment will languish. The overall pattern, however, will show less volatility and lower risk.

Persistent Trends Allow
Strategies to Work

We have also shown that a simple trend-following strategy, applied to currency or stock prices, can improve the quality of returns. Major market direction is the product of government policy, and that policy can persist for years. In order to control inflation, but not harm growth, the central bank will slowly increase interest rates and make money less available. If the first increase does not solve the problem, the central bank raises rates again, and then again, until the objective is reached. This can take years.

When the economy stagnates, the central bank takes the opposite approach and eases money, lowering interest rates slowly until its target of growth is reached. All the while it watches for signs of inflation, which indicate an overheated economy caused by overly accelerated growth.

These long-term goals translate into trends that can be identified by simple technical tools. It is not necessary to invest in complex strategies when the most basic ones can be very robust.

Asset Allocation

It is the allocation of the portfolio to each world market that is most difficult. There is safety, and improvement, by simply diversifying equally across a broad number of markets and entirely avoiding the need to decide which ones are likely to be the best in the next year or two. However, attention must be given to the relative volatility of each market.

In a broad way, world markets can be classified into "primary" and "emerging." The primary markets represent major economies and have somewhat comparable risk and reward profiles, over the long term. The emerging markets have consistently much greater volatility relative to their potential returns, less liquidity, and a larger element of unpredictability, regardless of the statistics given by their recent economic data. Emerging markets offer valuable opportunity, clear diversification, and unknown risk. They should be part of an aggressive portfolio, but only a small part.

New Tools to Facilitate Trade

Only a few years ago it would have been interesting to analyze world market diversification, but not practical to implement. Even professional investment managers would have needed special operations and regulatory permission to buy and sell the stocks of most other countries. Now there are very few barriers. Most primary dealers, institutions, brokerage houses, and banks can place orders anywhere at any time; money flows around the world, gets converted to the needed currencies, and finally appears on a consolidated statement at the end of the day and on a monthly summary.

But selecting individual stocks in unfamiliar countries is not easy. Worse still, a few stocks may not represent the direction of the nation's economy. It may be easy to form the opinion that, over the next 20 years, the growth of China will result in the economic expansion of all countries in Southeast Asia, in particular those actively trading with China. It is far more difficult to pick one or two stocks in Thailand, Indonesia, or Malaysia that will benefit from China's expansion than to decide on a macropolicy.

To solve this problem, the principal U.S. and other exchanges have introduced WEBS, world funds, and closed-end world funds, all trying to aggregate the performance of the major stock issues of each country into a single index that represents its market as a whole. Rather than being forced to decide which stocks are going to be the best, you can invest in the economy as a whole of nearly all industrialized countries and take the safer macroapproach.

These new products have been developed because there is a need for them. We buy Japanese and German cars, and clothes from Asia and Europe, and we find that the strength and weakness of those economies affect the prices we pay out every day. Investments and earnings must be protected, not only from domestic inflation, but from a decline in our own economy relative to others. Not long ago, when Japan's economy was its strongest, the cost of its cars become too expensive in the United States, and manufacturing was forced to relocate to be more competitive.

World market diversification is no longer a special talent to be exercised by a small group of cloistered professionals. It is an essential and substantial part of an investment portfolio, not just a token portion. Investments in one country, even your own, do not provide long-term protection against inflation, or a shorter-term buffer for market declines, or in general, the safety that we all expect and deserve.

Appendix

Statistical Data
for World Markets

The tables and charts on the following pages show the annual returns and statistical data for most world markets. They provide an overview of performance and volatility, and allow, in a very rough way, a diverse international portfolio to be sketched out. The world markets listed below appear in alphabetical order by country. All charts are printed through the courtesy of Bloomberg, L.P.

Argentina	Finland
Australia	France
Austria	Germany
Belgium	Greece
Brazil	Hong Kong
Canada	Hungary
Chile	India
China	Indonesia
Colombia	Ireland
Czech Republic	Israel
Denmark	Italy
Egypt	Japan
European Index Eurotrack	Malaysia

Mexico
Netherlands
New Zealand
Norway
Pakistan
Peru
Philippines
Poland
Portugal
Russia
Singapore
South Africa

South Korea
Spain
Sri Lanka
Sweden
Switzerland
Taiwan
Thailand
Turkey
United Kingdom
United States
United States (International Stocks)
Venezuela

Country:	Argentina
Currency:	Argentine Peso
Index:	Argentina Stock Market General
Description:	Capitalization-weighted index of all shares traded in Argentina. No derivatives available.

Years' end	Index		Argentine peso value	U.S. dollar	
	Values	Returns		Values	Returns
1988	4.14				
1989	717.09	17221.01%			
1990	2202.88	207.20%			
1991	17856.00	710.58%	0.993	17981.87	
1992	13427.50	−24.80%	0.998	13454.41	−25.18%
1993	20607.20	53.47%	0.998	20650.57	53.49%
1994	15855.60	−23.06%	0.998	15887.37	−23.07%
1995	16237.80	2.41%	1.001	16229.69	2.15%

Total return		392117.39%		−9.74%
Compounded rate of return		226.11%		−2.53%
Standard deviation		6455.89%		36.60%
Risk-adjusted ratio		0.04		−0.07
Correlation with the U.S.		0.34		0.17

Other indices: MERVAL
Capitalization weighted index of 22 major equities traded in Argentina.
Value as of December 31, 1989: 37.27.
Value as of December 31, 1995: 518.96.
No derivatives available.

BURCAP
Capitalization weighted index of the MERVAL components, weighted proportional to their market capitalization at base date.
Value as of December 31, 1992: 426.33.
Value as of December 31, 1995: 674.36.
No derivatives available.

PRICE GRAPH for ARGENTINA STK MK GENERAL

CLOSE/MID		
Last	17588.17	on 01/05/96
High	25470.99	on 05/29/92
Ave	11391.787	
Low	5.07	on 02/17/89

14JUL89 15DEC 11MAY90 12OCT 15MAR91 16AUG 17JAN92 12JUN 13NOV 16APR93 17SEP 11FEB94 15JUL 16DEC 12MAY95 13OCT

Figure A-1. *Argentina Stock Market General.*

Country:	Australia					
Currency:	Australian Dollar					
Index:	Australian All Ordinaries Index					
Description:	Capitalization weighted index of stocks traded at the Australian Stock Exchange. Base level of 500 as of December 31, 1979. Futures and options available.					

Years' end	Index		Australian dollar value	U.S. dollar	
	Values	Returns		Values	Returns
1987	1318.85		1.384	952.87	
1988	1487.50	12.79%	1.169	1272.56	33.55%
1989	1649.84	10.91%	1.267	1301.72	2.29%
1990	1279.82	−22.43%	1.296	987.38	−24.15%
1991	1651.40	29.03%	1.312	1258.70	27.48%
1992	1549.90	−6.15%	1.450	1068.66	−15.10%
1993	2173.60	40.24%	1.472	1476.53	38.17%
1994	1912.70	−12.00%	1.290	1482.92	0.43%
1995	2203.00	15.18%	1.346	1636.39	10.35%

Total return	67.04%	71.73%
Compounded rate of return	6.62%	6.99%
Standard deviation	21.01%	22.66%
Risk-adjusted ratio	0.32	0.31
Correlation with the U.S.	0.59	0.41

Other indices: Australian All Mining Index
Capitalization weighted index of all stocks of the mining sector, traded at the Australian Stock Exchange.
Base level of 500 as of December 31, 1979.
Value as of December 31, 1995: 998.3.
No derivatives available.

Australian Twenty Leaders Index
Capitalization weighted index of the 20 major stocks traded in Australia.
Base level of 500 as of December 31, 1979.
Value as of December 31, 1995: 1201.
Options available.

Figure A-2. Australian *All Ordinaries Index.*

	Austria
Country:	Austria
Currency:	Austrian Shilling
Index:	Creditanstalt Bankverein
Description:	Base level of 100 as of March 3, 1984.
	Capitalization weighted index of 25 domestic companies traded in Vienna.
	No derivatives available.

Years' end	Index		Austrian shilling value	U.S. dollar	
	Values	Returns		Values	Returns
1988	234.70		12.490	18.79	
1989	493.07	110.09%	11.890	41.47	120.69%
1990	440.06	−10.75%	10.550	41.71	0.58%
1991	374.63	−14.87%	10.720	34.95	−16.22%
1992	312.96	−16.46%	11.385	27.49	−21.34%
1993	429.46	37.23%	12.230	35.12	27.74%
1994	395.17	−7.98%	10.900	36.25	3.24%
1995	344.91	−12.72%	10.108	34.12	−5.88%

Total return	46.96%	81.59%
Compounded rate of return	5.65%	8.90%
Standard deviation	47.11%	49.00%
Risk-adjusted ratio	0.12	0.18
Correlation with the U.S.	0.30	0.28

Other indices: Austrian Traded ATX Index
Capitalization weighted index of the most traded stocks in Vienna.
Base level of 1000 as of January 2, 1991.
Value as of December 31, 1995: 959.79.
Futures and options available.

Vienna Stock Exchange Share Index
Capitalization weighted index of domestically listed companies.
Base level of 100 as of December 31, 1967.
Value as of December 31, 1995: 387.36.
No derivatives available.

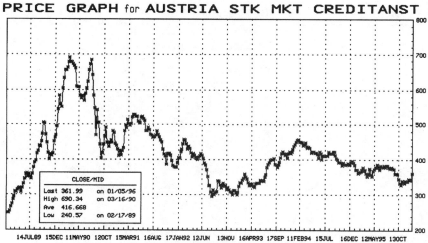

PRICE GRAPH for AUSTRIA STK MKT CREDITANST

CLOSE/MID	
Last 361.99	on 01/05/96
High 690.34	on 03/16/90
Ave 416.668	
Low 240.57	on 02/17/89

14JUL89 15DEC 11MAY90 12OCT 15MAR91 16AUG 17JAN92 12JUN 13NOV 16APR93 17SEP 11FEB94 15JUL 16DEC 12MAY95 13OCT

Figure A-3. Austrian Stock Market *Creditanstalt Bankverein.*

	Index		Belgian	U.S. dollar	
Years' end	Values	Returns	franc value	Values	Returns
1988	5565.56		37.23	149.49	
1989	6476.39	16.37%	35.61	181.87	21.66%
1990	4963.81	−23.36%	30.94	160.43	−11.79%
1991	5481.43	10.43%	31.29	175.18	9.19%
1992	5568.08	1.58%	33.27	167.36	−4.46%
1993	7543.12	35.47%	36.24	208.14	24.37%
1994	7248.64	−3.90%	31.82	227.80	9.44%
1995	8401.68	15.91%	29.53	284.51	24.90%

Country: Belgium
Currency: Belgian Franc
Index: Belgium Spot Market Return Index
Description: Base level of 1000 as of January 1, 1980.
Composition of all Belgian companies traded on the spot market.
No derivatives available.

	Values	Returns		Values	Returns
Total return		50.96%			90.32%
Compounded rate of return		6.06%			9.63%
Standard deviation		18.52%			14.42%
Risk-adjusted ratio		0.33			0.67
Correlation with the U.S.		0.56			0.68

Other indices: BEL 20
Capitalization weighted index of the 20 most capitalized Belgian stocks.
Base value of 1000 as of January 1, 1991.
Value as of December 31, 1995: 1559.63.
Futures and options available.

PRICE GRAPH for BELGIUM STK MKT BRUSSEL SE

CLOSE/MID	
Last 8600.37	on 01/05/96
High 8600.37	on 01/05/96
Ave 6409.754	
Low 4775.32	on 01/11/91

14JUL89 15DEC 11MAY90 12OCT 15MAR91 16AUG 17JAN92 12JUN 13NOV 16APR93 17SEP 11FEB94 15JUL 16DEC 12MAY95 13OCT

Figure A-4. *Belgium Spot Market Return Index,* Brussels Stock Exchange.

	Index		Brazilian	U.S. dollar	
Years' end	Values	Returns	real value	Values	Returns
1991	6.08		0.0004	15200.00	
1992	67.81	1015.30%	0.0045	15068.89	−0.86%
1993	3754.50	5436.79%	0.1167	32172.24	113.50%
1994	43539.00	1059.65%	0.8460	51464.54	59.97%
1995	42990.00	−1.26%	0.9717	44242.05	−14.03%
Total return		706972.37%			191.07%
Compounded rate of return		816.99%			30.62%
Standard deviation		2422.85%			58.85%
Risk-adjusted ratio		0.34			0.52
Correlation with the U.S.		−0.36			−0.55

Country: Brazil
Currency: Brazilian Real
Index: BOVESPA
Description: Capitalization weighted index of 52 Brazilian stocks traded in Sao Paulo. BOVESPA has been divided 9 times by a factor of 10 since January 1985. Futures available.

Other indices: Brazilian Stock Market Index I-SENN
Traded value weighted index of the 50 most traded Brazilian stocks.
Value as of December 31, 1992: 24.59.
Value as of December 31, 1995: 18892.
No derivatives available.

PRICE GRAPH for BRAZIL STK MKTS I-SENN

CLOSE/MID	
Last 18892	on 12/29/95
High 22990	on 09/30/94
Ave 10302.826	
Low 24.59	on 01/01/93

12MAR93 21MAY 30JUL 8OCT 17DEC 25FEB94 6MAY 15JUL 23SEP 2DEC 10FEB95 21APR 30JUN 8SEP 17NOV

Figure A-5. Brazilian Stock Market Index, *I-SENN*.

243

Country:	Canada
Currency:	Canadian Dollar
Index:	TSE 300
Description:	Capitalization weighted index of 300 major Canadian stocks.
	Base level of 1000 as of 1975.
	No derivatives available.

Years' end	Index		Canadian dollar value	U.S. dollar	
	Values	Returns		Values	Returns
1987	3160.05		1.300	2430.81	
1988	3389.99	7.28%	1.193	2842.28	16.93%
1989	3969.80	17.10%	1.159	3426.08	20.54%
1990	3256.80	−17.96%	1.160	2807.10	−18.07%
1991	3512.36	7.85%	1.155	3040.21	8.30%
1992	3350.44	−4.61%	1.271	2636.90	−13.27%
1993	4321.43	28.98%	1.325	3262.44	23.72%
1994	4213.61	−2.50%	1.403	3004.36	−7.91%
1995	4713.54	11.86%	1.365	3454.41	14.98%
Total return		49.16%			42.11%
Compounded rate of return		5.13%			4.49%
Standard deviation		14.39%			16.36%
Risk-adjusted ratio		0.36			0.27
Correlation with the U.S.		0.57			0.68

Other indices:

TSE 200
Capitalization weighted index of the 200 most highly capitalized Canadian stocks. Base level of 250 as of August 31, 1993. Value as of December 31, 1995: 282.93. No derivatives available.

TSE 100
Capitalization weighted index of the 100 most highly capitalized Canadian stocks. Base level of 250 as of August 31, 1993. Value as of December 31, 1995: 286.31. Futures and options available.

TSE 35 INTERIM INDEX
Capitalization weighted index of 35 major Canadian stocks. Value as of December 31, 1988: 180.51. Value as of December 31, 1995: 248.49. Futures available.

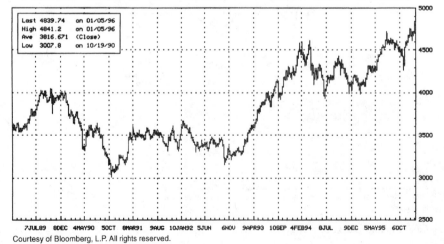

PRICE GRAPH for TS300 -- TSE 300 Index

Last 4839.74	on 01/05/96
High 4841.2	on 01/05/96
Ave 3816.671	(Close)
Low 3007.8	on 10/19/90

7JUL89 8DEC 4MAY90 5OCT 8MAR91 9AUG 10JAN92 5JUN 6NOV 9APR93 10SEP 4FEB94 8JUL 9DEC 5MAY95 6OCT

Figure A-6. Canada, *TSE 300*, Toronto.

	Country:	Chile
Currency:	Chilean Peso
Index:	Chile Stock Market General
Description:	Capitalization weighted index of the majority of stocks traded in Santiago.
	Base level of 100 as of December 30, 1990.
	No derivatives available.

Years' end	Index		Chilean peso value	U.S. dollar	
	Values	Returns		Values	Returns
1990	1166.57		337.09	3.46	
1991	2483.69	112.91%	374.5100	6.63	91.93%
1992	2733.46	10.06%	382.3300	7.15	7.81%
1993	3915.49	43.24%	428.4700	9.14	27.82%
1994	5426.46	38.59%	402.9200	13.47	47.38%
1995	5739.97	5.78%	407.1300	14.10	4.68%

Total return	392.04%	307.39%
Compounded rate of return	37.53%	32.43%
Standard deviation	42.93%	35.59%
Risk-adjusted ratio	0.87	0.91
Correlation with the U.S.	0.19	0.09

Other indices: Chile Stock Market Selection
Capitalization weighted index of 40 major stocks traded in Santiago.
Value as of December 31, 1989: 7.74.
Value as of December 31, 1995: 100.
No derivatives available.

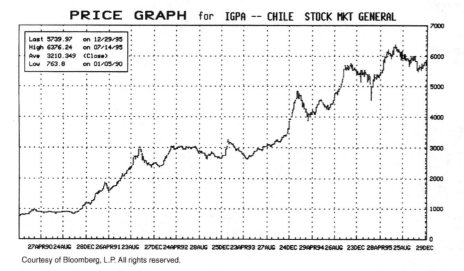

PRICE GRAPH for IGPA -- CHILE STOCK MKT GENERAL

Last 5739.97	on 12/29/95
High 6376.24	on 07/14/95
Ave 3210.349	(Close)
Low 763.8	on 01/05/90

27APR90 24AUG 28DEC 26APR91 23AUG 27DEC 24APR92 28AUG 25DEC 23APR93 27AUG 24DEC 29APR94 26AUG 23DEC 28APR95 25AUG 29DEC

Figure A-7. *Chile Stock Market General.*

Country: China
Currency: Chinese Renminbi
Index: CLSA Index China B
Description: Index compiled by Credit Lyonnais Securities Asia.
B shares for purchase by foreign investors.
No derivatives available.

Years' end	Index		China renminbi value	U.S. dollar	
	Values	Returns		Values	Returns
June 1992	1689.67		6.580	256.79	
1992	1069.62	−36.70%	7.580	141.11	−45.05%
1993	1450.67	35.62%	8.700	166.74	18.17%
1994	918.94	−36.65%	8.446	108.80	−34.75%
1995	688.32	−25.10%	8.317	82.76	−23.94%
Total return		−59.26%			−67.77%
Compounded rate of return		−22.63%			−27.64%
Standard deviation		34.65%			27.74%
Risk-adjusted ratio		−0.65			−1.00
Correlation with the U.S.		−0.01			0.08

Other indices: CLSA Index China World
Index compiled by Credit Lyonnais Securities Asia, including 30 stocks, base 1000 as of January 3, 1995.
Value as of December 31, 1995: 831.02.
No derivatives available.

China Stock Exchange SHANG A
Weighted index of A shares, using volumes as weighting factor.
Base 100 as of December 19, 1990.
Value as of December 31, 1995: 575.19.
No derivatives available.

China Stock Exchange SHANG B
Weighted index of B shares, using volumes as weighting factor.
Base 100 as of January 21, 1992.
Value as of December 31, 1995: 47.69.
No derivatives available.

VALUE GRAPH for CHINA CLSA INDEX CHINA B

CLOSE/MID	
Last 688.32	on 12/29/95
High 1694.66	on 06/19/92
Ave 1065.626	
Low 688.32	on 12/29/95

28AUG92 6NOV 15JAN9326MAR 4JUN 13AUG 22OCT 31DEC11MAR9420MAY 29JUL 7OCT 16DEC24FEB95 5MAY 14JUL 22SEP 1DEC

Figure A-8. China, *CLSA Index China B.*

Country: Colombia
Currency: Colombian Peso
Index: Colombia Stock Market BOG-BOLSA
Description: Composed of shares from 20 companies with the highest volume in the past 2 years. Base level of 100 as of December 31, 1991. No derivatives available.

Years' end	Index		Columbian peso value	U.S. dollar	
	Values	Returns		Values	Returns
1991	358.09		650.0000	0.55	
1992	499.87	39.59%	735.0000	0.68	23.45%
1993	749.44	49.93%	802.3300	0.93	37.35%
1994	889.91	18.74%	831.2000	1.07	14.62%
1995	756.44	−15.00%	988.1600	0.77	−28.50%
Total return		111.24%			38.95%
Compounded rate of return		20.56%			8.57%
Standard deviation		28.65%			28.40%
Risk-adjusted ratio		0.72			0.30
Correlation with the U.S.		−0.77			−0.85

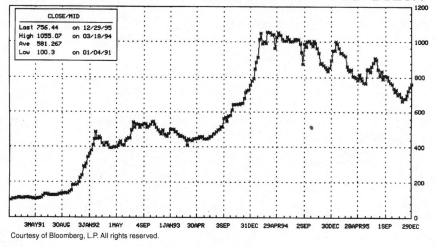

PRICE GRAPH for COLOMBIA STK MKT BOG-BOLSA

CLOSE/MID		
Last 756.44	on 12/29/95
High 1055.07	on 03/18/94
Ave 581.267	
Low 100.3	on 01/04/91

3MAY91 30AUG 3JAN92 1MAY 4SEP 1JAN93 30APR 3SEP 31DEC 29APR94 2SEP 30DEC 28APR95 1SEP 29DEC

Figure A-9. *Colombia Stock Market BOG-BOLSA.*

	Country:	Czech Republic
	Currency:	Czech Koruna
	Index:	HNWOOD 30 Index
	Description:	Base level of 1000 as of September 7 1993.
		Capitalization weighted index of 30 Czech stocks.
		No derivatives available.

| Years' end | Index | | Czech koruna value | U.S. dollar | |
	Values	Returns		Values	Returns
September 1993	1000.00		28.810	34.71	
1993	2246.00	124.60%	30.100	74.62	114.97%
1994	1530.00	−31.88%	27.910	54.82	−26.53%
1995	1260.00	−17.65%	26.580	47.40	−13.53%
Total return		26.00%			36.57%
Compounded rate of return		6.83%			9.31%
Standard deviation		86.53%			78.22%
Risk-adjusted ratio		0.08			0.12
Correlation with the U.S.		−0.21			−0.21

Other indices: PX 50 Prague Stock Exchange Equity Index.
Base level of 1000 as of April 5, 1994.
Value as of December 31, 1995: 425.9.
No derivatives available.

Czech National Bank CNB-120
Capitalization weighted index of 120 Czech stocks.
Based at 1000 on December 16, 1993 and rebased at 1000 on March 1, 1995 following the second tranche of privatizations.
Value as of December 31, 1995: 740.
No derivatives available.

VALUE GRAPH for CZECH HNWOOD-30

CLOSE/MID	
Last 1260	on 12/15/95
High 3717	on 02/04/94
Ave 1768.339	
Low 992	on 09/17/93

5NOV93 31DEC 25FEB94 22APR 17JUN 12AUG 7OCT 2DEC 27JAN95 24MAR 19MAY 14JUL 8SEP 3NOV

Figure A-10. Czech Republic, *HNWOOD-30 Index.*

Country:	Denmark
Currency:	Danish Krone
Index:	Denmark Stock Market Index
Description:	Base level of 100 as of January 1, 1983.
	Capitalization weighted index of 257 companies traded in Copenhagen.
	No derivatives available.

Years' end	Index		Danish krone value	U.S. dollar	
	Values	Returns		Values	Returns
1988	289.00		6.858	42.14	
1989	363.22	25.68%	6.591	55.11	30.76%
1990	314.80	−13.33%	5.779	54.47	−1.15%
1991	352.56	11.99%	5.920	59.55	9.33%
1992	261.59	−25.80%	6.300	41.52	−30.28%
1993	365.64	39.78%	6.793	53.83	29.63%
1994	349.32	−4.46%	6.083	57.43	6.70%
1995	366.30	4.86%	5.560	65.88	14.72%
Total return		26.75%			56.33%
Compounded rate of return		3.44%			6.59%
Standard deviation		22.58%			20.74%
Risk-adjusted ratio		0.15			0.32
Correlation with the U.S.		0.43			0.44

Other indices:	KFX Copenhagen Share Index
	Capitalization weighted index of the most liquid stocks traded in Copenhagen
	(20 in 1996).
	Base level of 100 as of July 3, 1989.
	Value as of December 31, 1995: 106.14.
	Futures available.

PRICE GRAPH for KFX -- KFX COPENHAGEN SHARE IDX

Last 106.14	on 12/29/95
High 118.3	on 02/04/94
Ave 97.824	(Close)
Low 70.59	on 10/30/92

27APR90 28SEP 1MAR91 26JUL 27DEC 29MAY92 30OCT 26MAR93 27AUG 28JAN94 1JUL 25NOV 28APR95 29SEP

Figure A-11. Denmark, *KFX Copenhagen Share Index.*

	Country:	Egypt
	Currency:	Egyptian Pound
	Index:	Hermes Egypt Stock Market Index
	Description:	Index composed of 42 most liquid companies, representing ten major business sectors. Base level of 2000 as of July 1, 1992. No derivatives available.

Years' end	Index		Egyptian pound value	U.S. dollar	
	Values	Returns		Values	Returns
June 30, 1992	2000.00		3.250	615.38	
1992	2415.71	20.79%	3.290	734.26	19.32%
1993	3772.54	56.17%	3.373	1118.62	52.35%
1994	9492.02	151.61%	3.393	2797.94	150.12%
1995	7508.30	−20.90%	3.396	2210.99	−20.98%
Total return		275.42%			259.29%
Compounded rate of return		39.20%			37.68%
Standard deviation		73.55%			73.05%
Risk-adjusted ratio		0.53			0.52
Correlation with the U.S.		−0.79			−0.75

Other indices: EFG Index
Capitalization weighted index published by the Financial Brokerage Group, subsidiary of the Egyptian Financial Group, including 40 most traded stocks on the Egyptian Stock Market.
No derivatives available.
Base level of 1000 as of January 1, 1993.
Value as of December 31, 1995: 3269.35.
No derivatives available.

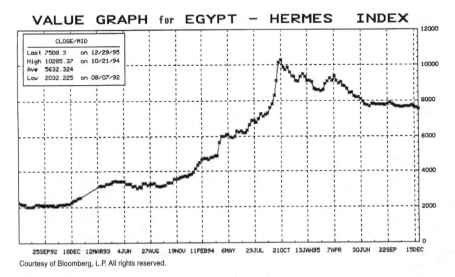

VALUE GRAPH for EGYPT – HERMES INDEX

CLOSE/MID		
Last	7508.3	on 12/29/95
High	10285.37	on 10/21/94
Ave	5632.324	
Low	2032.225	on 08/07/92

25SEP92 18DEC 12MAR93 4JUN 27AUG 19NOV 11FEB94 6MAY 29JUL 21OCT 13JAN95 7APR 30JUN 22SEP 15DEC

Figure A-12. Egypt, *Hermes Egypt Stock Market Index.*

Country: European Stocks–United Kingdom
Currency: German Mark (Base Currency of the Index)
Index: FT-SE EUROTRACK 100
Description: Capitalization weighted index of the most capitalized European stocks.
Base level of 1000 as of October 29, 1990.
No derivatives available.

Years' end	Index		German mark value	U.S. dollar	
	Values	Returns		Values	Returns
1990	936.60		1.497	625.65	
1991	1079.41	15.25%	1.520	710.14	13.50%
1992	1083.35	0.37%	1.621	668.24	−5.90%
1993	1473.36	36.00%	1.739	847.39	26.81%
1994	1333.16	−9.52%	1.550	860.38	1.53%
1995	1490.41	11.80%	1.438	1036.59	20.48%
Total return		59.13%			65.68%
Compounded rate of return		9.74%			10.63%
Standard deviation		17.16%			13.43%
Risk-adjusted ratio		0.57			0.79
Correlation with the U.S.		0.30			0.51

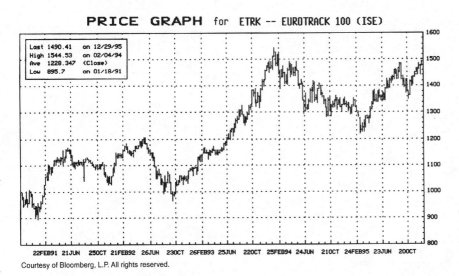

PRICE GRAPH for ETRK -- EUROTRACK 100 (ISE)

Last 1490.41 on 12/29/95
High 1544.53 on 02/04/94
Ave 1228.347 (Close)
Low 895.7 on 01/18/91

22FEB91 21JUN 25OCT 21FEB92 26JUN 23OCT 26FEB93 25JUN 22OCT 25FEB94 24JUN 21OCT 24FEB95 23JUN 20OCT

Figure A-13. Europe, *FT-SE Eurotrack 100,*

	Country:	Finland
	Currency:	Finnish Markka
	Index:	HEX General Index
	Description:	Base level of 1000 as of December 28, 1990.
		Capitalization weighted index of all the companies traded in Helsinki (90 in 1996).
		No derivatives available.

| Years' end | Index | | Finnish markka value | U.S. dollar | |
	Values	Returns		Values	Returns
1990	1000.00		3.632	275.33	
1991	781.50	−21.85%	4.142	188.68	−31.47%
1992	829.00	6.08%	5.265	157.45	−16.55%
1993	1582.12	90.85%	5.809	272.36	72.97%
1994	1846.68	16.72%	4.739	389.69	43.08%
1995	1712.17	−7.28%	4.363	392.43	0.70%
Total return		71.22%			42.53%
Compounded rate of return		11.35%			7.34%
Standard deviation		43.79%			43.30%
Risk-adjusted ratio		0.26			0.17
Correlation with the U.S.		−0.51			−0.53

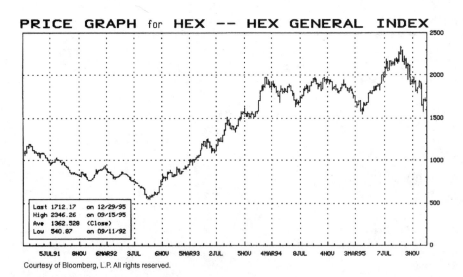

PRICE GRAPH for HEX -- HEX GENERAL INDEX

Last 1712.17 on 12/29/95
High 2346.26 on 09/15/95
Ave 1362.528 (Close)
Low 540.87 on 09/11/92

5JUL91 8NOV 6MAR92 3JUL 6NOV 5MAR93 2JUL 5NOV 4MAR94 8JUL 4NOV 3MAR95 7JUL 3NOV

Figure A-14. Finland, *HEX General Index.*

Country:	France
Currency:	French Franc
Index:	CAC 40
Description:	Base level of 1000 as of December 31, 1987.
	Composition of 40 companies listed in Paris.
	Futures and option available.

Years' end	Index Values	Index Returns	French franc value	U.S. dollar Values	U.S. dollar Returns
1987	1000.00		5.33	187.69	
1988	1573.94	57.39%	6.06	259.73	38.38%
1989	2001.08	27.14%	5.77	346.81	33.58%
1990	1505.10	−24.79%	5.10	295.12	−14.90%
1991	1765.66	17.31%	5.19	340.20	15.28%
1992	1857.78	5.22%	5.52	336.55	−1.07%
1993	2268.22	22.09%	5.40	420.04	24.81%
1994	1881.15	−17.06%	5.33	352.94	−15.98%
1995	1871.97	−0.49%	4.90	382.03	8.24%

Total return	82.70%	103.55%
Compounded rate of return	8.15%	9.29%
Standard deviation	26.21%	20.76%
Risk-adjusted ratio	0.31	0.45
Correlation with the U.S.	0.42	0.57

Other indices: SBF 120
Capitalization weighted index of the 120 most liquid French stocks.
Base value of 1000 as of December 28, 1990.
Value as of December 31, 1995: 1283.5.
No derivatives available.

SBF 250
Capitalization weighted index of the 250 most liquid French stocks.
Base value of 1000 as of December 28, 1990.
Value as of December 31, 1995: 1232.86.
No derivatives available.

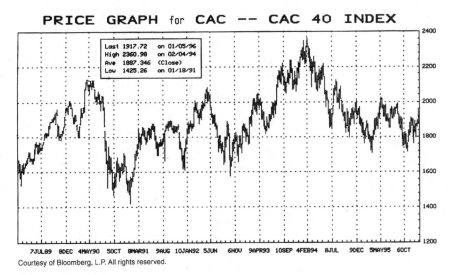

PRICE GRAPH for CAC -- CAC 40 INDEX

Last 1917.72	on 01/05/96
High 2360.98	on 02/04/94
Ave 1887.346	(Close)
Low 1425.26	on 01/18/91

7JUL89 8DEC 4MAY90 5OCT 8MAR91 9AUG 10JAN92 5JUN 6NOV 9APR93 10SEP 4FEB94 8JUL 9DEC 5MAY95 6OCT

Figure A-15. France, *CAC 40*.

Country:	Germany
Currency:	German Mark
Index:	DAX
Description:	Base level of 1000 as of December 31, 1987
	Total return index of 30 selected German stocks
	Futures and options available

| Years' end | Index | | German mark value | U.S. dollar | |
	Values	Returns		Values	Returns
1987	1000.00		1.571	636.62	
1988	1327.87	32.79%	1.774	748.73	17.61%
1989	1790.37	34.83%	1.690	1059.70	41.53%
1990	1398.23	−21.90%	1.497	934.02	−11.86%
1991	1577.98	12.86%	1.520	1038.14	11.15%
1992	1545.05	−2.09%	1.621	953.03	−8.20%
1993	2266.68	46.71%	1.739	1303.66	36.79%
1994	2106.58	−7.06%	1.550	1359.52	4.28%
1995	2253.88	6.99%	1.438	1567.59	15.30%

Total return		125.39%			146.24%
Compounded rate of return		10.69%			11.92%
Standard deviation		23.57%			19.10%
Risk-adjusted ratio		0.45			0.62
Correlation with the U.S.		0.44			0.55

Other indices: CDAX Performance Index.
Total return index of all domestic stocks traded in Frankfurt.
Base value of 100 as of December 31, 1987.
Value as of December 31, 1995: 215.7.
No derivatives available.

Commerzbank Index.
Capitalization weighted index of leading German stocks.
Base value of 100 as of December 31, 1953.
Value as of December 31, 1995: 2358.9.
No derivatives available.

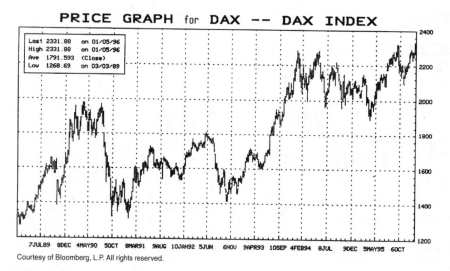

Figure A-16. Germany, *DAX*.

Country:	Greece
Currency:	Greek Drachma
Index:	ASE Composite Index
Description:	Capitalization weighted index of 76 Greek stocks.
	No derivatives available.

Years' end	Index		Greek drachma value	U.S. dollar	
	Values	Returns		Values	Returns
1991	935.00		175.850	5.32	
1992	672.31	−28.10%	215.500	3.12	−41.33%
1993	958.66	42.59%	250.120	3.83	22.86%
1994	868.91	−9.36%	240.150	3.62	−5.60%
1995	914.15	5.21%	237.670	3.85	6.30%
Total return		−2.23%			−27.66%
Compounded rate of return		−0.56%			−7.78%
Standard deviation		29.95%			27.22%
Risk-adjusted ratio		−0.02			−0.29
Correlation with the U.S.		0.18			0.31

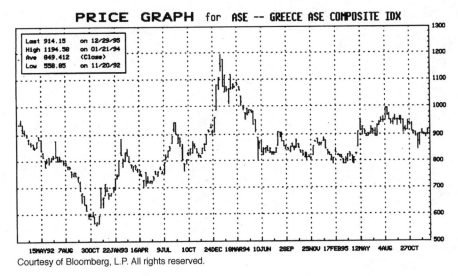

PRICE GRAPH for ASE -- GREECE ASE COMPOSITE IDX

Last	914.15	on 12/29/95
High	1194.58	on 01/21/94
Ave	849.412	(Close)
Low	558.85	on 11/20/92

15MAY92 7AUG 30OCT 22JAN93 16APR 9JUL 1OCT 24DEC 18MAR94 10JUN 2SEP 25NOV 17FEB95 12MAY 4AUG 27OCT

Figure A-17. Greece, *ASE Composite Index.*

Country:	Hong Kong
Currency:	Hong Kong Dollar
Index:	Hang Seng Index
Description:	Capitalization weighted index of 33 stocks representing about 70% of the Hong Kong market capitalization.
	Base level of 975.45 as of January 13, 1984.
	Futures and options available.

| Years' end | Index | | Hong Kong dollar value | U.S. dollar | |
	Values	Returns		Values	Returns
1987	2302.75		7.764	296.59	
1988	2687.44	16.71%	7.808	344.19	16.05%
1989	2836.57	5.55%	7.810	363.22	5.53%
1990	3024.55	6.63%	7.801	387.71	6.74%
1991	4297.33	42.08%	7.781	552.32	42.46%
1992	5512.39	28.27%	7.744	711.87	28.89%
1993	11888.40	115.67%	7.723	1539.39	116.24%
1994	8191.04	−31.10%	7.738	1058.62	−31.23%
1995	10073.40	22.98%	7.733	1302.74	23.06%
Total return		337.45%			339.23%
Compounded rate of return		17.82%			17.87%
Standard deviation		42.18%			42.42%
Risk-adjusted ratio		0.42			0.42
Correlation with the U.S.		0.12			0.12

Other indices:	Hong Kong Stock Exchange All Ordinaries
	Capitalization weighted index of all stocks traded in Hong Kong.
	Value as of December 31, 1992: 2951.06.
	Value as of December 31, 1995: 4770.57.
	No derivatives available.

PRICE GRAPH for HSI -- HANG SENG STOCK INDEX

Last	10529.9	on 01/05/96
High	12599.23	on 01/07/94
Ave	5934.563	(Close)
Low	2022.15	on 06/09/89

7JUL89 8DEC 4MAY90 5OCT 8MAR91 9AUG 10JAN92 5JUN 6NOV 9APR93 10SEP 4FEB94 8JUL 9DEC 5MAY95 6OCT

Figure A-18. Hong Kong, *Hang Seng.*

	Country:	Hungary
	Currency:	Hungarian Florint
	Index:	Budapest Stock Market Index—BTI
	Description:	Experimental index of 20 Hungarian stocks.
		Base level of 1000 as of January 2, 1991.
		No derivatives available.

Years' end	Index		Hungarian florint value	U.S. dollar	
	Values	Returns		Values	Returns
1990	1000.00				
1991	808.79	−19.12%			
1992	796.48	−1.52%			
1993	1228.73	54.27%	100.660	12.21	
1994	1470.10	19.64%	110.690	13.28	8.80%
1995	1528.92	4.00%	139.470	10.96	−17.46%
Total return		52.89%			−10.19%
Compounded rate of return		8.86%			−3.52%
Standard deviation		27.65%			18.57%
Risk-adjusted ratio		0.32			−0.19
Correlation with the U.S.		−0.49			−1.00

Figure A-19. *Hungary Stock Market BTI.*

	Country:	India
	Currency:	Indian Rupee
	Index:	SENSEX 30
	Description:	Weighted index of 30 most representative indian stocks. Calculation based on the "weighted aggregates" method: each share weighted by the number of outstanding equities. No derivatives available.

Years' end	Index		Indian rupee value	U.S. dollar	
	Values	Returns		Values	Returns
1987	442.17		12.860	34.38	
1988	666.26	50.68%	15.020	44.36	29.01%
1989	778.64	16.87%	16.890	46.10	3.93%
1990	1048.29	34.63%	18.120	57.85	25.49%
1991	1908.85	82.09%	25.790	74.02	27.94%
1992	2615.37	37.01%	28.950	90.34	22.06%
1993	3362.60	28.57%	31.500	106.75	18.16%
1994	3929.90	16.87%	31.370	125.28	17.36%
1995	3110.49	−20.85%	35.170	88.44	−29.40%
Total return		603.46			106.69%
Compounded rate of return		27.62%			12.54%
Standard deviation		29.62%			19.38%
Risk-adjusted ratio		0.93			0.65
Correlation with the U.S.		−0.17			−0.62

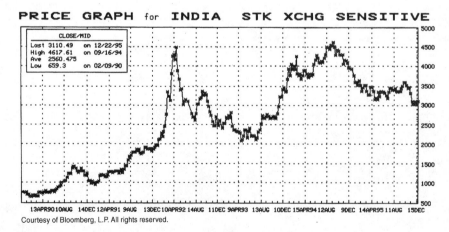

PRICE GRAPH for INDIA STK XCHG SENSITIVE

CLOSE/MID		
Last	3110.49	on 12/22/95
High	4617.61	on 09/16/94
Ave	2560.475	
Low	659.3	on 02/09/90

13APR90 10AUG 14DEC 12APR91 9AUG 13DEC 10APR92 14AUG 11DEC 9APR93 13AUG 10DEC 15APR94 12AUG 9DEC 14APR95 11AUG 15DEC

Figure A-20. India Stock Exchange, *SENSEX 30*.

	Index		Indonesian	U.S. dollar	
Country:	Indonesia				
Currency:	Indonesian Rupiah				
Index:	Jakarta Composite Index				
Description:	Capitalization weighted index of all stocks traded in Jakarta. Based on August 10, 1982. No derivatives available.				

Years' end	Index		Indonesian rupiah value	U.S. dollar	
	Values	Returns		Values	Returns
1991	247.39		1995.00	0.12	
1992	274.33	10.89%	2067.00	0.13	7.03%
1993	587.88	114.30%	2102.00	0.28	110.73%
1994	469.64	−20.11%	2199.00	0.21	−23.64%
1995	513.84	9.41%	2287.00	0.22	5.20%

Total return		107.70%		81.19%
Compounded rate of return		20.05%		16.02%
Standard deviation		58.87%		58.96%
Risk-adjusted ratio		0.34		0.27
Correlation with the U.S.		−0.02		−0.02

PRICE GRAPH for JCI -- JAKARTA COMPOSITE INDEX

Last 513.847 on 12/29/95
High 612.888 on 01/07/94
Ave 397.585 (Close)
Low 224.706 on 11/01/91

15FEB91 14JUN 18OCT 14FEB92 19JUN 16OCT 19FEB93 18JUN 15OCT 18FEB94 17JUN 14OCT 17FEB95 16JUN 13OCT

Figure A-21. Indonesia, *Jakarta Composite Index.*

Country:	Ireland
Currency:	Irish Punt
Index:	Ireland Stock Market Index
Description:	Base level of 1000 as of April 1, 1988. No derivatives available.

Years' end	Index		Irish punt value	U.S. dollar	
	Values	Returns		Values	Returns
1989	1765.87		0.641	2752.99	
1990	1201.77	−31.94%	0.561	2141.55	−22.21%
1991	1380.23	14.85%	0.572	2411.95	12.63%
1992	1227.35	−11.08%	0.614	1999.35	−17.11%
1993	1888.94	53.90%	0.710	2661.89	33.14%
1994	1850.76	−2.02%	0.645	2867.20	7.71%
1995	2232.45	20.62%	0.625	3573.04	24.62%
Total return		26.42%			29.79%
Compounded rate of return		3.98%			4.44%
Standard deviation		29.57%			22.17%
Risk-adjusted ratio		0.13			0.20
Correlation with the U.S.		0.49			0.59

PRICE GRAPH for ISEQ -- IRISH OVERALL INDEX

Last 2232.45 on 12/29/95
High 2264.43 on 12/08/95
Ave 1844.899 (Close)
Low 1261.8 on 02/19/93

23APR93 2JUL 10SEP 19NOV 28JAN94 8APR 17JUN 26AUG 4NOV 13JAN95 24MAR 2JUN 11AUG 20OCT 29DEC

Figure A-22. Ireland, *Irish Overall Index.*

	Country:	Israel
	Currency:	Israeli Shekel
	Index:	MAOF 25
	Description:	Base level of 100 as of January 1, 1992.
		Weighted average of the top 25 stocks listed in Tel Aviv.
		Calculated Sunday to Thursday.
		No derivatives available.

Years' end	Index		Israeli shekel value	U.S. dollar	
	Values	Returns		Values	Returns
1991	100.00		2.285	43.76	
1992	204.79	104.79%	2.764	74.09	69.30%
1993	247.67	20.94%	2.984	83.00	12.02%
1994	175.48	−29.15%	2.995	58.59	−29.41%
1995	215.26	22.67%	3.135	68.66	17.19%
Total return		115.26%			56.90%
Compounded rate of return		21.13%			11.92%
Standard deviation		55.46%			40.47%
Risk-adjusted ratio		0.38			0.29
Correlation with the U.S.		0.05			0.14

Other indices: Israel Stock Market General
Weighted average of all the stocks listed in Tel Aviv.
Calculated Sunday to Thursday.
Base level of 100 as of January 6, 1992.
Value as of December 31, 1995: 190.82.
No derivatives available.

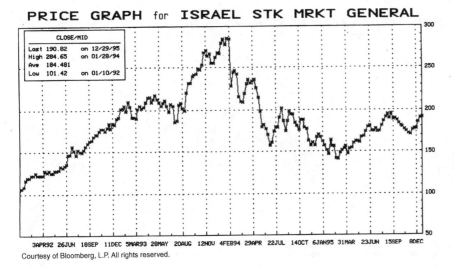

PRICE GRAPH for ISRAEL STK MRKT GENERAL

CLOSE/MID		
Last	190.82	on 12/29/95
High	284.65	on 01/28/94
Ave	184.481	
Low	101.42	on 01/10/92

3APR92 26JUN 18SEP 11DEC 5MAR93 28MAY 20AUG 12NOV 4FEB94 29APR 22JUL 14OCT 6JAN95 31MAR 23JUN 15SEP 8DEC

Figure A-23. *Israel Stock Market General.*

	Country:	Italy
	Currency:	Italian Lira
	Index:	BCI Stock Market Index
	Description:	Base level of 100 as of 1972.
		Capitalization weighted index of leading Italian stocks.
		No derivatives available.

Years' end	Index		Italian lira value	U.S. dollar	
	Values	Returns		Values	Returns
1987	487.99		1169.250	0.42	
1988	589.72	20.85%	1308.000	0.45	8.03%
1989	687.44	16.57%	1269.000	0.54	20.15%
1990	516.57	−24.86%	1130.000	0.46	−15.61%
1991	507.79	−1.70%	1140.000	0.45	−2.56%
1992	446.33	−12.10%	1477.000	0.30	−32.16%
1993	619.47	38.79%	1719.000	0.36	19.25%
1994	632.48	2.10%	1621.500	0.39	8.24%
1995	589.60	−6.78%	1587.500	0.37	−4.78%

Total return		20.82%		−11.01%
Compounded rate of return		2.39%	−1.45%	
Standard deviation		20.34%		17.79%
Risk-adjusted ratio		0.12		−0.08
Correlation with the U.S.		0.18		0.27

Other indices: MIB 30
Capitalization weighted index of 30 leading Italian stocks traded in Milano.
Base level 10000 as of January 1993.
Value as of December 31, 1995: 14132.
Futures and options available.

MIB Telematico
Capitalization weighted index of all the Italian stocks traded in the electronic market.
Base level 10000 as of July 16, 1993.
Value as of December 31, 1995: 9543.
No derivatives available.

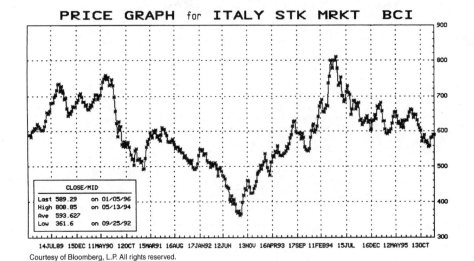

PRICE GRAPH for ITALY STK MRKT BCI

CLOSE/MID	
Last 589.29	on 01/05/96
High 808.85	on 05/13/94
Ave 593.627	
Low 361.6	on 09/25/92

14JUL89 15DEC 11MAY90 12OCT 15MAR91 16AUG 17JAN92 12JUN 13NOV 16APR93 17SEP 11FEB94 15JUL 16DEC 12MAY95 13OCT

Figure A-24. Italy, *BCI Stock Market.*

	Japan
Country:	Japan
Currency:	Japanese Yen
Index:	NIKKEI 225
Description:	Price weighted index of 225 top Japanese stocks traded at the First Section in Tokyo. Base level of 176.21 as of May 16, 1949. Futures and options available in Osaka, Singapore and Chicago.

Years' end	Index		Japanese yen value	U.S. dollar	
	Values	Returns		Values	Returns
1987	21564.00		121.250	177.85	
1988	30159.00	39.86%	125.050	241.18	35.61%
1989	38915.00	29.03%	143.800	270.62	12.21%
1990	23848.00	−38.72%	135.750	175.68	−35.08%
1991	22983.80	−3.62%	124.900	184.02	4.75%
1992	16924.90	−26.36%	124.860	135.55	−26.34%
1993	17417.20	2.91%	111.850	155.72	14.88%
1994	19723.10	13.24%	99.580	198.06	27.19%
1995	19868.20	0.74%	103.510	191.94	−3.09%
Total return		−7.86%			7.93%
Compounded rate of return		−1.02%			0.96%
Standard deviation		26.15%			24.56%
Risk-adjusted ratio		−0.04			0.04
Correlation with the U.S.		0.42			0.23

Other indices:

Tokyo Price Index (TOPIX)
Capitalization weighted index of all the companies traded at the Tokyo First Section. Base level of 100 as of January 4, 1968. Value as of December 31, 1995: 1577.7. Futures and options available in Tokyo.

NIKKEI 300
Capitalization weighted index of major stocks traded at the Tokyo First Section. Base level of 100 as of October 1, 1982. Value as of December 31, 1995: 296.33. Futures and options available in Osaka and Singapore.

JASDAQ
Capitalization weighted index of all the OTC stocks, except Bank of Japan. Base level of 100 as of October 28, 1991. Value as of December 31, 1995: 54.14. No derivatives available.

TSE Second Section
Capitalization weighted index of all the companies traded at the Tokyo Second Section. Base level of 100 as of January 4, 1968. Value as of December 31, 1995: 2062.11. No derivatives available.

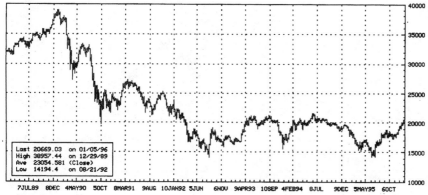

PRICE GRAPH for NKY —— NIKKEI 225 INDEX

Last 20669.03 on 01/05/96
High 38957.44 on 12/29/89
Ave 23054.581 (Close)
Low 14194.4 on 08/21/92

7JUL89 8DEC 4MAY90 5OCT 8MAR91 9AUG 10JAN92 5JUN 6NOV 9APR93 10SEP 4FEB94 8JUL 9DEC 5MAY95 6OCT

Figure A-25. Japan, *Nikkei 225.*

Country: Malaysia
Currency: Malaysian Ringgit
Index: Kuala Lumpur Composite Index
Description: Capitalization weighted index of 100 major stocks traded in Kuala Lumpur.
Base level of 95.83 as of January 3, 1977.
Futures available.

Years' end	Index		Malaysian ringgit value	U.S. dollar	
	Values	Returns		Values	Returns
1987	261.18		2.489	104.93	
1988	357.38	36.83%	2.710	131.87	25.67%
1989	562.27	57.33%	2.701	208.17	57.86%
1990	505.92	−10.02%	2.703	187.20	−10.07%
1991	556.22	9.94%	2.722	204.34	9.15%
1992	643.96	15.77%	2.619	245.88	20.33%
1993	1275.32	98.04%	2.691	474.01	92.78%
1994	971.21	−23.85%	2.553	380.42	−19.74%
1995	995.17	2.47%	2.540	391.85	3.00%

Total return		281.03%		2.73%
Compounded rate of return		18.20%		17.90%
Standard deviation		39.51%		37.05%
Risk-adjusted ratio		0.46		0.48
Correlation with the U.S.		0.20		0.20

Other indices: Kuala Lumpur Second Board
Capitalization weighted index of all stocks traded at the 2nd board of Kuala Lumpur.
Value as of December 31, 1992: 139.86.
Value as of December 31, 1995: 298.66.
No derivatives available.

Kuala Lumpur EMAS Index
Capitalization weighted index of all stocks traded at the main board of Kuala Lumpur.
Value as of December 31, 1992: 162.07.
Value as of December 31, 1995: 279.47.
No derivatives available.

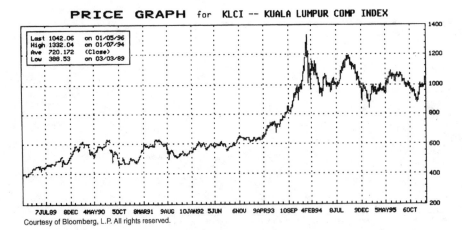

PRICE GRAPH for KLCI -- KUALA LUMPUR COMP INDEX

Last	1042.06	on 01/05/96
High	1332.04	on 01/07/94
Ave	720.172	(Close)
Low	388.53	on 03/03/89

7JUL89 8DEC 4MAY90 5OCT 8MAR91 9AUG 10JAN92 5JUN 6NOV 9APR93 10SEP 4FEB94 8JUL 9DEC 5MAY95 6OCT

Figure A-26. Malaysia, *Kuala Lumpur Composite Index.*

	Index		Mexican	U.S. dollar	
Years' end	Values	Returns	peso value	Values	Returns
1989	418.93		2.684	156.11	
1990	628.79	50.09%	2.948	213.29	36.63%
1991	1431.46	127.65%	3.066	466.88	118.89%
1992	1760.15	22.96%	3.121	563.97	20.79%
1993	2602.63	47.86%	3.107	837.67	48.53%
1994	2375.66	−8.72%	5.075	468.11	−44.12%
1995	2778.47	16.96%	7.695	361.07	−22.87%
Total return		563.23%			131.29%
Compounded rate of return		37.07%			15.00%
Standard deviation		46.89%			57.59%
Risk-adjusted ratio		0.79			0.26
Correlation with the U.S.		0.35			0.20

Country: Mexico
Currency: Mexican Peso
Index: Mexico Bolsa Index (or IPC, Indice De Precios y Cotizaciones)
Description: Capitalization weighted index of the leading stocks traded in Mexico.
Base level of 0.78 as of October 30, 1978.
No derivatives available.

Other indices: INMEX
Capitalization weighted index of the leading stocks traded in Mexico.
Base level of 100 as of December 30, 1991.
Value as of December 31, 1995: 185.
No derivatives available.

PRICE GRAPH for MEXBOL – MEXICO BOLSA INDEX

Last 3011.05 on 01/05/96
High 3040.5 on 01/05/96
Ave 1479.443 (Close)
Low 205.5 on 03/10/89

7JUL89 8DEC 4MAY90 5OCT 8MAR91 9AUG 10JAN92 5JUN 6NOV 9APR93 10SEP 4FEB94 8JUL 9DEC 5MAY95 6OCT

Figure A-27. Mexico *Bolsa Index.*

Country: Netherlands
Currency: Dutch Guilder
Index: Amsterdam EOE Index
Description: Base level of 100 as of February 1, 1983.
                Capitalization weighted index of 25 leading Dutch stocks.
                Futures and options available.

Years' end	Index		Dutch guilder value	U.S. dollar	
	Values	Returns		Values	Returns
1987	202.00		1.767	114.32	
1988	259.33	28.38%	2.002	129.54	13.31%
1989	301.00	16.07%	1.909	157.72	21.75%
1990	229.21	−23.85%	1.689	135.71	−13.95%
1991	277.05	20.87%	1.713	161.77	19.21%
1992	285.84	3.17%	1.819	157.18	−2.84%
1993	414.27	44.93%	1.947	212.73	35.34%
1994	414.27	0.00%	1.734	238.85	12.28%
1995	485.35	17.16%	1.609	301.74	26.33%

Total return		140.27%		163.95%
Compounded rate of return		11.58%		12.90%
Standard deviation		20.59%		15.87%
Risk-adjusted ratio		0.56		0.81
Correlation with the U.S.		0.48		0.63

Other indices: CBS All Shares
                  Capitalization weighted index of all stocks traded in Amsterdam excluding investment trusts.
                  Base level of 100 as of December 31, 1984.
                  Value as of December 31, 1995: 321.5.
                  No derivatives available.

                  Dutch Top 5
                  Capitalization weighted index of 5 major stocks traded in Amsterdam and worldwide.
                  It is the smallest equity index in the world.
                  Base level of 602 as of December 29, 1989.
                  Value as of December 31, 1995: 810.77.
                  Futures and options available.

Figure A-28. Netherlands, *CBS All Shares.*

Country:	New Zealand
Currency:	New Zealand Dollar
Index:	New Zealand Stock Exchange 40 (Previously Barclays Index)
Description:	Capitalization weighted index of 40 major stocks traded in New Zealand. Base level of 100 as of January 31, 1957. Futures available.

Years' end	Index Values	Index Returns	New Zealand dollar value	U.S. dollar Values	U.S. dollar Returns
1987	1959.81		1.582	1238.60	
1988	1839.94	−6.12%	1.582	1162.84	−6.12%
1989	1988.39	8.07%	1.679	1184.09	1.83%
1990	1202.86	−39.51%	1.702	706.80	−40.31%
1991	1504.78	25.10%	1.851	813.03	15.03%
1992	1565.50	4.04%	1.941	806.70	−0.78%
1993	2188.07	39.77%	1.789	1223.13	51.62%
1994	1914.24	−12.51%	1.565	1222.82	−0.03%
1995	2149.82	12.31%	1.530	1405.55	14.94%

Total return	9.70%		13.48%
Compounded rate of return	1.16%		1.59%
Standard deviation	24.14%		25.68%
Risk-adjusted ratio	0.05		0.06
Correlation with the U.S.	0.56		0.39

PRICE GRAPH for NZSE40 — NZSE TOP 40 INDEX

Last 2184.8 on 01/05/96
High 2454.96 on 09/08/89
Ave 1793.919 (Close)
Low 1142.21 on 01/18/91

7JUL89 8DEC 4MAY90 5OCT 8MAR91 9AUG 10JAN92 5JUN 6NOV 9APR93 10SEP 4FEB94 8JUL 9DEC 5MAY95 6OCT

Figure A-29. *New Zealand Stock Exchange Top 40.*

Country:	Norway
Currency:	Norwegian Krone
Index:	OBX
Description:	Base level of 200 as of January 1, 1987.
	Capitalization weighted index of 26 companies traded in Copenhagen.
	Futures and options available.

Years' end	Index Values	Index Returns	Norwegian krone value	U.S. dollar Values	U.S. dollar Returns
1987	181.90		6.220	29.24	
1988	268.95	47.86%	6.565	40.97	40.09%
1989	408.96	52.06%	6.602	61.94	51.21%
1990	350.91	−14.19%	5.870	59.79	−3.49%
1991	320.60	−8.64%	5.985	53.57	−10.40%
1992	264.53	−17.49%	6.948	38.08	−28.92%
1993	385.51	45.73%	7.537	51.15	34.34%
1994	403.37	4.63%	6.764	59.63	16.58%
1995	407.06	0.91%	6.346	64.14	7.56%
Total return		123.78%			119.34%
Compounded rate of return		10.59%			10.32%
Standard deviation		29.66%			27.43%
Risk-adjusted ratio		0.36			0.38
Correlation with the U.S.		0.23			0.21

Other indices:	OBX Total Index
	Capitalization weighted index of all the Norvegian stocks.
	Base level of 100 as of January 1, 1987.
	Value as of December 31, 1995: 732.96.
	No derivatives available.

PRICE GRAPH for OBX -- OBX STOCK INDEX

Last	421.22	on 01/05/96
High	519.35	on 08/03/90
Ave	373.775	(Close)
Low	212.99	on 08/28/92

7JUL89 8DEC 4MAY90 5OCT 8MAR91 9AUG 10JAN92 5JUN 6NOV 9APR93 10SEP 4FEB94 8JUL 9DEC 5MAY95 6OCT

Figure A-30. Norway, *OBX*.

Country:	Pakistan
Currency:	Pakistani Rupee
Index:	Pakistan Karachi Stock Index (KSE)
Description:	Source: Khadim Shah Bukhari & Co.
	No derivatives available.

Years' end	Index		Pakistani rupee value	U.S. dollar	
	Values	Returns		Values	Returns
1989	575.86		21.420	26.88	
1990	591.32	2.68%	21.890	27.01	0.48%
1991	1672.78	182.89%	24.540	68.17	152.34%
1992	1243.71	−25.65%	25.700	48.39	−29.01%
1993	2164.26	74.02%	30.120	71.85	48.48%
1994	2049.11	−5.32%	30.800	66.53	−7.41%
1995	1501.10	−26.74%	34.250	43.83	−34.12%
Total return		160.67%			63.02%
Compounded rate of return		17.31%			8.49%
Standard deviation		81.91%			70.38%
Risk-adjusted ratio		0.21			0.12
Correlation with the U.S.		0.33			0.30

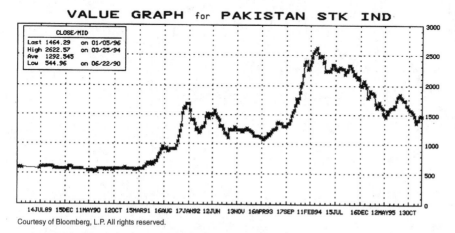

Figure A-31. *Pakistan Karachi Stock Index.*

	Peru
Country:	Peru
Currency:	Peruvian New Sol
Index:	Peru Stock Market General
Description:	Capitalization weighted index of 55 Peruvian stocks.
	Base level of 1000 as of December 31, 1991.
	No derivatives available.

Years' end	Index		Peruvian new sol value	U.S. dollar	
	Values	Returns		Values	Returns
1991	100.00		1.2000	83.33	
1992	372.95	272.95%	1.6330	228.38	174.06%
1993	930.47	149.49%	2.1650	429.78	88.18%
1994	1414.92	52.07%	2.1850	647.56	50.67%
1995	1243.37	−12.12%	2.3220	535.47	−17.31%
Total return		1143.37%			542.57%
Compounded rate of return		87.78%			59.21%
Standard deviation		124.17%			79.78%
Risk-adjusted ratio		0.71			0.74
Correlation with the U.S.		−0.56			−0.67

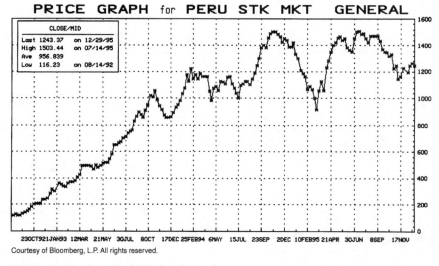

PRICE GRAPH for PERU STK MKT GENERAL

CLOSE/MID
Last 1243.37 on 12/29/95
High 1503.44 on 07/14/95
Ave 956.839
Low 116.23 on 08/14/92

230CT92 1JAN93 12MAR 21MAY 30JUL 8OCT 17DEC 25FEB94 6MAY 15JUL 23SEP 2DEC 10FEB95 21APR 30JUN 8SEP 17NOV

Figure A-32. *Peru Stock Market General.*

Country:	Philippines
Currency:	Philippine Peso
Index:	Philippines Composite Index
Description:	Capitalization weighted index of most representative stocks traded in the Philippines. No derivatives available.

Years' end	Index Values	Index Returns	Philippines peso value	U.S. dollar Values	U.S. dollar Returns
1989	1104.50				
1990	651.42	−41.02%			
1991	1151.87	76.82%	26.050	44.22	
1992	1256.22	9.06%	25.350	49.56	12.07%
1993	3196.08	154.42%	27.550	116.01	234.08%
1994	2785.81	−12.84%	24.530	113.57	−2.11%
1995	2594.18	−6.88%	26.180	99.09	−12.75%
Total return		134.87%			231.29%
Compounded rate of return		15.29%			22.35%
Standard deviation		72.60%			68.28%
Risk-adjusted ratio		0.21			0.33
Correlation with the U.S.		0.22			−0.27

PRICE GRAPH for PCOMP -- PHILIPPINES COMPOSITE IX

Last	2594.18	on 12/29/95
High	3327.86	on 01/07/94
Ave	1733.764	(Close)
Low	514.8	on 10/05/90

23MAR90 24AUG 25JAN91 21JUN 22NOV 24APR92 25SEP 26FEB93 23JUL 24DEC 27MAY94 21OCT 24MAR95 25AUG

Figure A-33. *Philippines Composite Index.*

Country:	Poland
Currency:	Polish Zloty
Index:	Poland Stock Market, Warsaw
Description:	Base level of 1000 as of April 16, 1991.
	Daily capitalization weighted index.
	No derivatives available.

| Years' | Index | | Polish | U.S. dollar | |
end	Values	Returns	zloty value	Values	Returns
1990	1000.00				
1991	919.10	−8.09%			
1992	1041.60	13.33%	1.750	595.20	
1993	12439.00	1094.22%	2.150	5785.58	872.04%
1994	7473.10	−39.92%	2.417	3092.27	−46.55%
1995	7585.90	1.51%	2.466	3076.82	−0.50%

Total return		658.59%	416.94%
Compounded rate of return		49.97%	72.91%
Standard deviation		493.46%	517.57%
Risk-adjusted ratio		0.10	0.14
Correlation with the U.S.		−0.24	−0.24

Other indices: Polish Stock Market, Warsaw WIG 20
Daily capitalization weighted index representing 20 top Polish companies.
Base level of 1000 as of April 16, 1994.
Value as of December 31, 1995: 791.9.

VALUE GRAPH for POLAND STOCK MKT WARSAW

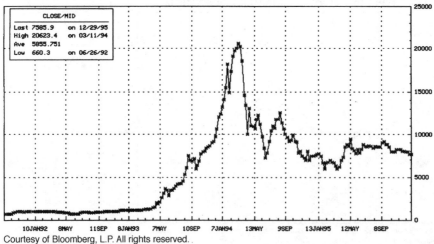

CLOSE/MID	
Last 7585.9	on 12/29/95
High 20623.4	on 03/11/94
Ave 5855.751	
Low 660.3	on 06/26/92

Figure A-34. *Poland Stock Market Warsaw.*

Country:	Portugal				
Currency:	Portuguese Escudo				
Index:	Portugal Stock Market Index PSI				
Description:	Base level of 3000 as of December 31, 1992.				
	Capitalization weighted index of 20 most liquid Portuguese stocks.				
	No derivatives available.				

Years' end	Index		Portuguese escudo value	U.S. dollar	
	Values	Returns		Values	Returns
1992	3000.00		147.000	20.41	
1993	4288.09	42.94%	177.220	24.20	18.56%
1994	4157.25	−3.05%	159.000	26.15	8.06%
1995	3896.24	−6.28%	149.900	25.99	−0.59%
Total return		29.87%			27.36%
Compounded rate of return		9.10%			8.40%
Standard deviation		27.53%			9.59%
Risk-adjusted ratio		0.33			0.88
Correlation with the U.S.		−0.34			−0.69

Other indices: Lisbon BVL General Index
                       Value as of December 31, 1993: 848.
                       Value as of December 31, 1995: 877.69.

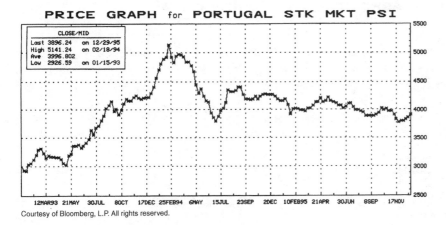

Figure A-35. Portugal Stock Market Index *PSI*.

| | Index | | Russian | U.S. dollar | |
Years' end	Values	Returns	ruble value	Values	Returns
June 1994	100.00		1989.000	0.05	
1994	202.89	102.89%	3550.000	0.06	13.68%
1995	183.98	−9.32%	4645.000	0.04	−30.70%
Total return		83.98%			−21.22%
Compounded rate of return		27.62%			−9.10%
Standard deviation		79.34%			31.38%
Risk-adjusted ratio		0.35			−0.29
Correlation with the U.S.		−1.00			−1.00

Country: Russia
Currency: Russian Ruble
Index: ASP General
Description: Base level of 100 as of June 20, 1994.
Capitalization weighted index of the most actively traded Russian companies.
No derivatives available.

Other indices: ASP Market Index
Capitalization weighted index of the 50 largest Russian stocks by market value.
Base level of 100 as of September 1, 1994.
Value as of December 31, 1995: 132.83.
No derivatives available.

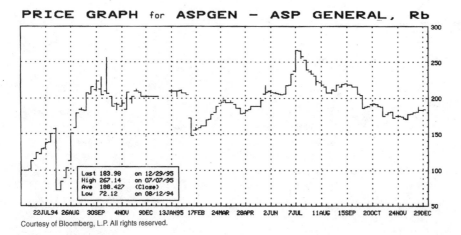

Figure A-36. Russia, *ASP General.*

	Country:	Singapore
	Currency:	Singapore Dollar
	Index:	Straits Times Industrial
	Description:	Price weighted index of 30 major stocks traded in Singapore.
		Base level of 100 as of December 30, 1966.
		No derivatives available.

Years' end	Index		Singapore dollar value	U.S. dollar	
	Values	Returns		Values	Returns
1987	823.58		1.997	412.41	
1988	1038.62	26.11%	1.946	533.72	29.42%
1989	1481.33	42.62%	1.891	783.36	46.77%
1990	1154.58	−22.06%	1.744	662.22	−15.46%
1991	1490.70	29.11%	1.631	913.98	38.02%
1992	1524.40	2.26%	1.643	928.10	1.54%
1993	2425.68	59.12%	1.610	1506.63	62.34%
1994	2239.56	−7.67%	1.458	1536.05	1.95%
1995	2266.54	1.20%	1.414	1602.59	4.33%

Total return	175.21%	288.59%
Compounded rate of return	13.49%	18.49%
Standard deviation	27.41%	26.94%
Risk-adjusted ratio	0.49	0.69
Correlation with the U.S.	0.42	0.41

Other indices: SES Singapore All Shares Index
Capitalization weighted index of all stocks traded in Singapore.
Base level of 100 as of January 2, 1975.
Value as of December 31, 1995: 555.39.
No derivatives available.

DBS 50
Capitalization weighted index of 50 major stocks traded in Singapore.
Base level of 100 as of January 2, 1975.
Value as of December 31, 1995: 560.98.
No derivatives available.

PRICE GRAPH for STI -- SING: STRAITS TIMES INDU

Last 2365.53 on 01/05/96
High 2482.91 on 01/07/94
Ave 1702.079 (Close)
Low 1079.5 on 10/12/90

7JUL89 8DEC 4MAY90 5OCT 8MAR91 9AUG 10JAN92 5JUN 6NOV 9APR93 10SEP 4FEB94 8JUL 9DEC 5MAY95 6OCT

Figure A-37. Singapore, *Straits Times Industrial.*

	Country:	South Africa
	Currency:	South African Rand
	Index:	Johannesburg All Market Index
	Description:	Capitalization-weighted index of all domestic stocks traded in Johannesburg. Base level of 100 as of October 2, 1978. No derivatives available.

Years' end	Index		South African rand value	U.S. dollar	
	Values	Returns		Values	Returns
1990	2719.00		2.563	1061.07	
1991	3440.31	26.53%	2.745	1253.30	18.12%
1992	3258.76	−5.28%	3.055	1066.70	−14.89%
1993	4892.99	50.15%	3.400	1439.11	34.91%
1994	5866.91	19.90%	3.538	1658.26	15.23%
1995	6228.42	6.16%	3.646	1708.52	3.03%
Total return		129.07%			61.02%
Compounded rate of return		18.03%			10.00%
Standard deviation		21.10%			18.53%
Risk-adjusted ratio		0.85			0.54
Correlation with the U.S.		−0.13			−0.05

Other indices: Johannesburg All Gold Index
Capitalization-weighted index of all domestic gold stocks traded in Johannesburg.
Base level of 100 as of October 2, 1978.
Value as of December 31, 1995: 1343.51.
No derivatives available.

Johannesburg Industrial Index
Capitalization-weighted index of 302 industrial stocks traded in Johannesburg.
Value as of December 31, 1991: 4000.
Value as of December 31, 1995: 7987.22.
No derivatives available.

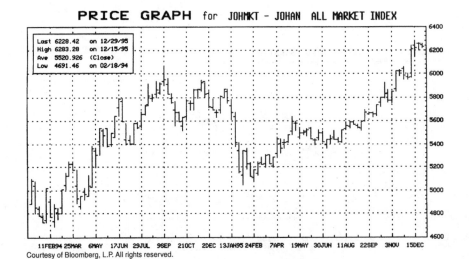

PRICE GRAPH for JOHMKT - JOHAN ALL MARKET INDEX

Last 6228.42 on 12/29/95
High 6283.28 on 12/15/95
Ave 5520.926 (Close)
Low 4691.46 on 02/18/94

11FEB94 25MAR 6MAY 17JUN 29JUL 9SEP 21OCT 2DEC 13JAN95 24FEB 7APR 19MAY 30JUN 11AUG 22SEP 3NOV 15DEC

Figure A-38. South Africa, *Johannesburg All Market Index.*

Country:	South Korea
Currency:	South Korean Won
Index:	Korea Composite Index
Description:	Capitalization-weighted index of all stocks traded in Korea.
	Base level of 100 as of January 4, 1980.
	No derivatives available.

Years' end	Index		South Korean won value	U.S. dollar	
	Values	Returns		Values	Returns
1987	525.11		795.900	0.66	
1988	907.20	72.76%	687.400	1.32	100.03%
1989	909.72	0.28%	681.400	1.34	1.16%
1990	696.11	−23.48%	719.200	0.97	−27.50%
1991	610.92	−12.24%	765.300	0.80	−17.52%
1992	678.44	11.05%	786.500	0.86	8.06%
1993	866.18	27.67%	808.100	1.07	24.26%
1994	1027.37	18.61%	786.500	1.31	21.87%
1995	882.94	−14.06%	770.200	1.15	−12.24%
Total return		68.14%			73.75%
Compounded rate of return		6.71%			7.15%
Standard deviation		30.74%			39.91%
Risk-adjusted ratio		0.22			0.18
Correlation with the U.S.		−0.18			−0.13

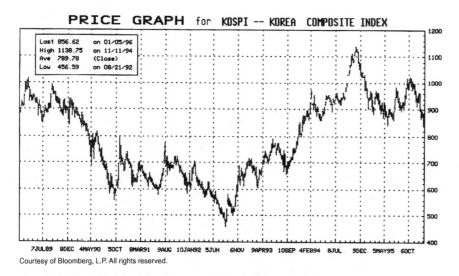

PRICE GRAPH for KOSPI -- KOREA COMPOSITE INDEX

Last 856.62	on 01/05/96
High 1138.75	on 11/11/94
Ave 789.78	(Close)
Low 456.59	on 08/21/92

7JUL89 9DEC 4MAY90 5OCT 8MAR91 9AUG 10JAN92 5JUN 6NOV 9APR93 10SEP 4FEB94 8JUL 9DEC 5MAY95 6OCT

Figure A-39. South Korea, *Korea Composite Index, KOSPI.*

	Spain
Country:	Spain
Currency:	Spanish Peseta
Index:	IBEX 35
Description:	Base level of 3000 as of December 29, 1989.
	Capitalization-weighted index of 35 leading Spanish stocks.
	Futures and options available.

Years' end	Index Values	Index Returns	Spanish peseta value	U.S. dollar Values	U.S. dollar Returns
1987	2407.10		109.000	22.08	
1988	2727.50	13.31%	114.650	23.79	7.73%
1989	3000.00	9.99%	109.200	27.47	15.48%
1990	2248.80	−25.04%	95.800	23.47	−14.55%
1991	2603.30	15.76%	96.800	26.89	14.57%
1992	2344.57	−9.94%	115.100	20.37	−24.26%
1993	3615.22	54.20%	143.200	25.25	23.94%
1994	3087.68	−14.59%	131.580	23.47	−7.05%
1995	3630.76	17.59%	121.670	29.84	27.17%
Total return		50.84%			35.13%
Compounded rate of return		4.67%			3.40%
Standard deviation		24.62%			18.67%
Risk-adjusted ratio		0.19			0.18
Correlation with the U.S.		0.47			0.74

Other indices: Madrid Stock Exchange Index
Weighted index of all the stocks traded in Madrid.
Base value of 100 as of December 31, 1985.
Value as of December 31, 1995: 320.07.

PRICE GRAPH for IBEX -- IBEX 35 INDEX

Last 3693.53 on 01/05/96
High 3980.53 on 02/04/94
Ave 2917.625 (Close)
Low 1861.9 on 10/09/92

7JUL89 8DEC 4MAY90 5OCT 8MAR91 9AUG 10JAN92 5JUN 6NOV 9APR93 10SEP 4FEB94 8JUL 9DEC 5MAY95 6OCT

Figure A-40. Spain, *IBEX 35.*

Country:	Sri Lanka			
Currency:	Sri Lankan Rupee			
Index:	Sri Lanka Stock Market, Colombo All Share			
Description:	Weighted index of all the shares traded in Colombo.			
	Calculation based on the "weighted aggregates" method: each share weighted by the number of outstanding equities.			
	No derivatives available.			

Years' end	Index		Sri Lankan rupee value	U.S. dollar	
	Values	Returns		Values	Returns
1992	605.31		45.750	13.23	
1993	974.62	61.01%	49.500	19.69	48.81%
1994	985.24	1.09%	49.670	19.84	0.74%
1995	663.73	−32.63%	53.500	12.41	−37.46%
Total return		9.65%			−6.23%
Compounded rate of return		2.33%			−1.60%
Standard deviation		39.04%			35.35%
Risk-adjusted ratio		0.06			−0.05
Correlation with the U.S.		−0.61			−0.68

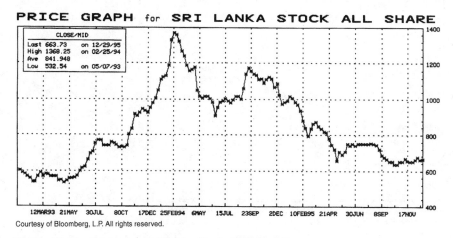

PRICE GRAPH for SRI LANKA STOCK ALL SHARE

CLOSE/MID		
Last 663.73	on 12/29/95	
High 1368.25	on 02/25/94	
Ave 841.948		
Low 532.54	on 05/07/93	

12MAR93 21MAY 30JUL 8OCT 17DEC 25FEB94 6MAY 15JUL 23SEP 2DEC 10FEB95 21APR 30JUN 8SEP 17NOV

Figure A-41. Sri Lanka, *Sri Lanka Stock All Shares.*

	Index		Swedish	U.S. dollar	
Country:	Sweden				
Currency:	Swedish Krone				
Index:	Affarsvarlden General Index				
Description:	Base level of 100 as of December 28, 1979.				
	Capitalization weighted index of 115 Swedish stocks.				
	No derivatives available.				

Years' end	Index Values	Returns	Swedish krone value	U.S. dollar Values	Returns
1988	1014.00		6.130	165.42	
1989	1262.00	24.46%	6.206	203.35	22.93%
1990	870.00	−31.06%	5.633	154.45	−24.05%
1991	917.60	5.47%	5.550	165.33	7.05%
1992	912.60	−0.54%	7.100	128.54	−22.26%
1993	1402.80	53.71%	8.360	167.80	30.55%
1994	1470.80	4.85%	7.420	198.22	18.13%
1995	1735.70	18.01%	6.657	260.73	31.54%
Total return		71.17%			57.62%
Compounded rate of return		7.98%			6.72%
Standard deviation		25.90%			23.53%
Risk-adjusted ratio		0.31			0.29
Correlation with the U.S.		0.41			0.58

Other indices: OMX Stockholm Index
Capitalization weighted index of 30 most traded Swedish stocks.
Base level of 500 as of September 30, 1986.
Value as of December 31, 1995: 1351.85.
Futures and options available.

PRICE GRAPH for SWEDEN STK MKT   AFFARSVARL

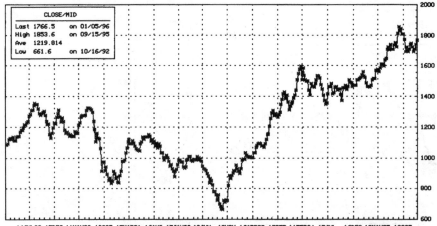

CLOSE/MID	
Last 1766.5	on 01/05/96
High 1853.6	on 09/15/95
Ave 1219.814	
Low 661.6	on 10/16/92

14JUL89 15DEC 11MAY90 12OCT 15MAR91 16AUG 17JAN92 12JUN 13NOV 16APR93 17SEP 11FEB94 15JUL 16DEC 12MAY95 13OCT

Figure A-42. Sweden, *Affarsvarlden General Index.*

Country:	Switzerland
Currency:	Swiss Franc
Index:	Swiss Market Index (SMI)
Description:	Base level of 1500 as of June 30, 1988.
	Capitalization weighted index of the largest Swiss stocks (23 in 1996).
	Futures and options available.

Years' end	Index		Swiss franc value	U.S. dollar	
	Values	Returns		Values	Returns
June 30, 1988	1500.00		1.506	996.02	
1989	1778.10	18.54%	1.541	1153.86	15.85%
1990	1383.10	−22.21%	1.277	1083.09	−6.13%
1991	1670.10	20.75%	1.362	1226.66	13.26%
1992	2107.00	26.16%	1.468	1435.78	17.05%
1993	2957.60	40.37%	1.489	1986.97	38.39%
1994	2628.80	−11.12%	1.309	2008.86	1.10%
1995	3297.70	25.45%	1.154	2856.88	42.21%
Total return		119.85%			186.83%
Compounded rate of return		11.91%			16.25%
Standard deviation		22.30%			17.77%
Risk-adjusted ratio		0.53			0.91
Correlation with the U.S.		0.57			0.60

Other indices:	Swiss Performance Index (SPI)
	Capitalization weighted index of 350 Swiss stocks.
	Base value of 1000 as of June 1, 1987.
	Value as of December 31, 1995: 2123.43.
	No derivatives available.

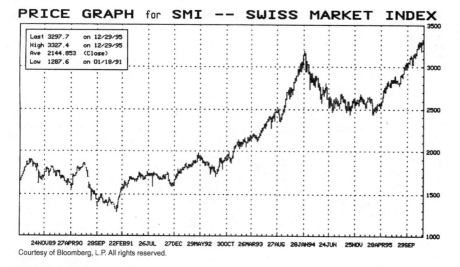

PRICE GRAPH for SMI -- SWISS MARKET INDEX

Last 3297.7 on 12/29/95
High 3327.4 on 12/29/95
Ave 2144.853 (Close)
Low 1287.6 on 01/18/91

24NOV89 27APR90 28SEP 22FEB91 26JUL 27DEC 29MAY92 30OCT 26MAR93 27AUG 28JAN94 24JUN 25NOV 28APR95 29SEP

Figure A-43. Switzerland, *Swiss Market Index, SMI.*

Country:	Taiwan
Currency:	Taiwan Dollar
Index:	Taiwan Weighted Index
Description:	Capitalization weighted index of all stocks traded in Taiwan.
	Based in 1966.
	No derivatives available.

Years' end	Index		Taiwan dollar value	U.S. dollar	
	Values	Returns		Values	Returns
1989	9624.18		26.160	367.90	
1990	4530.16	−52.93%	27.110	167.10	−54.58%
1991	4540.55	0.23%	25.750	176.33	5.52%
1992	3377.06	−25.62%	25.400	132.96	−24.60%
1993	6070.56	79.76%	26.670	227.62	71.20%
1994	7111.10	17.14%	26.290	270.49	18.83%
1995	5158.65	−27.46%	27.280	189.10	−30.09%

Total return	−46.40%	−48.60%
Compounded rate of return	−8.52%	−9.07%
Standard deviation	46.59%	44.53%
Risk-adjusted ratio	−0.18	−0.20
Correlation with the U.S.	−0.02	−0.00

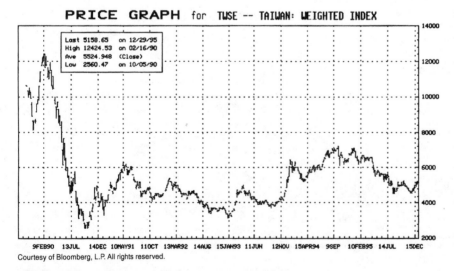

PRICE GRAPH for TWSE -- TAIWAN: WEIGHTED INDEX

Last 5158.65 on 12/29/95
High 12424.53 on 02/16/90
Ave 5524.948 (Close)
Low 2560.47 on 10/05/90

9FEB90 13JUL 14DEC 10MAY91 11OCT 13MAR92 14AUG 15JAN93 11JUN 12NOV 15APR94 9SEP 10FEB95 14JUL 15DEC

Figure A-44. Taiwan, *Taiwan Weighted Index (TWSE).*

		Index		Thai	U.S. dollar	
Years' end		Values	Returns	baht value	Values	Returns

Country: Thailand
Currency: Thai Baht
Index: SET
Description: Capitalization weighted index of all stocks traded in Thailand.
Base level of 100 as of April 30, 1975.
No derivatives available.

Years' end	Index Values	Index Returns	Thai baht value	U.S. dollar Values	U.S. dollar Returns
1987	284.94		795.900	0.36	
1988	386.73	35.72%	687.400	0.56	57.15%
1989	870.49	125.09%	681.400	1.28	1.27%
1990	612.86	−29.60%	719.200	0.85	−33.30%
1991	711.36	16.07%	765.300	0.93	9.08%
1992	893.42	25.59%	786.500	1.14	22.21%
1993	1682.85	88.36%	808.100	2.08	83.33%
1994	1360.09	−19.18%	786.500	1.73	−16.96%
1995	1280.81	−5.83%	770.200	1.66	−3.84%

Total return		349.50%	3.65%
Compounded rate of return		20.67%	21.16%
Standard deviation		53.38%	54.58%
Risk-adjusted ratio		0.39	0.39
Correlation with the U.S.		0.36	0.36

Other indices: SET 50
Capitalization weighted index of 50 major stocks traded in Bangkok.
Base level of 100 as of August 16, 1995.
Value as of June 30, 1996: 96.13.
No derivatives available.

PRICE GRAPH for SET -- THAI STOCK EXCHG OF THAI

Last	1364.23	on 01/05/96
High	1789.16	on 01/07/94
Ave	963.141	(Close)
Low	429.18	on 03/10/89

7JUL89 8DEC 4MAY90 5OCT 8MAR91 9AUG 10JAN92 5JUN 6NOV 9APR93 10SEP 4FEB94 8JUL 9DEC 5MAY95 6OCT

Figure A-45. Thailand, *SET.*

Country: Turkey
Currency: Turkish Lira
Index: Turkey Stock Market Composite
No derivatives available.

Years' end	Index		Turkish lira value	U.S. dollar	
	Values	Returns		Values	Returns
1991	3664.00		5396.00	0.68	
1992	4004.18	9.28%	8540.00	0.47	−30.95%
1993	20682.90	416.53%	14570.00	1.42	202.76%
1994	27257.10	31.79%	38430.00	0.71	−50.04%
1995	40024.60	46.84%	60150.00	0.67	−6.18%
Total return		992.37%			−2.00%
Compounded rate of return		81.80%			−0.50%
Standard deviation		194.23%			117.29%
Risk-adjusted ratio		0.42			0.00
Correlation with the U.S.		−0.11			−0.02

Other indices: Turkey Stock Market Industrial
Value as of December 31, 1992: 4914.5.
Value as of December 31, 1995: 46247.2.

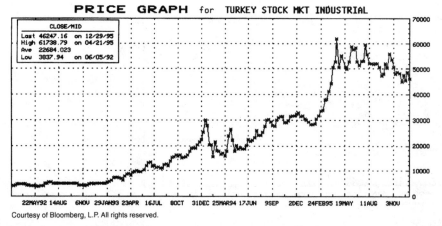

PRICE GRAPH for TURKEY STOCK MKT INDUSTRIAL

CLOSE/MID
Last 46247.16 on 12/29/95
High 61738.79 on 04/21/95
Ave 22684.023
Low 3837.94 on 06/05/92

Figure A-46. *Turkey Stock Market Industrial.*

| | | | | U.S. dollar | |
| Country: | United Kingdom | | | | |

Country: United Kingdom
Currency: British Pound
Index: Financial Times Stock Exchange 100
Description: Base level of 1000 as of January 3, 1984.
Capitalization weighted index of 100 leading British stocks.
Futures and options available.

| Years' end | Index | | British pound value | U.S. dollar | |
	Values	Returns		Values	Returns
1987	1712.70		0.530	3230.15	
1988	1793.40	4.71%	0.552	3247.85	0.55%
1989	2422.70	35.09%	0.620	3906.60	20.28%
1990	2143.40	−11.53%	0.518	4136.76	5.89%
1991	2493.10	16.32%	0.535	4663.84	12.74%
1992	2846.50	14.18%	0.662	4299.64	−7.81%
1993	3418.40	20.09%	0.677	5050.69	17.47%
1994	3065.50	−10.32%	0.639	4796.59	−5.03%
1995	3689.30	20.35%	0.645	5716.94	19.19%

Total return	115.41%		76.99%
Compounded rate of return	10.07%		7.40%
Standard deviation	15.99%		11.13%
Risk-adjusted ratio	0.63		0.66
Correlation with the U.S.	0.78		0.68

Other indices: Financial Times Stock Exchange MID 250
Capitalization weighted index of 250 most highly capitalized stocks, outside of the FTSE-100, traded in London.
Base level of 1412.6 as of December 31, 1985.
Value as of December 31, 1995: 4021.3.
No derivatives available.

Financial Times Stock Exchange Actuaries 350
Capitalization weighted index comprising of all the components of FTSE-100 and FTSE-250. It represents about 90% of the market's capitalization.
Base level of 682.94 as of December 31, 1985.
Value as of December 31, 1995: 1830.6.
No derivatives available.

PRICE GRAPH for UKX -- FT-SE 100 Index

Last 3704.5 on 01/05/96
High 3723 on 01/05/96
Ave 2715.497 (Close)
Low 1974.1 on 09/28/90

7JUL89 8DEC 4MAY90 5OCT 8MAR91 9AUG 10JAN92 5JUN 6NOV 9APR93 10SEP 4FEB94 8JUL 9DEC 5MAY95 6OCT

Figure A-47. United Kingdom, Financial Times *FTSE-100*.

Country: United States
Currency: U.S. Dollar
Index: Dow Jones Industrial Average
Description: Price weighted average of 30 blue chips listed at the NYSE.
The most popular stock index in the world, created by Charles Dow.
No derivatives available.

Years' end	Values	Returns
1987	1938.80	
1988	2168.60	11.85%
1989	2753.20	26.96%
1990	2633.66	−4.34%
1991	3168.83	20.32%
1992	3301.11	4.17%
1993	3754.09	13.72%
1994	3834.44	2.14%
1995	5117.12	33.45%

Total return	163.93%
Compounded rate of return	12.90%
Standard deviation	12.89%
Risk-adjusted ratio	1.00

Other indices: Standard & Poor's 500
Capitalization weighted index of 500 stocks representing all major industries.
Base level of 10 as of 1941.
Value as of December 31, 1995: 615.93.
Futures and options available.

Standard & Poor's 100
Capitalization weighted index of 100 highly capitalized stocks which options are listed on the CBOE.
Base level of 100 as of January 2, 1976.
Value as of December 31, 1995: 585.92.
Options available.

Besides the very small selection of most representative indices indicated above, the following indices are also watched by investors.

Dow Jones Transportation Average
Dow Jones Utilities Average
Dow Jones Composite Average
Standard & Poor's 400 Midcap Index
Standard & Poor's 600 Smallcap Index
Standard & Poor's Financials Index
Standard & Poor's Industrials Index
Standard & Poor's Transportations Index
Standard & Poor's Utilities Index
Standard & Poor's 1500 Supercomposite
NYSE Composite Index
NYSE Financials Index
NYSE Industrials Index
NYSE Transportations Index
NYSE Utilities Index
Philadelphia Value Line Index
Wilshire 5000
NASDAQ Composite Index
NASDAQ Financials Index

NASDAQ Industrials Index
NASDAQ Transportations Index
NASDAQ Telecom Index
NASDAQ Insurance Index
NASDAQ Bank Index
NASDAQ 100 Stocks Index
NASDAQ National Market Industrial Index
AMEX Major Market Index
AMEX Market Value Index
AMEX Institutional Index
AMEX Computer Tech Index
AMEX Oil Index
Philadephia Utility Index
Philadephia Gold And Silver Index
Russell 1000 (CBOE)
Russell 2000 (CBOE)
Russell 3000 (CBOE)

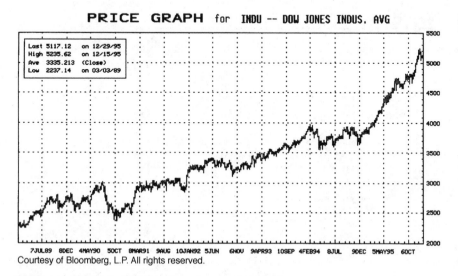

Figure A-48. United States, *Dow Jones Industrial Average.*

Country:	United States (International Stocks)	
Currency:	U.S. Dollar	
Index:	AMEX International Index	
Description:	Capitalization weighted index of 50 ADRs from Europe and Pacific Rim. Each ADR must have a worldwide market value of at least $100 million. Base level of 200 as of January 2, 1987. No derivatives available.	

Years' end	Value	Return
1989	333.30	
1990	290.65	−12.80%
1991	330.83	13.82%
1992	296.71	−10.31%
1993	376.43	26.87%
1994	415.30	10.33%
1995	466.75	12.39%
Total return		40.04%
Compounded rate of return		5.77%
Standard deviation		15.31%
Risk-adjusted ratio		0.38
Correlation with the U.S.		0.46

Other indices:	NASDAQ ADR Index
	Index representing about 100 ADRs traded at the NASDAQ.
	Value as of December 31, 1989: 136.98.
	Value as of December 31, 1995: 245.58.
	No derivatives available.

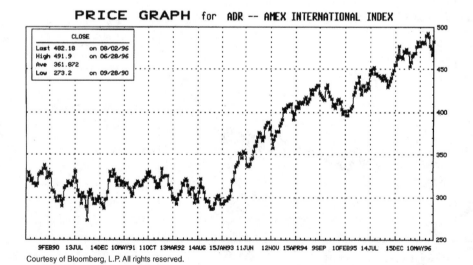

PRICE GRAPH for ADR -- AMEX INTERNATIONAL INDEX

CLOSE		
Last 482.18	on 08/02/96
High 491.9	on 06/28/96
Ave 361.872	
Low 273.2	on 09/28/90

9FEB90 13JUL 14DEC 10MAY91 11OCT 13MAR92 14AUG 15JAN93 11JUN 12NOV 15APR94 9SEP 10FEB95 14JUL 15DEC 10MAY96

Courtesy of Bloomberg, L.P. All rights reserved.

Figure A-49. *AMEX International Index.*

	Country:	Venezuela
	Currency:	Venezuelan Bolivar
	Index:	Venezuela Stocks Market Capital General
	Description:	Capitalization weighted index of Venezuelan stocks.
		Replaced the original stock market index on December 31, 1994.
		Base level of 1000 as of December 31, 1993.
		No derivatives available.

Years' end	Index		Venezuelan bolivar value	U.S. dollar	
	Values	Returns		Values	Returns
1993	1000.00		106.2500	9.41	
1994	1348.63	34.86%	170.0000	7.93	−15.71%
1995	2019.39	49.74%	286.0000	7.06	−11.00%
Total return		101.94%			−24.98%
Compounded rate of return		42.11%			−13.39%
Standard deviation		10.52%			3.33%
Risk-adjusted ratio		4.00			−4.01
Correlation with the U.S.		Insufficient Data			Insufficient Data

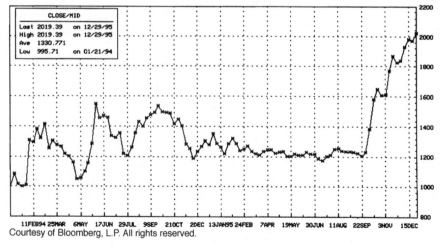

PRICE GRAPH for VENEZUELA STOCK CAPTL GNRL

CLOSE/MID		
Last 2019.39	on 12/29/95
High 2019.39	on 12/29/95
Ave 1330.771	
Low 995.71	on 01/21/94

11FEB94 25MAR 6MAY 17JUN 29JUL 9SEP 21OCT 2DEC 13JAN95 24FEB 7APR 19MAY 30JUN 11AUG 22SEP 3NOV 15DEC

Figure A-50. *Venezuela Stock Market Capital General.*

Index

About the Authors

ALBERTO VIVANTI is associated with Kredietbank Luxemburg, an investment and private banking group where he is in charge of asset management activities for international clients in Switzerland. Vivanti is the author of a book and numerous articles on technical analysis, and he is active in the area of professional education, frequently participating in conferences and seminars.

PERRY KAUFMAN is a well-known trader and analyst with more than 25 years' experience in the investment profession. He is the founder of Kaufman, Diamond & Yeong, international consultants to financial institutions. The co-founder of *The Journal of Futures Markets*, he has six books to his credit, including *Smarter Trading* with McGraw-Hill.